THE CHICAGO CUBS

THE
CHICAGO
CUBS
STORY OF A
CURSE

RICH
COHEN

FARRAR, STRAUS AND GIROUX | NEW YORK

Farrar, Straus and Giroux
18 West 18th Street, New York 10011

Library of Congress Cataloging-in-Publication Data
Names: Cohen, Rich, author.
Title: The Chicago Cubs : story of a curse / Rich Cohen.
Description: First Edition. | New York : Farrar, Straus and Giroux, [2017] |
    Includes bibliographical references.
Identifiers: LCCN 2017025511 | ISBN 9780374120924 (Hardcover) |
    ISBN 9780374717315 (Ebook)
Subjects: LCSH: Chicago Cubs (Baseball team)—History. | Cohen, Rich.
Classification: LCC GV875.C6 C635 2017 | DDC 796.357/640977311—dc23
LC record available at https://lccn.loc.gov/2017025511

Designed by Abby Kagan
Chapter-opening illustrations by Mark Stutzman

Our books may be purchased in bulk for promotional, educational, or
business use. Please contact your local bookseller or the Macmillan Corporate
and Premium Sales Department at 1-800-221-7945, extension 5442, or by e-mail at
MacmillanSpecialMarkets@macmillan.com.

www.fsgbooks.com
www.twitter.com/fsgbooks • www.facebook.com/fsgbooks

1 3 5 7 9 10 8 6 4 2

TO AARON, NATE, MICAH, AND ELIA,
who will grow up
with the nonsensical idea that
the Chicago Cubs are often a great baseball team

That team will break your heart.

—**Herb Cohen**

CONTENTS

THE CHICAGO CUBS

What you want is always out of reach. Sometimes it's miles out of reach, sometimes you can almost touch it. If you do touch it, you will realize, after a week or two, that it's not really what you want, that what you really want is still out of reach. This is what I was thinking as I arrived at the press window for the first game of the 2016 National League Championship Series. Wrigley Field beneath a Cub-blue sky. Chicago was playing Los Angeles best of seven to determine who would go on to the World Series, which the Cubs had not won since 1908.

Sports Illustrated had gotten me a press pass. I had written several stories about the Cubs for the magazine, but I'm not really a sports reporter. I did not know the etiquette. I dressed as I'd always dressed for a Cubs game—like a Cubs fan. At the window, before issuing my credential, the woman behind the glass said, "Take that off."

"Take what off?"

"The Cubs hat."

"Why?"

"Because you're a reporter—you're supposed to be neutral."

"I'm not neutral," I said. "I haven't been neutral since third grade."

"If you want your credential," she said, "take it off. There's no rooting in the press box."

I went to my first game when I was eight years old. My favorite part was coming out of the tunnel, the field stretched before me as the grasslands must have stretched before the first trapper to make it beyond the Alleghenies. Something about all that greenery in the middle of the city. Only when you see it do you realize it's what you've been craving. But what really got me was the players, scattered, playing long toss, the way they threw, how the ball exploded from their hands. If I can ever do anything that well, I told myself, I'll be happy.

My pass got me onto the field. I'd never been at Wrigley this late in the season. Every other year, save a handful, the Cubs were basically done by late September. The field was crowded with reporters and celebrities. They gossiped and schmoozed but got quiet when Kris Bryant, the Chicago third baseman, went into the batting cage. Bryant had just finished his second big league season. He'd won the Rookie of the Year in his first and would win the MVP for 2016. He's lanky and lean, with bright blue eyes, and he smiles all the time. He learned to hit from his father, a minor leaguer who never made it, who'd himself learned from Ted Williams. In Bryant, you see the end of a chain that goes back to a golden age. He bends his knees at the plate, watching the ball all the way to the end of his bat. He swings from his heels, grinning as he makes contact. People in the left-field bleachers call to fans in the street, "Bryant's up." Dozens assemble, adults who have brought their gloves, hoping to snag one of the monster shots he sends onto Waveland Avenue.

I ran into Theo Epstein, the forty-two-year-old president of the Cubs, the man who'd built the team into a contender. Epstein is a star, having taken over as general manager of the Boston Red Sox when he was just twenty-eight and leading them to their first championship in eighty-six years. In 2011, he moved on to Chicago as a climber will move from Everest to K2. If he won here, he'd have beaten the game's two most storied curses. Yet it was different. He's from Boston and grew up a Red Sox fan—a local boy made good. He arrived in Chicago as an outsider. Winning with him would be just as sweet but not quite as pure. Why had it taken a Red Sox fan to finally turn the Cubs around?

He was making his way through the crowd, chatting and shaking hands. He's sharp faced, as fit as one of his players, with dark hair buzzed at the sides and dark, intelligent eyes. He shook my hand. I know his father, Leslie, a terrific novelist. We talked. I said, "They made me take off my Cubs hat."

"Who did?"

"The people at the press window."

"Where is it now?" he asked.

"In my bag."

"Keep it in your lap as we play," he said. "If things go wrong, you can squeeze it for luck."

■ ■ ■

The press box is above home plate at Wrigley Field, a two-story glassed-in booth with long tables and enough seats to accommodate a few hundred reporters. The ambience has not changed much since the 1932 World Series, when Babe Ruth supposedly pointed to center field, then hit a home run to the exact place he had been pointing—the famous called shot. The last time I'd been here it was empty. Now it was packed, with over a dozen reporters from Japan alone. I ended up in the "auxiliary press box," a section of seats in the grandstand up near the rafters on the left-field line.

Jon Lester was the Cubs' starting pitcher. He has a mean game face, bald and bearded; he's a bulldog, a left-handed ace. He kept the Dodgers off the bases—the Cubs took an early lead. They were ahead 3 to 1 in the eighth inning, but, as all true Cubs fans know, this is the witching hour, the time when everything goes to hell, when a routine grounder slips through Leon Durham's legs, when Steve Bartman, the fan seated along left field, goes for the foul ball. Just like that, the Dodgers loaded the bases, the air leaked out of the balloon. You could hear it whine. Joe Maddon, the Cubs' manager, brought in his reliever, Aroldis Chapman, a big Cuban who throws in excess of 100 mph. He struck out two batters, but the third man hit the ball into the gap, driving in two runs.

The game was tied—but that's not how it felt to me. It felt as if we were a dozen runs behind and the cause was hopelessly lost and the slaughter rule would have to be invoked. What can I say? It's the nature of my condition, the disease incubated by forty summers at Wrigley Field. I am a Cubs fan. I get to the park expecting to lose, curious only about how it will happen. But the fans in the upper deck that night, especially those under thirty, did not seem downcast or forlorn. In fact, more than a few seemed confident, even happy. They began to chant. I could not make it out at first. Then I could: "We don't quit! We don't quit! We don't quit!" I laughed. Those fools! I said to myself. Do they know nothing of history? We do quit. That's who we are. We are the team that has not won a championship in 108 years, that is often eliminated from the playoffs by late August, that always finds a way to not get it done. Woebegone, befuddled, bewildered. We are the Cubs.

Being a Cubs fan has created my cast of mind. I am not unhappy; I am fatalistic. I know how to live in the moment. I know how to enjoy what I can while I can because I know that disaster is coming. It started with that first game my father took me to when I was eight. 1976. The Cubs were terrible. August, so humid the sky was weeping. The Cubs were playing the great Cincinnati Reds, the Big Red Machine. I do not remember the details, only that at some point we were optimistic and ahead and could not lose . . . and then we'd been beaten and it was all over. That was the first time I'd seen a drunk adult, the first time I'd heard a heckler. He was screaming in the left-field bleachers, flecks of peanut at the corners of his mouth, double-fisted, frosty malts sloshing: "Why don't you get a different fuckin' job, Biittner, ya bum!"

Chicago was outhit 11 to 8 and lost 8 to 3—classic Cubs math. We walked to the car in silence. We were on the highway before my father turned to me and said, "I want you to promise me something. I want you to promise me you will not become a Cubs fan."

"Why?"

"Because the Cubs do not win," he explained. "And because of that, a Cubs fan will have a diminished life determined by low expectations. Look at me. I know I am going to succeed. You know why? Because I'm a Yankees fan. We win and expect to win. But a Cubs fan knows he will lose. He's sitting there, waiting for it to happen. He'll settle for less as a result. His team has taught him that all human endeavor ends in failure. That team will screw up your life."

Of course, this left me with only one option. I became the most diehard of diehards, a Cubs fanatic, the biggest fan not only on my street but in my town, which, seeing as it was a Cubs-crazy town, made me among the biggest Cubs fans in the world. I collected the baseball cards and read the books, memorized statistics, hearsay, history. It was not just the team I loved. It was the lore, some worldly, some mystical. At night, as I lay in bed, the names of great players went through my mind like a litany. Cap Anson, Orval Overall, Billy Herman, Eddie Waitkus, who was shot in room 1297A of the Edgewater Beach Hotel by a Baseball Annie.

Though I grew up in the 1970s and 1980s, I could speak with confidence of things that had happened to the team in the 1890s, 1910s, 1920s. I loved the decades when the Cubs were good, but I loved the bad times too. No one I knew had ever seen the Cubs win a World Series. Even the oldest people in my town spoke of it as something from the ancient past, the way they might speak about Mrs. O'Leary's cow or the Republican convention that nominated Abraham Lincoln.

Of course, I fantasized about watching a winning team in Wrigley Field. It was the best place in the world to see a game. A brick-and-ivy jewel—never was new, never gets old. But can you imagine actually seeing a meaningful game there? I longed for a championship, but feared it too. Winning the World Series would change everything. Being a Cubs fan made you different, special, better. Wearing that blue cap told the world that you were holier, had escaped the wheel of profit and loss. The others, obsessed with their trophies and parades, were shallow. We were deep. A Cubs fan understood the futility of ambition. He was a kind of Buddhist. He knew that a different team had won last year and that a different team will win next year, so why the gloating? A Cubs fan learns to enjoy those moments of respite, when the world stands before him in all its beauty—bases empty, two outs, Rick Reuschel cruising. A Cubs fan appreciates every August afternoon, because, for him, there is no October. In other words, my father was right. The Cubs ruined me. But what do you expect? Everyone knows that team had been cursed.

■ ■ ■

I'm not sure how much of this is true, so bear with me. It's lore. In 1934, a flatbed truck that was carrying goats to the stockyards hit a root buckle, sending a baby goat onto the road, where it was found by a cop, who brought it into a bar on Madison Street. By the end of the day, William Sianis, the owner of the bar, was feeding the goat from a baby bottle. He changed the name of his joint to the Billy Goat Tavern. Tethered inside the front door, the billy goat, now called Murphy, ate peanuts and drank beer. Sianis took Murphy to events all over the city—political rallies, hockey games—in hopes of being written up, getting publicity.

The Cubs reached the World Series in 1945—that was the last

time. Game 4 was played at Wrigley Field. Sianis got two tickets, one for him, one for the goat. There are pictures of Murphy in line, a blanket thrown across his back that reads WE GOT DETROIT'S GOAT. So far, so good. The trouble began when Sianis and Murphy took their seats: box 65, tier 12, seats 6 and 7. There were complaints. It grew into a dispute, which was taken to an usher, carried to another employee, then brought to the executive suite, where P. K. Wrigley, the owner of the franchise, decided the tavern owner could stay but the goat had to go. Asked for a reason, Wrigley told Sianis, "Because your goat smells."

Sianis issued the famous curse that night: As long as the goat is not allowed into the park, the Cubs will not win. The team lost the 1945 World Series in seven games. Sianis sent Wrigley a telegram. It posed a question that has haunted Cubs fans ever since: "Who smells now?"

At first, the curse was regarded as a joke, but over time people began to wonder. The strange turns that kept the team out of the postseason, many of them occurring in strange ways, demanded explanation. In September 1950, after yet another dispiriting season, Wrigley wrote to Sianis, begging forgiveness. "Please extend to [the goat] my most sincere and abject apologies . . . and ask him to not only remove the 'Hex' but to reverse the flow and start pulling for us." The curse was finally lifted by Sianis in 1969, then lifted again by Sianis's nephew Sam in 1973, but of course the original billy goat was dead by then. In 1984, Dallas Green, the Cubs' general manager, asked Sam Sianis, who took over when his uncle died, to remove the hex for good. "All is forgiven," said Green. "Please bring the goat." In 1994, when the Cubs got off to a 3–9 start, manager Tom Trebelhorn had the greatest Cub of all, Ernie Banks, walk along the warning track with Sam Sianis and his new goat, Socrates, beside a procession of chanting monks. The team finished in last place.

Which raises a question: Do we really believe in a curse? Do I really believe in a curse? Of course not. I'm a monotheist, a modern. I take no truck with voodoo goblins and affronted goats. And yet there really is no way to look at Cubs history without asking the question: Are we cursed? Maybe belief in the curse is the curse. Maybe it's the mind-set that has hexed the team. It's been a ready-made excuse, a way for players and owners to explain away failure. It did not even start with Sianis and Murphy. It actually goes back much farther, to the beginning of the franchise.

You began to see them everywhere—T-shirts and hoodies and hats, all making reference to 1908, the last year the Chicago Cubs won the World Series. They began to proliferate after the 2008 season. Many fans expected the Cubs to win that year, if only for the bloody logic of it. A hundred years in the wilderness seemed like enough. Cubs announcer Jack Brickhouse had famously said, "Any team can have a bad century." Well, we were past that now, into a second hundred years. No one had ever been this bad this long, and there was a need to describe that misery in numbers.

I saw the first shirt at Wrigley Field in 2009. A kid was wearing it as he walked with his father along the concourse. It shocked me, which is why I fixed on it. Across the top, in huge letters: CHICAGO CUBS, WORLD CHAMPIONS. In smaller letters below: 1908. It made me see the absurdity of my situation.

One day, my son came to breakfast in a shirt that said DON'T HATE ON '08. I didn't buy it for him; these things just seem to materialize. Of course, to my son and hundreds of thousands of other fans, it was a gag, a joke. It was like a late-night comic saying, "You're like Johnny Carson, you're so old." Because they are dumb and have no idea what 1908 really means. Broadcasters tried to explain it by talking about some of the things the game did not have when the Cubs last won a championship—television, airplanes—but that too missed the point. The year 1908 is not just a marker, a place of origin. Not just the distant shore, the world we left behind. It's a story of its own.

The Cubs were first known as the White Stockings, a charter member of the National League in 1876. On the positive side, that team won six of the first eleven pennants. On the negative, that team, specifically its leader and star, Cap Anson, established the color line that was to segregate baseball until 1947. Anson did it by refusing to let his team play if there were any black athletes on the field. Many consider this—the game's original sin—as the true source of the curse.

In 1905, the franchise, which had been owned by Albert Spalding, the great pitcher, was purchased by the sportswriter Charlie Murphy for $125,000. Murphy borrowed a lot of that money from Charles Taft, a Cincinnati financier and the half brother of William Howard Taft, who'd soon become president. The team, which had been called the Orphans and the Remnants, had been struggling, but began to improve almost as soon as Murphy took over. Because the new owner was Irish, reporters started calling them the Spuds. It bothered Murphy, city officials, fans. It felt like a slur. Then, one morning, as *The Chicago Daily News* was about to go to press, a publisher came into the newsroom and told the sports editor to change the headline—"Spuds" is offensive. Needing a word to fit the space, the editor switched Spuds to Cubs.

The name stuck because it expressed the character of the team. Cute and small but showing signs of ferocity. It began with manager Frank Selee, whom Murphy hired away from the Boston Beaneaters, where he'd won five National League pennants. Selee, a forerunner to the modern front-office guru, was short, more bald than not, with an impressive handlebar mustache. Though he never made it in the majors himself, he had a preternatural ability to spot talent. He would stand near the field, watching practice. After ten minutes, he could tell who should be in, who should be out, and where each person should play. As soon as he arrived in Chicago, he began putting together the pieces of one of the greatest teams of all time. When you see a kid in that 1908 T-shirt, that's what you're seeing—the legacy of Frank Selee.

That team did not play in Wrigley Field—they played in Chicago's first great temple to the game, the West Side Grounds at South Wolcott and West Polk. It was the latest in modern ballpark construction, brick and steel, a lyric bandbox, eccentric, less like Wrigley Field, which is all about symmetry, than like the Polo Grounds in New York, where the field was stuffed into a container that did not want it—a diamond in a rectangle. It meant a ridiculously short home run (216 feet) if you hit the ball down the line and an astonishing long home run (535 feet) if you went dead center. Sixteen thousand people could fit in the West Side Grounds. More watched from the rooftops across Polk

Street. There were eighteen luxury boxes—soft chairs, a velvet curtain to close out the sun and the dark-hatted masses. For two generations, Chicago baseball meant the West Side Grounds. It's where thousands of fans learned that it's thrilling to win but clarifying to lose. It's where Ring Lardner became a sports reporter. It's where Albert Spalding tolled a gong when he wanted his manager to change pitchers. It might even have been a model for the most fantastic landscape of all, Emerald City, capital of Oz. In the late 1800s, L. Frank Baum, author of the Oz novels, was living in Humboldt Park, a few blocks from the West Side Grounds. He could see the pennants above the rooftops, hear the cheers when something went right. Now and then, he bought a ticket. The trip from dreary Polk Street through the tunnel into the great green light-filled bowl, where men in uniforms chased each other around the bases trying to get home, is the trip from Kansas to Oz told another way.

Frank Selee built his great team around the shortstop, because the shortstop is the key. He covers the most ground in the infield, takes charge on a double play, chases the fly into shallow left. He needs good hands and a good arm and to be constantly on the move—not fast, but quick, a magician. Selee heard about Joe Tinker when Joe Tinker was playing for the Portland Webfoots of the Pacific Northwest League. He got him for $200, brought him to Chicago for what they used to call a "look-see." He was a hick when he turned up, a face in a Walker Evans photo, redolent of the snowy West—with clear blue eyes, freckles, jug ears. Born in Muscotah, Kansas, in 1880, he learned the game on vacant lots. At sixteen, he was playing for the third-best team in Kansas City—the John Taylors. From there, he went to the Bruce Lumbers, then to the Kansas City Schmeltzers. A scout saw him while looking for someone else—so began his hopscotch through the minors. Denver. Great Falls. Helena. The whistle blows, the engine groans, the train flashes through the outskirts. He was a third baseman in the bush leagues, but Selee moved him to short—because of his hands.

He played 133 games at shortstop for the Cubs in 1902. He was twenty-one. He was joined by twenty-year-old Johnny Evers, who grew up in Troy, New York. Some say Evers was the smallest man to ever play in the majors. Not height, heft. He was of medium height but willowy, as slender as a string. A few teammates refused to play with him, afraid he might be killed in a collision. But Evers turned out to be durable. He was like a piece of iron. Hammer him and nothing happened. (If you see a man that small, you can bet that he's the toughest player on the field.) Recalling his first day with the Cubs, Evers said, "As I climbed aboard [the team bus] the first day, Jack Taylor, the pitcher, looked me over very carefully and cut me to the quick with, 'He'll leave in a box car tonight.' He meant that I wouldn't do at all. Some years later, I must admit, it gave me great pleasure to still be with the Chicago club when Taylor was released, and I refreshed his memory by remarking, 'Well, I'm still here, Jack, and I see you're getting the gate.'"

Evers was the epitome of the "dead-ball era" of the national game, the sport as it had been played before the proliferation of the home run, when the ball was supposedly different and did not have the same jump. It was exceedingly hard to hit out of the park—dead—meaning a team had to make its way by singles and doubles and stolen bases, nickel and dime them to death. It was all about finding holes in the defense—"Hit 'em where they ain't," as Wee Willie Keeler, a star of the era, famously said. It was all about control. Evers held his hands closer to the middle of the bat than the bottom, slapping the ball into the gaps. His face was like his game—tough and small, ridges and bones. He looked angry when he played. He was a screamer and a spiker and hurt players on the base paths. You'd see the slide, then the cloud of dirt, which resolves into Evers throwing punches. He once needed a police escort to get out of Ebbets Field in Brooklyn. He'd thrown a bottle at a heckler but missed and hit a kid. His teammates called him the Crab. By the middle of that rookie season, Tinker and Evers had formed a bond, come to understand each other so intimately that no words were necessary. They'd play together for more than ten years. You can hate a man with all of your heart—they did come to hate each other—but working that perfectly in tandem is a kind of love.

Of course, the real anchor of that infield was Frank Chance. He was bigger than the others, a genuine six footer. He'd come out of the west, a rich kid from Fresno, California. Selee moved him from catcher to first base. Perhaps to compensate for his soft background, Chance made himself into a brawler. (Gentleman Jim Corbett, the heavyweight champion of the world, said Chance was the best amateur fighter he'd ever seen.) Later, when nominating himself as team manager, Chance listed among his qualifications that he could "whip anyone on this club." He played that way too—a right-handed slugger who crowded the plate, daring pitchers to throw inside. It was a tactic that boosted his power and shortened his career. He holds the most gruesome record in Cubs history—hit by pitch 137 times, many of those coming as bean balls (shots to the head). It became a lasting image of Chicago's golden age. Frank Chance, as handsome as a screen star, as perfectly weathered as a beautiful old house, broad shouldered and serene, ten feet off the bag, moving with the pitch.

Two days after Chance debuted at his new position, the infield turned its first double play. A hard grounder scooped up by the shortstop, flipped to the second baseman, who, catching the ball as he crossed the bag, threw to first. Tinker to Evers to Chance. Before it was over, they'd turn hundreds of double plays—other infields turned more, but few looked as good doing it.

If we remember them, it's for the poem, written by the columnist Franklin Pierce Adams, a wounded baseball fan:

> These are the saddest of possible words:
> "Tinker to Evers to Chance."
> Trio of bear cubs, and fleeter than birds,
> Tinker and Evers and Chance.
> Ruthlessly pricking our gonfalon bubble,
> Making a Giant hit into a double—
> Words that are heavy with nothing but trouble:
> "Tinker to Evers to Chance."

Frank Selee planted the seeds, then got sick. The players noticed. He looked a little green around the eyes, black circles turning yellow. Something dragging him down. Even his mustache looked sad. He was told he had consumption. If he wanted to survive, he'd have to move to a better climate, lead a calmer life. He went west, settling in a Colorado sanitarium. But he could not stop thinking about baseball. He pooled his money, found a partner, bought an interest in a minor league team. At first, he was going to enjoy games from a distance, then decided to watch a few from the dugout, then went all in. He died in 1909, forty-nine years old. He was elected to the Baseball Hall of Fame in 1999.

Frank Chance took over as player-manager. This used to be

common—the manager being someone in the lineup. How else could you really know what was going on? It was an arrangement that grew naturally from the sandlots, where the best player, the most ambitious, the player willing to get everyone together, became the captain, then the captain came to be called the manager.

A football coach stalks the sidelines in down coat, sweater vest, sensible pants. Diagramming a play during a time-out, an NBA coach wears Armani. Only in baseball does the head man dress like a player, in stirrups and jersey, as if, at any moment, he might run out there—because the first great managers did in fact lead from the front. The uniforms they wear are a relic from that earlier time. It was the notion of a bench manager that seemed silly. Carry an extra man on the payroll, a man with no function other than to watch from afar? Nuts. When these characters began to turn up in the early 1900s, "bench manager" was a pejorative, like "backseat driver." The earliest were retired players; they could no longer make it on the field, but their leadership was valued. Probably the first modern bench manager—he did not take the job until the National League was twenty years old—was Cap Anson, who led from the bench for a single season in New York. Others followed. Some had been good players; some had hardly played at all. A mediocre player often turned out to be a better manager. A superstar usually can't teach what comes naturally. The biggest busts in managerial history have been some of the best players—Buddy Bell with the Royals, Alan Trammell with the Tigers. Such men, presented with a slumping hitter, might say, "Just hit the fucking ball."

Pete Rose was the last player-manager. I remember when he got the job with the Reds in 1984. It thrilled me. Charlie Hustle returning, at the end of his career, to the city where he'd started so many years before, to break Ty Cobb's all-time hit record. I remember Rose coming out to the mound with a lineup card before the historic game, how rotund he looked in tight white pants. I remember the hit too, number 4,192, a soft liner that bounded when it hit the fake grass, how he raised his arms and how the players, some of them nearly as young as his son, Pete Rose, Jr., whom I later saw play in the minors—he had his father's face and jaw and shape but played just eleven games in the show—swarmed him.

Frank Chance would lead the Cubs from 1905 till 1912. His Cubs teams won 768 games, four National League pennants, and two World Series. And it wasn't just that they won, but how they did it—with smarts and determination, the grittiest kind of small ball. It was as if he'd lent them his hard-nosed personality. These days, after a player singles, you often see him chatting amicably with the opposing first baseman. If Chance caught you doing that, or even shaking hands, you got fined.

He was strict, but also supportive of his players. He followed the oldest code: If you're on a person's side, you stay on that person's side. He became known as "the Peerless Leader." If you read old Chicago newspapers, you see him referred to that way without explanation, as none was needed.

He did more than just manage—he scouted players, suggested trades, and anchored the infield. He was like Theo Epstein if Theo Epstein also played first base and hit fifth. In 1906, Chance made the trade that completed the infield. If you don't remember the name of the acquisition, the third baseman, it's because he was left out of the famous poem. That's the power of light verse.

Harry Steinfeldt didn't follow a traditional path into the majors. No college, no glorious turn on the town team. He started as a performer in Al. G. Field Minstrels instead, singing and playing banjo in blackface in towns around the Southwest. The Minstrels had a ball team that played the best local clubs to drum up publicity. Steinfeldt—he'd grown up in St. Louis—was the standout Minstrel ballplayer. Great arm, great bat, and one of those hard faces that baseball people love, sharp-angled symmetry, a cold stare. Scouts came to see him. His first pro contracts took him to the Houston Magnolias, then to the Fort Worth Panthers, then to the Galveston Sandcrabs. He made his big league debut with Cincinnati in 1898. He was a good player, but people hated him, though no one seems to remember why. Cincinnati wanted to trade him, but word got out. Certain players are seen as locker room poison. But Chance had played with him in the off-season and liked him and was convinced Steinfeldt would be the difference.

He's what we need, Chance told his owner.

Murphy made inquiries, came back. I asked around, he said. Your guy's a disaster. Find someone else.

Chance insisted. It went back and forth. Murphy relented. Steinfeldt joined the Cubs in 1906, when he was twenty-eight years old. Though mostly forgotten, he was probably the best bat on the greatest regular-season team ever, leading the 1906 Cubs in hits and RBIs. As predicted, he completed the infield. Played close to the line at third, in on the grass, pulling would-be triples right out of the air, turning would-be bunt singles into harmless outs. You never again heard a thing about his personality. He'd play six seasons in Chicago. Bill James ranked him the fifty-seventh best third baseman of all time.

Other players:

Ed Reulbach, a right-handed pitcher, turned away from hitters as he went into his motion, hiding the ball behind his raised left leg until the last possible moment. For a hitter, the ball seemed to vanish, then reappear. This technique, later mastered by Fernando Valenzuela and Rick Sutcliffe, is known as "shadowing." It made Reulbach—"Big Ed"—one of the game's best pitchers. He led the National League in winning percentage in 1906, 1907, 1908. He threw forty-four consecutive scoreless innings in 1908, setting an NL record. But now and then, his control vanished. Observers said it was terrible, like watching a person forget how to walk. One moment, he's cruising, then he can't find the plate. Reulbach later said it was not his arm but his eyes. He was short-sighted and could usually get along squinting, but when the twilight shadows covered the grounds, the world beyond the mound turned into a blur. At such times, he was hurling the pill into the void, hoping for the best.

Jack Pfiester, a left-handed pitcher, was often tapped to shut down teams stocked with left-handed power. His fastball was so-so but he had a beautiful curve, one of those slow-breaking lollipops that hang before diving in for a strike. Pfiester had soft blue eyes and a smile that broke as slowly as his curve, a superior smile that made opponents want to open his skull with a baseball bat. In 1906, his ERA was 1.51. If you don't know baseball stats, that means, in the course of nine innings, he'd often give up no more than a run. If you got two men across when Pfiester was on the mound, you were probably going to win. He snapped a tendon in his throwing arm in 1908 and was sent to see the medical guru Bonesetter Reese. He was still good after that, but never as good.

Johnny Kling was the Cubs' catcher from 1900 to 1910. He'd been a playground legend in Kansas City, the sort of kid other kids invoke to end an argument. "That's not how Johnny Kling does it!" Even in old pictures, he looks modern, dark eyed, clean-cut, handsome. Kling deserves as much credit as anyone else. When he played, the Cubs won. When he didn't, they stumbled. It was the way he handled pitchers, worked batters, exploited weaknesses. There's the game, then the game inside the game—signals and motions, the catcher racing to the mound to cool down the spooked hurler. Base runners were cautious when Kling was behind the plate. He had a rocket arm and was the first catcher to consistently pick players off at first.

He created the look of the modern catcher just as much as Johnny Unitas created the look of the modern quarterback. He was the first big leaguer to throw from a crouch. He said he'd learned the trick from the Negro League catcher Buddy Petway. Because of Kling, we imagine the catcher on his shanks, glove held out as a target, lip fat with chew, hat backward, yelling through his wire mask. He loved mind games and was constantly yammering at batters. They knew him as Noisy Johnny. *Careful, Cy. Ed's wild today. I'm calling pitches, but, to be honest, I have no idea where it's going.* They also called him the Jew—because he either was Jewish or he married a Jew. Asked to name the best players he'd ever seen, Johnny Evers listed Ty Cobb, Honus Wagner, Christy Mathewson, and, of course, the Jew.

But that Cubs team is remembered less for its individuals than as a group. Tinker, Evers, and Chance went into the Hall of Fame as a unit, as if one player. There's nothing else like it in Cooperstown. They were masters at killing rallies, then manufacturing the single run needed to win. 1906, 1907, 1908. High summer in dead ball. Low-scoring games were the rule. In part because of the pitching—what was legal that would soon become illegal.

Pitchers were allowed to doctor the ball in pretty much any way they wanted. The spitter was legal. You'd cover one side of the ball with snot or some other slick substance—Vaseline, tobacco juice—then snap it on release. The resulting spin, and thus the path of the ball, was unpredictable even to the pitcher. Also in regular use: the shine ball, the emery ball, the mud ball. What's more, umpires had been told to keep a ball in play for as long as possible. The same ball might be in use for an entire game. By the middle innings, it was dingy, as brown as the infield dirt. By late in the game, it could be impossible to see the spit-covered rock as it hurtled toward you. And no stadium lights, which meant playing in the summer rain, in the gloaming, the ball crossing in semidarkness.

Low scores resulted. Games progressed like soccer matches, knotted deep into extra innings. To a modern fan, it sounds boring. We've grown fat in our home-run-drunk age. In fact, many people who experienced both that game and the game that followed said the dead-ball era was superior. Because there was desperation in every play, because the action was almost always taut, because the need to manufacture runs drove players to creative extremes. A lot of watching modern baseball is waiting. And eating. And walking to the bathroom. And waiting. And making a second trip to the bathroom, standing over the trough. Waving down the beer guy. Passing greasy bills to the peanut man. And waiting. And hoping. And screaming, "Let's Go Cubs!" And waiting. It was different then, because the score was almost always close and a plan was almost always afoot—a steal, a double steal, a delayed steal, the hidden-ball trick.

Christy Mathewson, the Giants' dead-ball-era ace, said a baseball game usually comes down to a handful of plays, maybe even a single play when the fate of the afternoon is determined. He called this moment "the pinch," which is why he called his memoir *Pitching in a Pinch*. Forget all the other innings—what matters is how you do when the decisive moment comes around. It's where we get the term "pinch hitter." That's whom you ask to get it done when it most needs doing. The Frank Chance Cubs dominated because they were the best team in the pinch. It was all about the infield working as a team, creeping in with the pitch, not conceding a single run.

What connects the 2016 Cubs to those earlier teams, what defines a franchise? In Chicago, it's always been about the infielders, a tradition that includes Addison Russell and Ryne Sandberg and Ernie Banks but started with Steinfeldt, Tinker, Evers, Chance. Whenever the Cubs have been good, they've played great defense. The entire Cubs infield started the 2016 All-Star Game. Ditto 1969. There was no All-Star Game in 1906, 1907, 1908, but most of that infield is in the Hall of Fame. And yet there's an interesting difference between 1906 and 2016—interesting because it says as much about changes in the culture as about changes in the game. Kris Bryant is currently at third base. Addison Russell is at shortstop. Javier Báez often at second. Anthony Rizzo at first. We're told that infield excels because they're great players but also because they have great chemistry. They love one another. If you watch that team, you've probably noticed how they're constantly smiling and touching. Their acrobatics are powered by affection. Steinfeldt, Tinker, Evers, and Chance were powered by antipathy, the extreme example being the shortstop and the second baseman. Despite playing side by side for years, despite turning all those double plays, they did not speak for decades. It started before an exhibition game in Indiana. The Cubs were supposed to share taxis to the ballpark. As a group of them waited in front of the hotel, Evers hopped into a cab by himself, slammed the door, took off. It irked Tinker, who confronted Evers in the clubhouse. Words were exchanged. A few hours later, on the afternoon of September 12, 1905, they got into a fistfight on the field.

Tinker pulled Evers aside the next day. "If you and I talk to each other, we're only going to be fighting all the time," he told the second baseman, "so don't talk to me, and I won't talk to you. You play your position and I'll play mine, and let it go at that."

"That suits me," Evers said.

■ ■ ■

What put the Cubs over the top, what made that team go supersonic?

Everyone worth asking gives the same answer. It was the crippled kid from Indiana, the mangled boy. He turned up in 1904, calm and doe-eyed with that wreck of a right hand, and it was blastoff . . .

The bad thing happened when he was five years old. He was at his uncle's farm in Nyesville, Indiana—flat country, ringed by fields—helping his brother load wheat into a reaper. The gears clogged. The boy reached in to clear the machine, sending the blades back into motion. His index finger, middle finger, and ring finger were sliced, left hanging by shreds of skin.

The boy's name was Mordecai Peter Centennial Brown— Centennial because he'd been born in 1876. He held the ruin of his right hand in his left as his uncle harnessed the horses for the ride to town. The uncle later said the boy "showed all kinds of bravery" as he waited. He was treated by a Dr. Gillum, who'd been a field surgeon during the Civil War. He'd seen worse. And still, a small boy with a mangled hand, three of five fingers severed. The doctor removed what remained of the index finger—no saving it—but was able to reattach the others. He bandaged the hand, then sent the boy home, telling him to leave it till the next appointment.

A few weeks later, Mordecai and his sister were playing with a pet rabbit, bathing it in an iron tub. "I was making it swim," Brown said later. "Suddenly I lost my balance and tumbled into the tub, my right hand smashing the bottom, breaking six bones, although I didn't know it then. 'Don't tell Dad,' I warned my sister, because I knew he'd tan me good and plenty. She promised and we rebandaged the hand any old way."

When Dr. Gillum removed the bandage, the fingers, having set improperly, were chaotically askew. What a mess! A nub plus four twisted fingers. There's been nothing to match that hand in baseball. It would become a kind of wonder, shown in the newspapers, diagrammed, explained. He was told to forget sports. How can you throw with fingers like that? He practiced just the same, taught himself in the field behind his house. He set up pine planks along the fence, counted off sixty feet six inches, turned and threw rocks, aimed for the knots, trying to drive them out of the planks. "If you can't afford to buy a ball, make one, use a potato, or anything that is round and weighs about the same as a baseball," Brown said later. "You can learn control with a potato or a turnip just as well as with an ordinary ball."

When he was fourteen, he quit school and went to work in the mine. His hand disqualified him from heavy labor. He became a checker, keeping a tally of every bit of mineral that came out of the ground. And he played for the company baseball team, rough, competitive games against teams from other mines, mills, and factories. It was the protozoan pond scum from which all professional sports emerged. Factory leagues with ringers, hometown umps, rickety bleachers filled with drunken crowds. The team captain used Brown only if he was short a player. When Brown played third base, he threw with a wicked spin, the natural and unavoidable effect of those misshapen fingers. It drove the first baseman nuts.

Legs O'Connell, an old-time veteran of bush league baseball then working in the mine, was fascinated by Brown and the spin he put on every ball without trying. He knew what it could mean if he were pitching. "He took a liking to young Brown and undertook the job of tutoring him in baseball," Ed Burkholder wrote in *Sport* magazine in 1953. "[O'Connell's] home was near the mine, and each day after work he would take Brown to his home and have him practice throwing the ball."

"If it hadn't been for Legs, I would never have been anything more than a water-boy or a mascot for a ball club," Brown said. "He was a hard teacher but he taught me how to overcome the handicap of my fingers and even put them to great advantage."

It has the contours of a fairy tale. The old ballplayer and the crippled boy playing catch in the fading light of an Indiana town. Brown threw sidearm, his knuckles nearly scraping the dirt, the ball released with a devastating spin. "Unlike other pitchers who used their thumb and index finger to apply pressure to the ball, Miner Brown spun his pitches off his awkward middle finger, causing the ball to sink and fade away from the batter," Cindy Thomson and Scott Brown write in *Three Finger: The Mordecai Brown Story*. "Some say he threw a natural knuckleball or a sinker, but the pitch he threw is difficult to describe. With fingers that gave Mordecai a grip that couldn't be duplicated, the ball likely tailed in such a fashion that batters had never seen before."

O'Connell spoke to the captain of the company team, but he refused to let Brown pitch. According to *Sport*, his big break finally came on July 17, 1898. The starting pitcher tripped while fielding a bunt, fracturing his arm. O'Connell said, "Give Brown a chance. He'll win the game for you." Brown shut down the other team—Brazil, Indiana—not letting a runner reach base for five innings. In the course of an afternoon, he became a local legend. A good player is prized, but a good player with a great story is beloved. He was recruited by a semipro team, then a bush league team. By the time he was called to the Class B team in Terre Haute, he was known as the Miner, or as Miner Brown, or as Three Finger Brown.

He made his major league debut with St. Louis in 1903. To many, he was a freak. Frank Chance saw his greatness right away. "Those three fingers of his put something on the ball that completely fooled us," he explained. The Cubs acquired Brown in an off-season trade. He made his first start in the West Side Grounds the following spring. He did not look like much. Short and doughy, a bland, forgettable face. He threw a fastball—he called it the speedy one—but its main purpose was to set up his array of junk—curveballs and sinkers. His best pitch was akin to a modern knuckle curve. It came in slow, looked fat and hittable just before it dropped into the dirt. Brown called it the hook. "Brown pitches the 'hook' overhand, releasing the ball at various points after his hand swings past his body," John Evers wrote in his memoir, *Touching Second*, published in 1910. "By the point at which he releases the ball he regulates the point at which it breaks in the air. He can make the ball either describe a wide fast arc, or by jerking his hand at the proper instant, make the ball go almost a straight line, perhaps fifty feet, and then dart suddenly down and outward."

"It was a great ball, that down-curve of his," Ty Cobb said. "I can't talk about all of baseball, but I can say this: It was the most deceiving, the most devastating pitch I ever faced."

Most of Brown's effects came naturally, from the shape of his hand. He couldn't not put spin on everything he threw. In a sense, any pitcher throwing junk is imitating grips perfected of necessity by Mordecai Brown. The great stylists of the game are replicating the Miner's deformity, even if they don't know it. What Brown could not achieve just by throwing, he accomplished by pushing his mangled fingers into even more distorted positions. It caused him tremendous pain, which he admitted only later. It hurt every time he threw, his great effects, like the effects of all great artists, achieved through bad luck, toil, and suffering. "Few persons ever knew what pain [these pitches] caused Brown," Randy Roberts and Carson Cunningham write in *Before the Curse: The Chicago Cubs' Glory Years*. "His forefinger, stiff and twisted, had to be bent back almost to the breaking point to get a firm grip on the ball."

Brown was 15–10 in his first season as a Cub, with a 1.86 ERA. He went 18–12 in 1905, then put together six straight twenty-win seasons. He'd go on to win 239 major league games. He should have been happy. They'd laughed at him. They'd said he would never even play for the company team. And look where he was! Look how far he'd come! He should have been happy, but was not. There was pathos in Miner Brown, a sadness that radiates from every picture taken of him on the mound. He did not celebrate what he'd accomplished with what he'd been given but mourned what he might have accomplished had he not been so unlucky. "Much has been written about the part my deformed fingers played in my career," he told a reporter. "Undoubtedly, they did have much to do with curves. I couldn't throw any other kind of ball. Yet those fingers were a tremendous handicap. Few know the excruciating pain I suffered when I had to grip the ball in certain ways. I always felt if I had had a normal hand, I would have been a great pitcher."

■ ■ ■

In 1906 and 1907, the Cubs blew through the National League, clinching the pennant weeks before the end of each season. In 1906, they posted the greatest season in baseball history (116–36) but lost the World Series to the White Sox. In 1907, they beat Detroit to win one of only three World Series in the life of the franchise. Which brings us back to the DON'T HATE ON '08 T-shirt. That's the season we invoke because it's the last time the Cubs won a championship and because it was the most exciting season ever played. The pennant race went wire to wire, with three teams—Chicago, Pittsburgh, New York—battling for first place.

On September 23, the Cubs played the Giants in the Polo Grounds. The stadium covered several acres between 155th and 157th Streets in upper Manhattan, along Eighth Avenue. It was torn down in 1964, but for generations it was a temple of the game, horseshoe shaped, beside the Harlem River. There was always a crowd in the street on game day, the elevated train raining down sparks. The stadium sat beside a great palisade: Coogan's Bluff, where hundreds gathered to watch from a distance.

The Cubs were a game behind New York. Christy Mathewson was pitching for the Giants. Matty, as he was known. Big and blond, well-spoken, a Bucknell graduate, a kind of Doc Holliday, a gentleman who'd fallen in among gunfighters. He'd be a charter inductee into the Baseball Hall of Fame—one of the first five picked. He dominated with all kinds of stuff but was most famous for his fadeaway pitch, a screwball that he saved for the pinch. It hurt so much to throw, he'd use it only if absolutely necessary. Fans called him "the Big Six," though no one is exactly sure why. It might've started with the sportswriter Sam Crane, who likened Mathewson to the Big Six company of the New York Fire Department, "the fastest to put out a blaze." Mathewson was theatrical. "He'd always wait until about ten minutes before game time," Brown said. "Then he'd come from the clubhouse across the field in a long linen duster like auto drivers wore in those days, and at every step the crowd would yell louder and louder."

The game started as a classic pitchers' duel. Hitters came up, hitters sat down. In the fourth inning, the Cubs broke through in a spectacular way. Tinker, normally a middling batter, always did well against Mathewson. The Big Six pitched him away, but Tinker reached out and got hold of a ball and drove it into center field. Mike Donlin, believing he could make the play, charged— he dove and missed and the ball shot past, rolling all the way to the fence. Meanwhile, there was Tinker, flying around the bases, sliding into home in a huge cloud of dust. An inside-the-park home run. Cubs 1, Giants 0.

Jack Pfiester was pitching for Chicago. He was good that day, not great. Giants outfielder Buck Herzog hit a ground ball to third. Steinfeldt, in a rush to make the play, threw wild. Donlin singled and Herzog scored. Cubs 1, Giants 1.

Then it was the bottom of the ninth, the hordes leaning on the rails, topcoats and bowlers, Coogan's Bluff. Dusk. Moose McCormick singled with two outs. That brought up Fred Merkle, who was playing for injured Giant's first baseman Fred Tenney. Merkle was nineteen years old, a Wisconsin kid in his first full season. He played in only thirty-eight games that year—he'd been sick, poisoned by the blue dye in his cheap baseball socks. It got into his blood and swelled up his foot. It could have killed him. In other words, Fred Merkle was having a bad year even before this happened.

He worked the pitcher, extended the count, sent foul balls into the seats, fans scrambling. When he finally got a decent pitch, he hit it into right. McCormick, who'd been running with the throw, made it to third. The stadium erupted, paper raining down from the upper deck. This is why baseball is never captured in highlights. As an individual play, that hit would not have been much. It's the context that makes it exciting—all that waiting, the tension building, then the release.

The umpire raised his arm, calling time. He had to shout to be heard. You don't notice the umpire until you want to send him a bottle of champagne, or have him killed. Hank O'Day, in navy blue, hands on his knees, set up behind the plate. He had connections to both teams. He'd been born in Chicago and grew up watching the Cubs, but had played for the Giants. He'd been gregarious in his playing days but had since entered the monastic order of umps. "These men in blue travel by themselves," Mathewson wrote, "live at obscure hotels apart from those at which the teams stop, and slip into the ball parks unobtrusively just before game time. They never make friends with the ball-players off the field for fear that there might be hint of scandal. Seldom do they take the same train with a club unless it cannot be avoided." Mathewson described O'Day as the stubborn kind of ump. "He is bullheaded. If a manager gets after him for a decision, he is likely to go up in the air and, not meaning to do it, call close ones against the club that has made the kick, for it must be remembered that umpires are only 'poor weak mortals after all.'"

O'Day dropped his arm.

Play ball!

First and third, two outs. Like a familiar chess scenario, a situation that occurs again and again, that's been gamed out, studied. It drew special notice from O'Day, because it represented a repetition, a chance for a do-over.

Two weeks earlier, at Exposition Field in Pittsburgh, O'Day had been umping during a nearly identical situation. Cubs versus Pirates, bases loaded, score tied, two outs, bottom of the tenth. Chief Wilson, Pittsburgh's Native American shortstop—in those days, any player with any Indian heritage was called "Chief"— singled. When the lead runner crossed home, the fans poured onto the field. The runner on first, Doc Gill, went halfway to second base, then, seeing the mob, dashed for the clubhouse. This had been a common practice. To avoid mayhem, runners broke off as soon as the lead runner crossed home and the winning run had seemingly been scored. Like a walk-off single. Johnny Evers screamed at the umps—on a force play, when the infielder merely has to touch second to get the out, the run does not count until the man on first completes the play by reaching second. Which Doc Gill never did. Evers got the ball and stepped on the bag for what should have been the third out of the inning, but O'Day had already left the field. Evers chased him down, shouting, "It's not over."

"It's finished," said O'Day. "Even if you made the play, the throw could never have beaten the [lead] runner."

"It doesn't matter if it beat the runner," said Evers. "Gill never touched second. It's a force out. The run doesn't count."

"You're wasting your time," said O'Day.

But O'Day could not stop thinking about it—thinking, considering, reconsidering. Evers was right. The run shouldn't have counted.

Now back to September 23, Polo Grounds, Cubs versus Giants. New York shortstop Al Bridwell came to the plate. Moose McCormick, the potential game-winning run, was on third, Fred Merkle on first, Pfiester pitching. Pfiester was tired—had been out there for hours. He hung a curve. Bridwell hammered it. McCormick raced in from third, scoring the winning run. Giants fans poured onto the field. Merkle, seeing the mob, broke off between first and second and ran for the clubhouse. Meanwhile, O'Day stayed in position, watching and waiting.

Evers screamed to Cubs center fielder Solly Hofman—*Gimme the ball. Gimme the goddamn ball.* "I had my eye on [Merkle], saw him stop, glance around at the fans pouring out of their seats, and start for the clubhouse," Evers explained. Hofman threw the ball in from the outfield, but sailed it. It went past Tinker and bounced. Giants pitcher Joe McGinnity, called "the Iron Man"—because he was big and durable and because he had worked in a foundry—knew what Evers was up to. "He got [the ball] first," Evers said, "but before he could get rid of the thing, [Tinker] and I had him and we wrestled around there for what seemed to be five minutes."

O'Day watched as fans streamed past on their way to the dugout, where they hoisted Mathewson on their shoulders for a triumphal parade. McGinnity got the ball, stood up, reared back, and heaved it. He later said he believed he'd thrown it out of the park, but Evers swears he found the fan who'd picked it up in center field. "I can see the fellow who caught it yet," Evers remembered, "a tall, stringy, middle-aged gent with a brown bowler hat on."

Evers asked for the ball. When the man refused, Rube Kroh, a Cubs pitcher, "hit [him] right on top of that stiff hat," Evers said, "drove it down over his eyes and as the gent folded up, the ball fell free."

Evers raced in from the outfield, weaving through fans, waving to O'Day, who watched as the Cubs infielder stepped on second. O'Day shouted, *Yer out! That's three! The run does not count. Score tied. Score tied. Game continues.*

O'Day went through the crowd, explaining. "For two hundred feet he walked through a raging mob, telling them the run did not count, while they shrieked, struck at him, pulled him and threatened his life," Evers writes. It was "one of the greatest examples of individual heroism the game has known."

Finally accepting that the game could not continue—a squad of police were in the infield, battling the mob—O'Day called for a postponement. Frank Chance, jersey covered with dirt and blood, shouted in O'Day's ear, making the case that, as the home team, the Giants were responsible for the condition of the field— the Cubs should therefore win by forfeit. O'Day said no, the league office would have to decide.

The decisive play, or failure to make that play, became known as Merkle's Boner, the most famous screwup in baseball history. Fred Merkle was only nineteen. He had a long major league career ahead of him. He'd play for several teams, including the Cubs. He would eventually become dignified and old. He'd see many things and go many places, but he would always be known for that one moment. It tagged him and he stayed tagged. "Merkle's Boner" was a newspaper headline that ruined his life.

When Merkle realized what had happened, he tried to quit the Giants. "I did not know at first what it was all about," he said, "but the meaning of it all suddenly dawned upon me, and I wished that a large, roomy, and comfortable hole would open up and swallow me."

"Lose me," Merkle told manager John McGraw. "I'm the jinx."

McGraw refused. "You stick," he said.

"Merkle moped," Mathewson wrote. "He lost flesh, and time after time begged McGraw to send him to a minor league or to turn him loose altogether, but McGraw just kept saying, 'You stick.'"

As word of O'Day's decision spread through the Polo Grounds, the crowd turned into a menace. "Rioting and wild disorder in which spectators and players joined, causing a scene never witnessed in New York before, marked the conclusion at the Polo Grounds yesterday of the game between the Giants and the Cubs," *The New York Herald* reported. "When hundreds of drunk and angry Giants fans learned what Chance and the Cubs were trying to pull, they headed for the Chicago clubhouse, intent on revenge."

The Cubs barricaded themselves in. Stunned to nervous silence, they changed into street clothes and were led out by a phalanx of New York police.

Late that night, after the crowds had gone, McGraw sent Merkle back out onto the field to step on second. That way, if they ask, you can say you touched it without having to lie.

The hearing was led by Harry Pulliam, president of the National League. Pulliam, who'd organized the first World Series, was a high-strung melancholic. The son of a Kentucky tobacco farmer, he wore candy-striped shirts that hid a deeply troubled heart. He formed a three-person panel to investigate and decide. Players testified, umps and managers. "Only one man in the whole Giants team told the truth," Mordecai Brown said. "Mathewson said Merkle positively did not touch second. That was the kind of fellow Mathewson was . . . a wonderful pitcher and a square fellow."

John McGraw pointed out the absurdity—regardless, there was no way the throw could have beaten the lead base runner. The Giants had won the game. Two panelists agreed, but the decision had to be unanimous. O'Day's ruling stood. It was a tie. The game would be replayed at the end of the season if necessary.

Merkle's Boner would have been forgotten had the Pirates beaten the Cubs on October 4, 1908. By winning that game, Chicago knocked Pittsburgh out and tied the Giants. The Merkle Game would have to be replayed. The National League Pennant would go to the winning team, who would then face the Tigers in the World Series. A huge crowd saw the Cubs off at Lake Shore Station. The team boarded the 20th Century Limited, the fast train to New York. The cars were swarmed when the train stopped in Elkhart, Indiana, 112 miles southeast of Chicago. The people there called for Miner Brown. He finally emerged. They demanded to see the hand—the mangled hand. He raised it slowly, somberly, showing his wounds as if they were stigmata.

■ ■ ■

In *Pitching in a Pinch*, Christy Mathewson begins his section on that one-game playoff with the most bravura—and longest— sentence ever written by a starting pitcher:

The New York Giants and the Chicago Cubs played a game at the Polo Grounds on October 8, 1908, which decided the championship of the National League in one afternoon, which was responsible for the deaths of two spectators, who fell from the elevated railroad structure overlooking the grounds, which made Fred Merkle famous for not touching second, which caused lifelong friends to become bitter enemies, and which, altogether, was the most dramatic and important contest in the history of baseball.

The Cubs took the subway to the Polo Grounds in street clothes, the autumn light of upper Manhattan, rail yards and river. No one recognized the young men, who looked around uneasily, like spies in an enemy camp. Brown kept his hand in his pocket, stashed like a pistol. All week he'd been receiving death threats. In many of them, he was given a choice: Sit out the game and live, or pitch and die. These letters were marked by a small black handprint, imprimatur of the Sicilian underworld.

Brown showed the letters to Chance.

"What do you want to do?" asked the manager.

"You know what I want to do," said Brown. "I want to pitch."

The scene in front of the stadium was like a painting by Bosch. The Polo Grounds held 25,000, but 250,000 had come out. They jammed the streets and fire escapes, the trestles and rooftops, the sycamores and utility poles—they swarmed Coogan's Bluff. Several were injured that day. Fell from a bridge, stumbled into the path of a train, tripped from a roost on the elevated tracks. It was not just a game people wanted to see—it was a morality play. The righteous Giants taking on the evil Cubs. The Chicago players were recognized as they neared the clubhouse. The fans began to hoot and boo. Chance was called a robber and a bandit. The Cubs changed in silence, then went onto the field to warm up. Every few minutes, a lunatic would drop out of the bleachers and charge the infield, only to be tackled by a cop. Several thousand fans stood in deep center field behind a fence. When it collapsed, they came running. The police beat them down and took them away.

A rumor spread among the Cubs. It was said that someone had tried to fix the game, cornered an umpire with a bankroll. Some said it was a freelancing mobster, a gonif who couldn't stand to see his team lose. Others said it was someone connected to Giants' manager John McGraw. There was an investigation after the season. Umpire Bill Klem told a detective that a man had indeed waved a bankroll at him beneath the stands, saying, "Here's $2,500. It's yours if you will give all close decisions to the Giants."

Violence roiled the stadium, waves of disturbance. "Fights immediately started all around in the stands," Mathewson wrote. "I remember seeing two men roll from the top to the bottom of the right-field bleachers, over the heads of the rest of the specta- tors." Two fans, arms linked, fell from the upper deck, seventy feet, to their death.

Al Spalding came east for the game, as did Charles Murphy. Harry Pulliam needed police protection. His ruling had turned him into a villain. He internalized the catcalls, brooded and stewed. He'd take a leave of absence after the season, spend time in a rest home, then return, but wasn't right. The following sum- mer, he'd shoot himself in the head in his room at the New York Athletic Club. The bullet went through his skull and hit the wall. He was alive when police found him. They asked him why he shot himself. "I'm not shot," he said, then lost consciousness. He died the next morning.

Frank Chance spoke to his team before the game. His advice was practical. He told each Cub to pick out a Giant and ride him, heckle him till he explodes. If you've got personal dirt on any of those boys, he said, now's the time to use it.

Chance took Brown aside. "Pfiester is starting," he said, "but be ready. You might get in sooner than you think."

John McGraw told Iron Man McGinnity to pick a fight with Frank Chance during warm-ups. Chance is a tough guy, McGraw explained. He'd never back down. *You'll both be tossed. You're dispensable. Chance is not.* McGinnity cursed and shoved Chance near the Cubs' bench as the fans screamed, but Chance just stood there smiling at him. When the fans did not get their fight, they went after the rest of the Cubs, denouncing them in the worst language. "I never heard anybody or any set of men called as many foul names as the Giants fans called us that day," Brown said.

Merkle was booed when he ran out. "By this time, Merkle had lost twenty pounds, and his eyes were hollow and his cheeks sunken," Mathewson wrote. "The newspapers showed him no mercy, and the fans never failed to criticize and hiss him when he appeared on the field. He stuck to it and showed up in the ball park every day, putting on his uniform and practicing."

Mathewson put the Cubs down one, two, three in the first. Then Pfiester came out for Chicago—sixty feet six inches from home plate but all alone. He was rattled from the start, by the violence of the crowd and the gravity of the situation. He hit the first batter, walked the second, struck out the third. Johnny Kling threw out a man trying to steal. The Giants' Mike Donlin doubled, scoring the first run for the Giants. Chance called time, walked to the mound. The infield gathered in a circle. Chance asked for the ball, held it in his hand, waved to the bullpen. The gate swung open. Giants fans stood in the way, would not move. Brown shoved them aside, headed across the grass, his shadow stretching before him. Two on, two out. He threw a few warm-ups, then struck out Art Devlin to end the inning.

The pinch came in the third, with Mathewson on the mound. He'd had one of the best seasons in baseball history (37–11, 1.43 ERA), but it did not help on the last day. Now and then, you just don't have it. He later said the Giants lost because "I never had less on the ball in my life." Tinker led off for Chicago. Mathewson stepped off the mound and called out to Giants center fielder Cy Seymour. He told him to move back—play deeper. Seymour either did not hear or did not agree. Instead of moving back, he actually took a step closer to the plate. "Tinker, with his long bat, swung on a ball intended to be a low curve over the outside corner of the plate," Mathewson wrote. "He pushed out a high fly to center field, and I turned with the ball to see Seymour take a couple of steps toward the diamond, evidently thinking it would drop somewhere behind second base. He appeared to be uncertain in his judgment of the hit until he suddenly turned and started to run back. That must have been when the ball cleared the roof of the stand and was visible above the sky line. He ran wildly. Once he turned, and then ran on again, at last sticking up his hands and having the ball fall just beyond them. He chased it and picked it up, but Tinker had reached third base by that time."

Kling lined to center, scoring Tinker and tying the game. Brown bunted, moving Kling to second. Sheckard flew out. Evers walked. Schulte doubled, driving in Kling, but with Chicago only one run ahead, the Giants remained optimistic. Frank Chance ended all such hope, going the opposite way with what Mathewson said was his best pitch of the afternoon. "A right-handed hitter naturally slaps a ball over the outside edge of the plate to right field," Mathewson explained, "but Chance pushed this one, on the inside, with the handle of his bat, just over [the right fielder's] hands and on into the crowd. The hit scored Evers and Schulte and dissolved the game right there. It was the 'break.'"

Miner Brown was pitching the best game of his life. The speedy one. The hook. Complete command. Brown versus Mathewson was one of the storied rivalries. They faced each other in so many big games it felt like love. Mathewson was said to be the better pitcher. A charter member of the Hall of Fame, whereas Brown had to wait eighteen years. Yet the Miner seemed to win all the big contests. In the three previous seasons, he'd gone 13 and 0 against Mathewson. The one-game playoff was a culmination. "Inning after inning, our batters were mowed down by the great pitching of Brown, who was never better," Mathewson wrote. "His control of his curved ball was marvelous, and he had all the speed. As the innings dragged by, the spectators lost heart, and the cowbells ceased to jingle, and the cheering lost its resonant ring. It was now a surly growl . . . None of the players spoke to one another as they went to the bench. Even McGraw was silent. We knew it was gone. Merkle was drawn up behind the water cooler. Once he said: 'It was my fault, boys.'"

As soon as Brown retired the last hitter, the Cubs, who had won the game 4–2, ran for the clubhouse, Giants fans hard on their heels. "Some of our boys got caught by the mob and beaten up,"

Brown said. "Chance was hurt most of all. A Giant fan hit him in the throat and the Husk's voice was gone for a day or two."

The mood in the Giants' clubhouse was somber, funereal, everyone quiet except for the center fielder, Cy Seymour, who was sobbing. It was not that they'd lost. It was that they'd already won—the game and the pennant rightfully belonged to them. It had been taken away by trickery. To a certain sect, *this* is the real source of the curse of the Cubs—why they'd never win another World Series. At the end of the season, Giants owner John Brush handed out rings to his players that said, THE 1908 NEW YORK GIANTS, THE REAL CHAMPIONS OF THE NATIONAL LEAGUE.

Meanwhile, the Cubs were once again barricaded in their clubhouse, the mob outside, trying to get in. Cops pushed through with pistols drawn. A terrible rumor spread: Fred Merkle has killed himself. "When it was safe we rode to our hotel in a patrol wagon," said Brown, "with two cops on the inside and four riding the running boards and the rear step."

The Cubs were on a train by midnight, city giving way to swamps, New Jersey, Pennsylvania, Ohio. They'd travel all night and reach Detroit by morning.

■ ■ ■

The Cubs scored ten runs in the first game of the World Series. They would take the championship in five. Chicago pitcher Orval Overall beat Wild Bill Donovan in the last game at Detroit's long-gone Bennett Park, low-slung with smokestacks all around. There were surely Cub fans at that game and among them surely a father and son, and the father would have pointed out each Chicago player to his son and spoken each name, like Homer naming the fleet captains in the *Iliad. Kling, Chance,* and *Tinker, Evers, Sheck-ard, Steinfeldt, Schulte,* and *Hofman.* That father would've dropped an arm across the shoulder of the boy and said, "Remember those names, son, for these are the Cubs, who will certainly win many more World Series in your lifetime."

As we know, that father would grow old and die and that boy would grow up and make predictions to his children and grow old and die, and his son would make predictions to children who would predict and grow old and die, and so on for more than a hundred years and still we would be waiting.

The Frank Chance Cubs did not simply vanish—they were in fact good for years and years. All told, they must be considered among the greatest baseball teams ever. They won 116 games in 1906; 107 in 1907; 99 in 1908. They won 104 games in 1909 and 1910. Between 1906 and 1913, they won 801 games, which remains a record.

When I was a kid, I was amazed, considering the ineptness of my team, just how many games the Cubs had won: 10,711 games through 2016, second only to the Giants. Because they'd been so good for so long so early. That's what made the coming drought especially pathetic—this was not some random franchise having a bad century. It was a charter franchise of the National League and among the most storied organizations in sports—a team that won and won and won. Until, one day, they stopped winning.

■ ■ ■

The members of Frank Chance's Cubs, who'd succeeded together, failed on their own.

Johnny Kling took off 1909 to play billiards—he won a National

Championship. He led the Cubs to their tenth pennant in 1910, but a lot of players blamed him for the World Series loss to the Philadelphia A's. The pitchers said Kling had failed to hide his signals, allowing Philadelphia hitters to steal signs—they knew what was coming. "The players were sore because they'd lost the Series and lost the extra money which many of them had counted on as their own before the games started," wrote Mathewson, "and they looked around for someone to blame." How could Kling stick around after that? He finished in Cincinnati, then returned to Kansas City, where he ran a pool hall.

Johnny Evers was in a car crash. He was driving and his best friend was killed. He had a nervous breakdown, was committed, then came back to win an MVP with the Boston Braves. He settled in Albany, New York, where he ran a sporting goods store. He died in 1947. He was bedridden the last five years of his life, paralyzed by a stroke.

Orval Overall died in 1947. Wildfire Schulte quit the game, worked with racehorses, moved to Oakland, and died in 1949. Jack Pfiester died in 1953. Ed Reulbach retired after the 1917 season, and settled in Maplewood, New Jersey, where he worked for a piano maker. He died of a heart attack in 1961. Joe Tinker managed several teams after his playing days, including the Reds and the Cubs. He worked as a boiler inspector for the Army Air Force during World War II, but never quit baseball. In 1950, he was living in Orlando, working as a scout. He went to see Johnny Evers before he died. The men, who had not spoken in years, fell into each other's arms, weeping.

Tinker to Evers to . . .

Frank Chance was undone by all the bean balls—hit in the

head repeatedly, before batting helmets. On July 1, 1911, he collapsed on the field. A blood clot was removed from his brain. He was told he could no longer play, but persisted in spite of this—for some, there is only the game. He sat out the remainder of 1911, played two games in 1912, then went to the New York Yankees. He appeared in twelve games in 1913, collecting just five hits. He moved to California and managed in the Pacific Coast league and died in 1924. He was forty-eight years old.

Three Finger Brown refused to quit, even as he lost effectiveness. He went 5–6 with the Cubs in 1912, then began wandering club to club with that mangled hand. By 1921, he was back in the minors, pitching for Terre Haute. You've heard about the player who wants to go out on top, quit at the peak, leaving fans with the best possible memories. Brown was another sort. He did not manage his exit; he fought for his life. He loved the game and would suffer any humiliation or diminishment to keep playing it.

He dropped down the ranks, majors to Class B, then finally back to the bush leagues, barnstorming teams where his name might draw a few hundred people to the park. In 1932, he played in an Old-Timers' Game with Cy Young, Honus Wagner, and Tris Speaker. He was pitching for an oil company by then, the Havolines, in an Indiana factory league. A kid named Sam Valentine later spoke of hitting against the aged Three Finger Brown. He was haggard, downright elderly. He limped to the mound beneath the weak arc lights as the factory workers cheered. Swimming in that uniform, raising his glove, turning the ball over in his hand. He could still pitch. Valentine said the ball seemed to hang between the mound and the plate, stop and linger, then suddenly close on the catcher's glove. Brown opened a Texaco station at the corner of Seventh Street and Cherry in Terre Haute, a few blocks from his house. His name was on a sign out front. Passersby were encouraged to come in and talk.

This was all that remained of the great 1908 Cubs: a mangled old man telling stories about Christy Mathewson as he checked your oil.

Twenty-five thousand years ago, Northern Illinois was buried in blue ice. As the earth shifted on its axis, the sun burned down, killing the last of the land monsters, the mastodons and giant sloths, cracking and buckling and melting that ice, swelling the streams into great rivers. Ten thousand years ago, water from those rivers collected in a tremendous basin, a freshwater sea, leaving the land flat and dry, bare at first, then covered with forest. Five hundred years ago, trees had been cleared from that forest to make way for a Potawatomi village. A century or so later, French trappers appeared from the east, looking for pelts and a way to the Pacific Ocean. They set up a trading post, which gave way to a farm, then a fort, then a town, which became Chicago.

Most of the industry in that city was located on the south and west sides, warehouses and docks on the lake, factories and mills on the Des Plaines and Chicago Rivers. The north was forest, then farms, then harbors where candles glowed in windows, then streets of wood houses where the middle class could live inside and outside the machine. West Addison Street was laid out in the 1800s; Waveland the same. Clark and Sheffield. Together they enclosed a five-acre block just west of Lake Michigan. By 1890, that land had been acquired by the Chicago Lutheran Theological Seminary, which turned it into a campus: church, dormitory, a house for the minister.

In 1909, a developer bought the property for $175,000, then leased it to Charles Weeghman, the lunch counter king of Chicago. In 1913, along with a few other businessmen, he set up a new major baseball league. The Federal League. He hired the architect Zachary Taylor Davis—who'd designed Comiskey Park for the White Sox—to build a stadium for his team. Weeghman Park. Davis designed the park to fit its surroundings—redbrick, small scale, cozy. It's been remade and added to over the years, but the soul of the place, the spirit, was there from the first.

Chicago of the Federal League—known first as the Dolphins, then as the Whales—played at 1060 West Addison for two seasons. The 1914 team consisted of castoff stars attracted by big-time money. Joe Tinker signed on as player-manager. Miner Brown came aboard in 1915 and the Whales won the Federal League pennant. Weeghman challenged the winner of the World Series—the Red Sox—to a championship, was rejected, then rejected a challenge by the champion of the Negro League—the Chicago American Giants. The Federal League was in trouble by then, a victim of a price war it had launched. Just about every owner was struggling. They sued for peace. The American and National Leagues pooled resources and paid the Feds $600,000 to disband. The more established Federal League teams were afforded special arrangements. The St. Louis Terriers were taken into the American League. The Chicago Whales merged with the Chicago Cubs, a trick accomplished by letting Weeghman buy the franchise from Charles Taft, who'd taken ownership from Charles Murphy. Weeghman paid Taft $500,000 for the Cubs, combined the team with the Whales, then moved them into Weeghman Park.

Charlie Weeghman was known as Lucky Charlie, a nickname that came to seem ironic. By 1918, the only kind of luck he had was bad. He had to take on partners to pay for the franchise. Then, whenever a bill came due, had to go back for more money, usually to the same partner, William Wrigley, Jr. In this way, when Charlie Weeghman declared bankruptcy in 1920, Wrigley found himself in possession of a baseball team.

Chicago is a serious city. Steak and diesel. Winter coming in. Its great men made their great fortunes slaughtering or trading or stacking or demolishing or hauling. How funny that the fortune behind its famous North Side ball team was frivolous and light, kids' stuff, made from candy.

William Wrigley started out selling soap. In 1874, he went on the road as a salesman for his father's Philadelphia factory. He was a twelve-year-old working mostly on commission, a boy in a stiff suit humping a sample case from farm to farm. He traveled with a four-horse team and got to know every town in the East. When the soap did not sell, he added baking soda to his line. When that didn't sell, he started throwing in chewing gum as a kind of incentive. For the kids. When the gum proved more popular than the soap or baking soda, he borrowed money, moved to

Chicago, built a small factory, and went into business for himself. One of his first products was called Youcanchu—say it slow—a banana-flavored gum. Other flavors followed: spearmint, juicy fruit. The new century was going to be about a unique kind of American energy, which was perfectly expressed by a jaw working away at a piece of gum. Wrigley arrived in Chicago in 1891. By 1900, he was a millionaire. Red faced and round, stuffed into a heavy wool suit. He had the good cheer and the infuriating wisdom of the self-made man. The sign over his desk quoted Ralph Waldo Emerson: NOTHING GREAT WAS EVER ACHIEVED WITHOUT ENTHUSIASM.

William Wrigley did not take full ownership of the Cubs till 1920, but was basically in charge by the summer of 1916. He might have fallen into it by accident, but that did not change the most important thing about him: He loved baseball. He understood the game and respected the players and wanted to win. That's the only way it works, the only way a franchise can succeed. A prudent owner, an owner in it to make money, an owner overly worried about attendance or concession sales will never have the long-term vision to build a great winner. Pro sports is a crazy endeavor, often a money-losing endeavor. Its best owners are driven by pride. That was William Wrigley. He refurbished the stadium, then, later, in the way of an honorable man, gave it his own name. Wrigley Field. When the team played poorly, he fumed. He looked everywhere for answers. *Why can't we win?* He came across a series of articles published in the *Chicago American* under the pseudonym Bill Bailey, which for years had been used by any reporter who wanted to write freely. Ring Lardner had used it when he was at the paper. These particular stories went after the Cubs—not just the team but how the franchise was being run.

Wrigley called the editor and demanded to speak to the author. A meeting was arranged. The sportswriter told his story. His name was William Veeck, Sr. He'd grown up in a town with a name that sounds like a synonym for nowhere: Boonville, Indiana. An autodidact, he never made it beyond ninth grade. He sat in the kitchen instead, teaching himself how to write. He became a newspaperman, which was a philosophical disposition as much as a career.

At some point, Wrigley said, "If you think you can do a better job of running my ball club, why go ahead."

Veeck took over in July 1919. He would serve as president of the Cubs—he operated in the way of a modern general manager—from 1920 till 1933, when he died of leukemia. In his first years on the job, he spent much of his time managing Wrigley's prized superstar, the lanky right-handed ace Grover Cleveland Alexander, who was turning out to be a tragic figure. It's like a story out of mythology and was in fact made into *The Winning Team*, a biopic in which a forty-one-year-old Ronald Reagan plays the pitcher at every age from eighteen to fifty.

The pitcher was born in 1887, during the Grover Cleveland administration, hence the name. He grew up in a farmhouse in Elba, Nebraska, 145 miles from Omaha. He worked in the fields when he was a boy, or else wandered with a handful of rocks, throwing them at fence posts. "When we wanted dinner," his mother said, "we'd send Grover out with a stone and he'd come back with a chicken." That's how he developed the fastball. What about the breaking ball? He said it came from the book *How to Curve a Baseball*. He looked at the pictures, mimicked the grips, let it fly. But no matter how hard he worked, he could not get the ball to break. He finally threw the book in the trash, but it sat there, mocking him. He fished it out and tried again. And again. And again. It finally clicked. He worked for the local telephone company, digging holes and stringing cable. That's how he's seen in the Reagan movie, young and handsome, atop a utility pole, pulling voices out of the air. In 1908, he was paid five bucks a game to pitch for various semipro teams, including St. Paul and Central City, railroad towns. Even then, he was remarked upon. When he was seventeen years old, a newspaper reporter described his pitches as "mysterious."

He was being called "Alex" by the time he turned up in Galesburg, Illinois, where he'd get his first chance to pitch against grown men. *The Galesburg Times* described him as "a blonde of the ruddy type with the build of a switch engine. Manager Jap Wagner figures that the big strawberry slinger floating up puzzles to the opposing batsmen already is a master and is much taken by his looks."

Alexander threw a no-hitter against Canton, Illinois, on July 22, 1909, then struck out nineteen batters in his next start. A few weeks after that, in what would be his first of many disasters, he was beaned while running the bases. He just lay there, stretched out on the green, green grass. He was unconscious for thirty-six hours. When he woke up in the hospital, he had a terrible headache and was seeing double. He shook his head, but his vision did not clear. "If you had put out your hand to shake with me," he later said, "I would have seen two hands." In the movie, this is shown as an expressionist effect, streets and cars, trees and teammates and pitched balls, shimmering in hazy duplicate. His world had become unintelligible. There's a scientific name for this condition, but all he knew was that he could not pitch. He went home, got in bed, and sulked. Then, one day, he shook his head and the double resolved into a single sharp image. He put on his glove and went back to work.

Alexander made his major league debut in the spring of 1911 with the Philadelphia Phillies, chestnut haired and red faced, like a man with a sunburn. He was straight as a post on the mound, shadow behind him, shadow before him, hitters standing in, hitters sitting down. He threw sidearm and worked fast. Get the ball, throw the ball. Get the ball, throw the ball. A modern big league game averages two hours and fifty-two minutes; Alexander was usually finished in ninety minutes. He could throw hard, but it was less his velocity than the way he changed speeds that bothered hitters. Control and of course that breaking ball—the wicked curve. He was 28–13 in his first major league season, one of the best rookie years ever. He pitched seven shutouts and was responsible for 35 percent of his team's victories. He was a classic type: the rawboned kid who's blown in from nowhere to devastate the best hitters in the game. You can't help but root for a kid like that, even if he's on the wrong team, because he's the promise of youth.

Mark Fidrych had a freshman season like this for the Detroit Tigers in 1976, going 19–9 with a 2.34 ERA and ten complete games. Dwight Gooden too—he won seventeen games for the New York Mets in 1984, with a 2.60 ERA. But Fidrych got hurt and Gooden became distracted, whereas Alexander just kept getting better. Between 1915 and 1917, he was astonishing. He won more than thirty games in each season. In 1915, he had a 1.22 ERA and struck out 241 batters—you'll never see that again. These feats are still more remarkable when you consider his home stadium, the Baker Bowl, a tiny park on Broad Street in industrial Philadelphia, astride the freight yards. Known as the Cigar Box, the Baker Bowl had a crazily short right field. A routine fly elsewhere was a home run here. The team's owner, William Baker, compensated by raising the fence, erecting the famous Baker Wall, which turned would-be home runs into doubles. It was like Fenway Park, only more so. Down the line, Fenway's left field ends 310 feet from home plate—short—and its compensating wall, the Green Monster, is 37 feet tall. Down the line, Baker's right field ended 280 feet from home—supershort—and its compensating wall was 60 feet—supertall. It was black and blank and made of industrial concrete. A ball hitting that wall sounded like a cannon shot. The fact that Alexander, a right-handed pitcher vulnerable to left-handed hitting, threw more than twenty shutouts in the Baker Bowl is astounding.

Why did the Phillies sell the game's greatest pitcher?

Because the owner of the Phillies needed cash and because, with America's entry into World War I looming, knew Alexander was likely to be drafted anyway. Simple logic: Sell while you still can. Wrigley paid $60,000 for the pitcher, an unprecedented sum. After a brief holdout, Alexander turned up at spring training, worked out with the Cubs, then, just as the season was about to begin, was indeed drafted into the army and told to report, at the end of April, to Camp Funston, near Manhattan, Kansas. It gave him enough time to start three games. He lost on opening day in St. Louis, won in Cincinnati, then pitched a two-hitter to win the Cubs home opener on April 26, 1918. He was at his best that day, deliberate and calm, perfect control. He waved his cap as he walked off the field, face slick with sweat, smiling. It was the last the world would ever see of Alexander as he'd been known. He was going away coherent and sane but would come back scrambled and crazy; was going away provincial and certain but would come back worldly and unsure; was going away simple and confident but would come back complicated and scared. He was going away young and would come back as old as anyone who's ever lived.

Alexander stood before his teammates after that last game, in uniform, head low, talking. He said, "I'm sorry to leave all you fellows, but it looks like a tough fight over there and as if a lot of us must go and help. I don't know whether I shall ever come back to play ball or not, but if I don't, I'll make it necessary for them to dig a lot of holes for the enemy before they get me." Within eight weeks, he'd been shorn, outfitted, and trained, and was marching in the ranks of the 342nd Field Artillery of the 89th Division of the U.S. Army. He was a sergeant, waiting for orders.

Meanwhile, the Cubs kept winning. The season had been shortened because of the war, the World Series rescheduled for September. The Cubs won the National League by ten and a half games, then played the Red Sox for the championship. The Cubs are already into the drought by this time, so we know they're going to lose, but that's not what's interesting. What's interesting is the premonition that World Series gave of the future, of how baseball would be played after the war. Amid the Red Sox ranks stood the revolutionary who would remake everything about the game.

When people think of Babe Ruth, it's the big fat man, the way he was at the end, when he turned up on quality film stock. He played himself in *Pride of the Yankees* when he was nearly fifty, portly and grand but squeezing into the old uniform, giving entire generations of future fans the wrong idea—that he was slovenly and out of shape and would never make it in the game today. But in 1918, Babe Ruth was young and fit and as great as any athlete who's ever played. A man among boys, a modern among ancients. He was like Chuck Berry. It's not just what he did but that he did so much of it first. He did not merely excel at the game, he remade it. He invented a new game as he played the old game. He was still a pitcher in 1918, maybe the best on the Boston staff. I'm not even going to look up his biography. I'm just going to tell it from memory, not because I will get it right but because I will get it wrong, the myth instead of the facts, which is what I want, as, in this case, the myth is everything.

Ruth grew up in an orphanage in Baltimore. His childhood was cruel. He was abused and angry and channeled that anger into the game he learned on the playground. He played for a minor league Baltimore team, then was sold to the Red Sox. A left-handed pitcher, a twenty-game winner. He could also hit. Because he was a pitcher, no one cared what he did at the plate, so they left him alone when he began to goof with a new swing. He sometimes said he'd copied it from Shoeless Joe Jackson, the White Sox slugger who was later banned for the 1919 World Series fix. Most major league swings were short and level—put the ball in play, don't strike out. Jackson swung big and along a rising arc, with the intention of putting the ball into the air. Ruth took that and exaggerated it. He was the first player with what we'd recognize as a modern swing, starting at the heels, ending in the sky, the follow-through winding his body like a coil. The old way, the drama ends when you make contact. The new way, contact is just something that happens in the long life of a big swing. Fans began to turn up early to watch Babe Ruth take batting practice. That swing was an object of beauty, and when he actually connected, the ball did not merely leave the field, it left the stadium, turned into a white dot in a blue sky, broke windows across the street. But Ruth in the cage was a sideshow act then—to entertain kids. The real story was still Ruth on the mound. He won two games in the 1918 World Series, and held the Cubs to sixteen scoreless innings.

■ ■ ■

The war had already been going for close to three years when America entered. Some of the most violent battles in history had been fought. Eight hundred thousand people died at Verdun, 1.2 million at the Somme. Hemingway said it was "like the stockyards of Chicago if nothing was done with the meat except to bury it." Alexander was on the Western Front, bundled up and terrified as the German artillery rained down. He'd read about Europe in books, but that was princes and towers and damsels in distress; this was mud and misery, trucks and canons, blood and wounded men. It all happened so fast. He was pitching for the Cubs in April, in basic training in May, on a troop ship in June, fighting in France in July. He kept running into other ballplayers. Clarence Mitchell, from Franklin, Nebraska, who'd played for the Reds and the Brooklyn Robins. Winnie Noyes, from Pleasanton, Nebraska, who'd had a sensational debut with Philadelphia but never made it back after the war. Otis Lambeth, who'd had strong seasons in Cleveland but also never made it back. These men arrived as celebrities, but that wore off fast. It was like having been someone important in a previous life. It almost meant something.

The Germans were exhausted by the autumn of 1918, falling before the onslaught of fresh American soldiers and equipment. By October, Alexander was in a trench on the frontier. It was the last major battle of the war. He was either digging or marching or shooting, dragging the big gun, or burying himself in a hole. His unit was shelled for seven straight days and nights, the mortars raining down, the treetops on fire. No one with him came out unchanged. It was the noise and the smoke and the fear, the nearness of death. Eddie Grant, who'd played for the Phillies, was killed in the Argonne in October 1918. Robert Troy, who'd pitched for the Tigers, died in Cazaux, France. Alexander went deaf in one ear, took shrapnel in the neck and face. He later said he was afraid that he was about to die every moment at the front. That never went away—the sense of being on the edge. Alexander would be remembered as one of the game's incorrigible drunks—hiding bottles in the clubhouse, stumbling on the mound—and this is where it started. He drank nothing stronger than beer before the war. Then one night, as the bombs fell, a man handed him a flask. He started drinking and never stopped.

The Allied armies broke through. The enemy collapsed. Blown-out roads, ruined towns. The Armistice was signed November 11. The war was over. Alexander sailed into New York, flags waving, the city appearing off the prow, drunk all the time. Then the long trip across the prairie, home to Nebraska, the final salute and farewell, and just like that he was back at spring training, trying to remember how he'd thrown that wicked curve.

No one is exactly sure when he started having seizures. He was diagnosed with epilepsy, but it seems to have started only after the war, possibly as a result of trauma. It could happen at any moment—walking alone, in the middle of a game. It came on like a migraine, a blue dot in a clear field, a shimmer on the visual periphery. There was a premonition, then he was on the ground, foaming and convulsing. The players would form a tight circle, shielding him from view. He let reporters and fans believe he'd been drunk, had blacked out or suffered a whiskey fit. In those days, being an alcoholic was socially acceptable; being epileptic was not. It was like being possessed, haunted by demons. Specs Toporcer, the first big league player to wear glasses, was on the field when Alexander had a seizure. "Pitching against the Phillies one afternoon, it struck him just as he was going into his windup," Toporcer said. "He automatically went through with the pitch, arching the ball to the plate, while Don Hurst, the Philly batter, froze in amazement. Curiously enough, the ball cut the heart of the plate for a called strike."

"Sometimes he'd have one of those spells out on the mound," said Alexander's teammate Pinky Whitney. "We'd get around him and pull his tongue out. And then he'd get up and throw the next ball right through the middle of the plate."

"He always carried a bottle of spirits of ammonia with him," Alexander's wife, Aimee, told a reporter. "They would take him into the locker room. Alex would whiff the ammonia, fight to get control of himself, then go right back out and pitch again."

The stories of his alcoholism were not untrue, nor exaggerated. He was indeed a wretched drunk. But this did not cause his seizures—it was probably his way of treating whatever underlying condition caused them. In other words, he did not suffer because he drank; he drank because he suffered. Of course, all Wrigley and Veeck cared about was, *Could he pitch?* He came back slow in 1919, opening the season with five straight loses, but eventually found the groove. There was only pitching now, and surviving long enough to pitch again.

There was another new situation to deal with after the war. Not only had his brain been remade—so had baseball. It's an old story: A man goes off to fight, believing he will return to the same game with the same rules, but while he's away, everything changes. It happened in 1920, which probably not coincidentally was also Alexander's last great season. He went 27–14, with a 1.91 ERA. It seems fitting that the man behind the change, tumult, and creative destruction was an apostate pitcher.

While Alexander was in Europe, the Red Sox worked out the deal that sent Babe Ruth to the Yankees, where manager Miller Huggins, recognizing the breakthrough represented by Ruth's swing, moved him off the mound into right field. He wanted Ruth's bat in the lineup every day. In 1919, Ruth hit twenty-nine home runs. He hit fifty-four in 1920. Before him, the most any-one had ever hit in a season was twenty-one. In 1920, Ruth, all by himself, hit more home runs than any team in the majors—that is, more home runs than all the players on any club combined. This was not just an aspect of the old game done bigger; it was a new game altogether.

Since the days of Cap Anson, baseball had been about singles and doubles and triples, putting the ball in play. It was called the dead-ball era only in retrospect, because there really was nothing dead about it. You could make the case that it was more alive than the game that followed, all about creativity, gamesmanship. Base-ball in its classical incarnation was personified by Ty Cobb. He used a thick bat that didn't taper at the handle, probed the de-fense for holes, placed the ball between fielders. He spent hours and hours perfecting many varieties of bunt. His real work began only when he got on base. He did not have to rely on other players to move him from second to home. He stole his way. His appear-ance matched his style, skinny and neat, carefully tucked, sharp-tongued, moody, and mean. Even when it seemed like he was doing nothing, he was setting up a play that might come off an hour or even a week hence. He changed his batting style to fit the situation. In 1912, in 609 plate appearances, he struck out just 30 times.

The home-run-besotted game that is still being played today was personified by Ruth. Not just the long balls, the personality: bighearted, sloppy, gregarious, warm. He did not just drive the ball out of the park; he drove it *way* out of the park. Dawn of the tape measure blast. He did not just hit a home run, but promised he would hit a home run. He was like Muhammad Ali—full of swagger and talk. He stood in the on-deck circle swinging three bats, which were fat at the top but skinny at the handle—harder to control but easier to whip through the strike zone. The sound the ball made off his bat was different. Sharp. Concussive. It screamed in pain. He did not love strikeouts but didn't fear them either. They were the price of power. He'd gladly trade three Ks for one home run. He led the league in strikeouts five times. In 1923, he struck out ninety-three times but led the league in home runs twelve times. In 1927, he hit sixty home runs. He'd happily trade five points of batting average for five dingers, though he hit both for power and for average.

Major league baseball was already in its forty-fifth season when he broke through. Why had this innovation been so long in coming? Was Babe Ruth that different, or had something else changed? Most people believe it was the ball—that it had been remade, juiced. Some suggested the string inside had been wound more tightly, turning it into a kind of superball. That's the conventional wisdom. That's why the pre-Ruth game is called the dead-ball era. Because that ball seemed flat in comparison—no fizz. But Albert Spalding, whose company manufactured every ball used in the majors, denied it. He said the design had not changed since 1910, when the cork center was added. If it was not the ball, maybe it was the new bats—tapered at the handle, heavy at the top. Once you started to swing, the bat seemed to go on its own. Easier to propel, harder to control—home runs and strikeouts. And there was the redesigned swing itself—the stance and the stroke that Ruth had been free to pioneer because he'd been a pitcher, and who really cares what a pitcher does at the plate?

But the greatest change probably *was* the ball—not its design, its condition. In the past, a ball was kept in play until it was lost in the stands or fell apart. By the late innings, it was the color of dirt, nearly impossible to see. It left a pitcher's hand and then vanished, not to be seen again until it was in the catcher's mitt. And there was that tremendous catalog of trick pitches—still in use and legal. Spitball, licorice ball, elm ball, shine ball, paraffin ball. Details varied but the intent was always the same: Change the spin, confuse the flight. A hitter expects it to break this way, it goes that way instead.

That changed on August 16, 1920. The Polo Grounds, where the Yankees played till Ruth's fame financed the new stadium across the Harlem River in the Bronx. Carl Mays was pitching for New York, afternoon shadows creeping in. He was a submarine pitcher, known for throwing junk, going after batters. He was pitching to Ray Chapman, the Cleveland Indians' shortstop. It was Chapman's ninth season in the majors. He was batting .308. The ball, which had spent the afternoon being banged around the grounds, was the color of smoke, indistinguishable from the gloaming. It was later decided that Chapman never saw the pitch. Because he did not move, just froze as it climbed. The sound of the ball hitting his head could be heard all over the park. People screamed, looked away. After hitting Chapman, it rolled back to the mound. Mays, not knowing he'd hit the batter, fielded it and threw to first baseman Wally Pipp, who understood what had happened when he saw Chapman drop to his knees, then fall on his face. Chapman got up somehow, was escorted across the field, stepped into the dugout, and collapsed. He was taken to a hospital, where part of his skull was removed. He died the next morning.

Ray Chapman is the only player ever killed in the course of a major league baseball game. After a series of emergency meetings, two rule changes were made. Since many blamed the state of the ball, umpires were told to replace the game ball as soon as it showed stain or any sign of wear. That's why you see the umpire, between pitches, turning the ball over in his hand, examining. At the slightest imperfection, the ball is replaced. Upward of one hundred baseballs will be used in the course of a single game. Since others blamed the pitch, believing Mays had doctored the ball, the spitball and its relatives were banned. No more nicking the ball on your belt buckle to alter its spin, no more roughing it with sandpaper (emery ball), or polishing one side of it on your jersey while slicking the other side with dirt (shine ball). Players who'd come up throwing such pitches were grandfathered, allowed to continue using them till the end of their careers, which had the perverse effect of creating a distinct class of feared specialists. There were seventeen pitchers on that list, including Dutch Leonard and Phil Douglas, who played for the Cubs. Burleigh Grimes stuck around longest, not retiring till 1934. By the mid-1920s, the game ball, which had been dirty by the third inning, was snow-white for Ruth and his disciples. Easier to see, easier to hit. In this way, the power surge was at least partly built on the dead body of Ray Chapman.

Of course, the main cause was probably just the Babe himself.

Not his swing so much as the success of that swing. After "Heartbreak Hotel," no one wanted to be Perry Como. They wanted to be Elvis Presley. After 1920, no one wanted to be Ty Cobb. They wanted to be Babe Ruth. The old game had been about precision, strategy, incremental progress. The new game was about power, the single blast that busts open the piñata.

Ty Cobb and hundreds of others who continued on in the classical way suddenly seemed obsolete. And hated it, Cobb most of all. He was a withering critic of the new style and its great exemplar, the fat man. It was not just what the change had done to Cobb's legacy, but what it had done to Cobb's sport. He considered the game that emerged with Ruth inferior, a move from elegance to vulgarity. It's how the great film directors of the silent era felt about the talkies. Too easy, too simple. It destroyed virtuosity. Writers dismissed this as jealousy. They said Cobb envied Ruth. You think I can't hit home runs? Cobb protested. Any fool can hit the ball out of the park. Putting it in play, putting the runners in motion, that's the trick.

Cobb said he did not hit home runs because it could be done only by sacrificing batting average. When a Detroit reporter seemed skeptical, Cobb said, "I'll show you something today. I'm going for home runs for the first time in my career."

On May 25, 1925, Ty Cobb hit three home runs against the St. Louis Browns. The next day, he hit two more. At that point, no one, not even Ruth, had hit five home runs in two days. Cobb then reverted to slap hitting. Because he believed that was the true baseball.

(A friend of mine, representing many skeptical fans, dismisses this as a fluke. "Yeah, yeah, I've heard the 'Cobb could hit home runs at will if he wanted to' story before," he told me. "He couldn't.

He just had a nice couple of days against the Browns, those perpetual patsies.")

The change in the game, how it went from dogged and small to flashy and big, was about more than baseball. It was the zeitgeist. The culture has a way of remaking its games to match its obsessions. Dead ball had been perfect for preindustrial, preglobal America. It was village and farm, the hick with the spitball, the yokel with the level swing. The game invented by Ruth was much more appropriate for the America coming into being, the twentieth-century America that would go everywhere and do everything and overwhelm everyone with its weapons. A bigger game for a bigger nation. Front-loaded and flashy like its cities and its factories and its music and its movies. All mechanism, machinery. Flamboyant, gaudy, easier to understand. Halfway to the modern NFL.

It was a bit of luck the way this new style remade baseball. In the course of a season, it set the stars of the previous generation in the distant past. It was like Noah's Flood, this cataract of home runs. It created two worlds: before and after, pre- and postlapsarian. It gave the game its mythology. It made old-time players—Albert Spalding, Cap Anson—seem like patriarchs whose feats are mysterious. You approach a statistic like 59—the number of games the pitcher Old Hoss Radbourn won for the Providence Grays in 1884—as you approach a statistic like 969—the number of years Methuselah lived in the book of Genesis.

■ ■ ■

It left Grover Alexander in a strange position. He was one of those odd figures whose careers spanned eras, who came up under one dispensation and lived deep into another. Like Al Jolson shopping at Walmart or Greta Garbo checking her e-mail. By 1921, his task had gone from outwitting slap hitters to dealing with a handful of dangerous sluggers, avoiding the big blow with a repertoire of pitches that were starting to lose steam. He probably only half understood what was happening. He was either drunk, about to be drunk, or hungover from the moment the bombs started falling in France till the moment he died. Baseball was the only thing that gave him focus. Every four or five days, he pitched. Otherwise, it was here-goes and who-knows and let's-hope-I-don't-get-arrested.

His game-day routine became particular and intense. If a home game was scheduled for 3:05, he'd turn up at the park around noon, reeking faintly of the night before, go out on the field, walk the perimeter, then head back to the clubhouse. He was tall and gaunt. The good looks of his early years clung to him like a tattered suit. When he stood, he stood slowly, as if unfolding a complicated device that stopped being new long ago.

At 2 p.m., he was sitting on a stool in front of his locker, staring at the clock. The other players kept their distance. With twenty minutes left, he made his creaky way to the trainer's room, sat on the table, and rubbed Sloan's Liniment into his pitching shoulder, feeling it burn. He'd go to the bathroom and wash his hands, scrubbing each finger with fanatical tenacity. Then back to his locker to put on his uniform—tuck in the jersey, pull up the socks and stirrups, tie the cleats, pull on the cap. With five minutes left, he'd smoke a Camel cigarette down to the knuckle. He was in the tunnel by 2:59, up the steps and on the mound by 3:00.

By 1922, he'd begun to fall apart. The seizures had gotten worse, as had the alcoholism. Now and then, he'd arrive at the park looking like he still needed to sleep it off. If questioned, he'd say he drank for the team. He pitched better hungover, he explained. At first, he imbibed only between starts. Then, one afternoon, he showed up drunk for a game. Rogers Hornsby, the Cubs manager, sent him out anyway. He pitched a one-hitter. It got worse. Sprees turned into binges. As if he could not stand to be sober even a minute. He'd skip practice, vanish. Reports came in. He'd been seen at a joint on N. Sedgwick, buying drinks for everyone. He'd been seen at a joint on N. Broadway, buying drinks for everyone. He'd been seen at a joint on S. Halsted, buying drinks for everyone. He'd be gone for days, then turn up in a jail in some little town with no memory of how he got there. He might be missing a few teeth, or a piece of his ear. Vomit and blood. It might have been booze, it might have been an epileptic fit. The players covered for him as best they could, as did reporters. In the papers, they'd merely say that once again Alex the Great had "broken training."

One day in 1926, he did not show up for the train taking the team on an East Coast trip. Even the club detective couldn't find him. The Cubs had a new manager, Joe McCarthy, who was not as tolerant as his predecessors. Alexander missed games in Pittsburgh, Brooklyn, and New York before appearing in gray Philadelphia. Asked to account for himself, he could not. The letter McCarthy wrote him on hotel stationery is in the Baseball Hall of Fame. In it, he told Alexander that he'd been suspended and was to return to Chicago and await decision on his future.

A few days later, Alexander was put on waivers. St. Louis, in the midst of a pennant race, with Rogers Hornsby at the helm, picked up the broken-down maestro, hoping he still had something left. Alexander pitched well through the summer, helping the

Cardinals into the postseason, but his greatest moments came in the 1926 World Series. He was thirty-nine years old and facing the Yankees of Gehrig and Ruth. New York won the first game. Alexander started Game 2, a surprise to many. He was a ruin, so old he came from another place in baseball time, but Hornsby said there was no one in the world he'd rather have in the pinch.

Alexander held the Yankees to four hits. Gehrig went 0 for 3 with a strikeout. Ruth went 0 for 4 with a strikeout. The Cardinals won 6–2. The Cardinals were facing elimination when Alex was asked to start again—Game 6, Yankee Stadium. Though depleted—his fastball nothing but a bluff—he shut down the Bombers. It was a culmination. Everything he'd ever learned put to use. You celebrate after a game like that, because you know, no matter what else happens, having just pitched nine innings and being nearly forty years old, that your season is over. The right arm is attached but barely—a noodle hanging by a thread.

Hornsby shocked everyone by sending Alexander out to the bullpen in the middle of Game 7. He did not tell his pitcher to warm up but did tell him to be ready. Alexander spent the afternoon beneath the bleachers with the other pitchers, kids half his age. With no TV or radio, the relievers had little idea what was happening in the game. St. Louis was leading 3–2 when Yankee outfielder Earle Combs led off the bottom of the seventh with a single. Mark Koenig sacrificed, advancing Combs. Ruth drew an intentional walk. Bob Meusel grounded out. Gehrig walked. With bases loaded and two outs, Tony Lazzeri, who, in his rookie year, had hammered American League pitching, came to the plate. A walk ties the game; a single to right puts the Yankees ahead. That's when Alexander got the call. He'd been asleep two minutes before. People later debated the question: Was Alex drunk, or just hungover?

He had little time to warm up. He just stood and walked, loping in from the outfield. Hornsby, who played second, and the rest of the infield, stood around Alex, who did most of the talking. He listed the names of every batter he'd have to face—not just in this inning but in the rest of the game. First Lazzeri. Then Joe Dugan, Pat Collins, and whoever pinch-hits for Herb Pennock in the eighth. Combs and Koenig in the ninth. "And if I get them all," he said, "when the big son of a bitch comes up, the best he can do is tie the ballgame."

Hornsby was holding the ball. He started to talk, then stopped and handed it to Alexander, saying, "Who am I to tell you how to pitch?"

Alexander stared at Lazzeri, who was taking practice swings outside the batter's box. Alex spoke to himself calmly, saying, "Take your time. He isn't feeling any too good up there. Let him stew." He'd beaten Lazzeri with breaking balls earlier in the World Series, so that's how he started. Curveball. Lazzeri watched it. Strike one. Then fastball. Alexander was an old man throwing heat. Lazzeri, at twenty-two, was a young man guessing heat. It was one of those perfect swings, frozen in the phosphorous flash, the crack of the bat, your heart in your mouth as it climbs and climbs. No one cheers. Everyone silent, watching and waiting. For a moment, either thing is possible—triumph or disaster. At the last instant, it hooks foul.

The umpire handed over a new ball, which the catcher threw to Alexander. He squeezed it and scuffed it, trying to forget what had almost happened. That's the key. Remember—no fastball.

Then forget. He came back with a curve, the breaking ball he'd learned from the book as a boy. Lazzeri chased it. Strike three. Alexander sat at the end of the bench, head down. "A few feet," he said, "made the difference between a hero and a bum."

He got the Yankees one, two, three in the bottom of the eighth, started the ninth with two groundouts, then faced Ruth, as he'd foreseen. He was careful with the Babe. All junk, all corners. Don't let the fat man beat you in his own house. He got two strikes, pushed him to the brink. No one wants to make the last out of the World Series. Then threw a changeup on the corner. Ruth took it. Ball three. Alex was incredulous. He walked halfway to the plate, then called to the ump.

"How much did it miss by?"

The ump held his hands apart.

"An inch," said Alexander. "You'd have thought you'd give an old guy like me a break."

He walked Ruth, then faced Meusel. He had a strategy for Meusel, but it did not matter, as Ruth took off running. Asked his thinking—it did not seem like a smart play—Ruth later said something like, With the way Alex was pitching, there was no way we'd get two hits off him. The only chance was I get myself into scoring position and we get lucky. It's a historical oddity—the 1926 World Series ended with Babe Ruth caught stealing. Of course, the real story was the hungover dominance of the epileptic shell-shocked former Chicago Cub.

That was his last good moment. By 1928, Alexander had lost his stuff. His wife left him shortly after his fastball. He was cut by the Cardinals, signed then cut by the Phillies. "Alex had been paid off for the season and when I entered his hotel room, he was in bed and all his money was stacked on top of the dresser," his wife said. "Bellboys who had been bringing him highballs took what they wanted from the poor guy." Here's how the *Chicago Tribune* reported the retirement: "Old Pete has petered his last out." *The Washington Post* did it like this: "Today Alexander takes the back trail that waits for all ball players . . . when their steely arms turn to lead."

He refused to quit, instead going on and on, pitching for ever poorer teams in ever smaller towns. He lived in rooming houses, went on benders, haunted dives, passed out in the streets. He was admitted to so many emergency rooms he could have written a guide. In 1938, when told he'd been elected to the Baseball Hall of Fame and would be given a plaque in Cooperstown, he said, "You can't eat off that plaque, can you?" At some point, he was working in Hubert's Dime Museum and Flea Circus in Times Square. He dressed in his old uniform and told stories about Babe Ruth and Tony Lazzeri.

By 1950, Alexander was living in a rented room on an upper floor of a private house in St. Paul, Minnesota. He woke early and walked the wide shaded streets, or stood at the edge of green lots, watching kids play ball. He was a shell of what he had been, hollowed out by life. It's amazing how many great players came to a bad end, destitute and alone, pitiful at the finish.

One day in November 1950, he retired to his room after lunch and never came back down. The man who ran the house, Ed Nevrivy, went up and knocked. When there was no answer, he opened the door, and there was Alexander, amid sparse furnishings and few possessions, on the ground, arms outstretched as if in greeting. "He had rolled off the bed and must have had a heart attack," Nevrivy told reporters. "He was face down on the floor and he must have hit his head when he fell because there was blood."

It's the back side of those Chicago afternoons when he stood them up and sat them down, when he was carried away on the shoulders of fans. As if he'd traded a decent life for a perfect moment lived long ago.

Here's to the wilderness! Here's to the endless trek by millions of Cubs fans across many barren decades of losing! Here's to Cubs teams that were sometimes good but never good enough! Here's to years of blown leads and late-season collapses and shocking turns of fortune! Here's to every Cub who dropped a routine fly ball or booted what should have been an easy double play! Here's to the many Texas League singles and ground rule doubles and seeing-eyed scorchers that tormented our defense! Here's to a futility that lasted so long we turned it into a religion, proof of a heavenly hand, proof of the special place occupied in this universe by the Cubs fan.

As of 1928, the Cubs had not won a world championship in

twenty years. That was not yet forever, but bad seasons were starting to accumulate. They had won National League pennants in 1910 and 1918, and would win more: 1929, 1932, 1935, 1938. But something always went wrong in the World Series. A botched lead, a blown play, the turn of witchcraft that was coming to characterize the franchise. The owner had already begun to compensate fans the way airlines used to compensate bumped fliers with extra bags of peanuts. We did not have the championship, but the executives were always careful to give us at least one world-class star we could hitch our dreams on: Rogers Hornsby, the last major leaguer to repeatedly hit .400, was a Cub from 1929 to 1932; Gabby Hartnett, a Hall of Fame catcher, who one afternoon had his picture taken at Wrigley Field with Al Capone—the gangster, who rarely missed a home game, is seen with laughing henchmen and a dark-eyed son—was with the team from 1922 to 1940. But Hack Wilson was the most colorful of the wilderness stars, not only because he was funny looking, charismatic, and strange, but also because his story, in its ups and downs, captures a universal fear—that we will forget how to do what we have always done, forget how to be ourselves.

"Hack, one of the idols of my youth, was an oddly built, stocky little barrel of a man, with clothes hangers in his shoulders and a watermelon in his gut," Bill Veeck, Jr., writes in *Veeck—As in Wreck*. "Below his waist he was so small that when I was twelve years old his shoes were too small for me."

He was a pocket Babe Ruth, the same story in miniature. He grew up in Ellwood City, a mill town outside Pittsburgh. His father took off, and his mother died. Like Babe, he was raised in orphanages. He quit school after sixth grade and went to work, successively, in a printers' shop, a foundry, a shipyard. He served as a printer's devil, a riveter, a sledgehammer jockey. All the lifting and pounding made him strong. He was five foot six by age fourteen, as tall as he'd ever need to get. He weighed close to two hundred pounds. He played baseball after work and on weekends. In 1921, he took it up full-time, signing with the Martinsburg Mountaineers in the Blue Ridge League. He set up deep in the batter's box, started his swing early, met the baseball with a rocketeer's trajectory. His bat was skinny and long but heavy at the end, like his sledgehammer. He called it Big Bertha. When he struck out, Big Bertha paid the price. In pictures, you see this freakishly proportioned man—he had an eighteen-inch neck and a size six shoe—heaving a bat into the air, or smashing it into the ground. Giants manager John McGraw spotted him playing for the Portsmouth Truckers in the Virginia League and tagged him as the next Babe Ruth—in those days, every baseball man was looking for the next Babe Ruth. Wilson flopped in New York, hitting just sixteen home runs in three seasons. When he arrived in Chicago in 1926—age twenty-six—it was as a kind of reclamation project, a last chance for the next big thing.

For whatever reason—maybe it was the friendly dimensions of Wrigley Field, maybe it was the guidance of manager Joe McCarthy—Wilson blossomed in Chicago. He hit .321 in his first season, 21 home runs, 109 RBIs. And became a cult hero. It was those big shoulders and that monster neck perched precariously atop those dancer's feet. It was his presence in the hot spots, how he loved to party—as drunk as Alexander, only sociable instead of brooding. A regular at the Hole in the Wall, Al Capone's place in Cicero. His temper, too, was titanic and righteous. He went into the stands one afternoon to beat up a heckler. Another time, he was calmly standing on first one moment, then racing like a lunatic into the Cincinnati Reds' dugout, swinging madly, taking on the entire team. Asked to explain himself, he said, "You should have heard what them sons of bitches was calling me." He got into a brawl with a visiting team at a train station because the bastards were giving him the high hat. And, of course, he could really play. On May 24, 1926, he hit one of the longest home runs ever hit at Wrigley Field, a towering drive that cleared the wall by thirty feet and just kept going. Over the right-field bleachers. Over Sheffield Avenue.

Wilson batted .345, hit 39 homers, and drove in 159 runs in 1929, leading the Cubs to their first pennant in over a decade. In the World Series, Chicago faced a Philadelphia A's team stocked with immortals: Jimmie Foxx, Al Simmons, Mickey Cochrane. Wilson had eight hits in that series, best of all Cubs batters, drove in four runs, tripled, and made several good plays in center field, but that's not what people talked about. What they talked about was Hack Wilson's disastrous Game 4, played in Philadelphia's Shibe Park on October 12, 1929. The Cubs, trying to even the series at two games apiece, were leading by eight runs going into the seventh. The pivot, the pinch.

Jimmie Foxx started it with a single for the A's. Bing Miller, Jimmy Dykes, and Joe Boley followed. A's infielder Max Bishop then drove a ball to deep center field. Wilson watched it merge with the sun, then disappear. It dropped softly behind him. A run scored, the inning continued. The centerfielder came to the plate, Mule Haas. You've never heard of him before and will never hear of him again. Once is enough. He hit another ball to deep center. Wilson, still kicking himself for the previous error, looked up, found it, started to run, looked up again, and it was gone. He raced around like a lunatic as the ball fell behind him then rolled to the fence. On the score sheet, it's an inside-the-park home run, but everyone knew it was really a colossal screwup by Hack Wilson. By the time the Cubs got out of the inning, Philadelphia had scored ten runs and the series was as good as over. Joe Mc-Carthy, the Cubs' manager, tried to talk Wilson down after the game, but Wilson was in no mood. He wanted to hate himself. "The poor kid simply lost the ball in the sun," McCarthy told reporters, "and he didn't put the sun there."

These days, when a player commits an important error, or series of errors, he's required to talk to the press soon after the game is over. Wilson had the advantage of a long train trip to consider and reconsider after the final game of the series, Game 5— reconsider, forgive himself, and move on. But that's not what he did. He was even more upset when he got off the train in Chicago. Fans and reporters were waiting. They shouted questions, but he did not answer. "The big fellow forced his way out of a crowd of admirers with tears streaming down his face," wrote an AP reporter. " 'Let me alone now, fellows,' he said as he choked and sobbed. 'I haven't anything to say except that I am heartbroken and that we did get some awful breaks.' "

There's something about those errors—they resonate more clearly than the great plays. In the end, the humiliations are more memorable than walk-off home runs. It's where we see ourselves in the game, where we come closest to its players. How do you recover from such a turn? How do you prevent a few bad plays from being the only thing history remembers about you? By giving it something else to remember.

Starting in April 1930, just a few months removed from the disasters of Game 4, Hack Wilson put together one of the greatest stretches in baseball history. Even now people refer to it as "the season." It wasn't just the doubles and triples and home runs, but how certain he seemed, as if he'd broken the code, licked the sport. Everything stopped when he came to the plate. Your eyes went to him. The staggering walk, the big bat, the vicious swing. He hit home runs in the second, third, fourth, sixth, ninth, tenth, and eleventh games of the season. He hit two more in St. Louis in the thirteenth game. Then continued. If you could diagram the balls he sent out of Wrigley, trace the path of each dinger, it would look like the finale of a fireworks show. Wilson hit .356, with 56 homers and 191 RBIs—a number that will never be equaled—in 1930. Lou Gehrig came closest, with 185 RBIs in 1931.

Wilson had come into that season with a head full of steam, determined to erase the shame of Shibe Park, Game 4. Which he did, burning from April to October but apparently using up all his fuel in the process. I was once standing beside a Cubs player when he was asked how long he'd stay in the game. "It depends on my performance," he said. "Some guys go on and on, but others just fall off the table." That's what happened to Hack Wilson. He hit .261 in 1931 with 13 home runs and just 61 RBIs. He was not hurt and had not quit the juice. It was the same player with the same bat in the same ballparks, but the magic was gone. He'd fallen off the table.

How does that happen? How does a great hitter forget how to hit? It is alarming. It means a person can slip from the groove of life. Some said the problem was as old as Grover Cleveland Alexander. All that whiskey finally caught up with the slugger. He arrived at spring training twenty pounds overweight in 1931. It affected his bat speed, his timing, his swing. ("I spent most of that off-season in tap rooms," he admitted.) Some said the ball had been changed—the center deadened and the stitches raised, giving pitchers a better grip, resulting in a general power failure. Or maybe it was just a loss of life force, energy. Wilson played hot, rode his temper, which can exhaust a man in the course of a long season—season after season. Driven by fury, he burned himself out. The sportswriter J. Roy Stockton visited Wilson in West Virginia at the end of 1931. "It must have been a combination of things," Wilson told him. "Probably the ball had something to do with it, but it couldn't make that much difference. Then, possibly, I was trying too hard to live up to my new contract and my 1930 record." But the fact is, and this is what terrifies, there is no good explanation. He had it, then lost it. That's all. The Cubs traded Wilson to Brooklyn in 1932. He played a handful of seasons with the Dodgers and was out of the game by 1935, before he was thirty-five years old. He was inducted into the Hall of Fame in 1979.

1945 was the last year the Cubs played in a World Series until 2016. The singer-songwriter Steve Goodman, from Park Ridge, Illinois, expressed the absurdity in world historic terms: "the last time the Cubs won a National League pennant / Was the year we dropped the bomb on Japan."

To those of us who grew up in the 1970s and '80s, 1945 seemed so ancient you might as well have been talking about the Great Chicago Fire. We glossed over it because 1945 was a war year, and wartime baseball floats beneath an asterisk. It was a freak show of faded veterans and green adolescents, the fifteen-year-old and the one-armed outfielder. The war with Japan officially ended

August 14, 1945, but some of the best players would not be back until the following season. The 1945 Cubs might have been good—Peanuts Lowrey was on that team, and so were Andy Pafko, Stan Hack, and Phil Cavarretta, who won the MVP—but they probably won the pennant only because some of the best Cardinals were still in the service. The Cubs faced the Tigers in the World Series. Asked to predict the outcome, the Chicago sportswriter Warren Brown said, "Neither team is good enough to win it."

Chicago won the first and third games in Detroit—black-and-white photos, doubles down the line—then headed to Wrigley for Game 4. You remember what happened. As the players take batting practice, the tavern owner enters with Murphy the goat. The rest unfolds like a movie made long ago, the plot determined by your forefathers. You can only sit and watch. The goat beneath the banner—WE GOT DETROIT's GOAT. Then wandering across the infield, chomping grass. Then arriving at his seat, the fans in the same section waving over an usher. You want to jump into the screen and shout, "Don't do it! Don't open your mouths. Don't you say a fucking word. Just sit there and watch the game," but it's too late. The usher is already carrying the complaint to another man who is carrying it to Phil Wrigley, who is saying, *No good, the goat goes.* You hear the cloven hoofs clattering on the concrete concourse, you see the faces of ignorant fans, hear the pathetic braying, then it is night at the Billy Goat Tavern and William Sianis is leaning across the bar, issuing the curse: *As long as the goat is not allowed into the park, the Cubs will not win.*

They lost Games 4 and 5 in Wrigley, won Game 6 in Detroit,

then returned to Chicago for Game 7. Detroit scored five runs in the first inning. The final score was Tigers 9, Cubs 3. Chicago shortstop Roy Hughes led off the bottom of the ninth inning with a single. Clyde McCullough struck out. Stan Hack flied out. Don Johnson grounded out. That was it for the next seventy-six years.

Eddie Waitkus, a tall, slender twenty-nine-year-old first baseman, played well that afternoon, his first game back in Chicago after having been traded to the Phillies. He'd just finished his second cocktail in the lobby of the Edgewater Beach Hotel when a bellboy told him a message was waiting at the desk.

It was written on hotel stationery:

Mr. Waitkus—

It's extremely important that I see you as soon as possible.

We're not acquainted but I have something of importance

to speak to you about. I think it would be to your advantage to let me explain it to you.

As I'm leaving the hotel the day after tomorrow, I'd appreciate it greatly if you could see me as soon as possible.

My name is Ruth Anne Burns, and I'm in room 1297A.

I realize that this is a little out of the ordinary, but as I said, it's rather important.

Please come soon. I won't take up much of your time, I promise.

Burns. The name sounded familiar. He asked the receptionist to check the register. Where is she from? Portland Street, East Cambridge, Massachusetts. Eddie's street, Eddie's town.

He called from a house phone.

The woman who answered sounded sleepy.

"This is Eddie Waitkus," he said.

"Come up to my room right away," she told him. "I have a surprise for you."

He looked at his watch. Midnight.

Eddie Waitkus was a standout in the National League. He remained a favorite of Cubs fans even after he was traded to the Phillies. He'd spent the better part of four seasons with Chicago. That's where he took on the trappings of a star. He wore finely tailored suits and beautiful shoes. He was well-read, sophisticated.

He knocked on the door. The woman was wearing a silky robe.

Waitkus walked past her into the room.

"What's it all about?" he asked.

"I have a surprise for you," she said, then went to the closet.

Ruth Ann Steinhagen was a twenty-three-year-old Baseball Annie. She'd grown up in Cicero, Illinois, where she fixated on one celebrity after another. First the actor Alan Ladd, then the outfielder Peanuts Lowrey, finally Waitkus. She said he was in another class altogether, above the others. She would stand outside the Cubs clubhouse, hoping to see him, get his autograph. He'd talked to her a few times. She began to read up on him in the sports pages. She lived with her parents then, and her sister. The walls of her room were covered with pictures of Eddie. She'd found a copy of his high school yearbook—that's where she got the name "Burns." She'd studied Lithuanian so she'd understand the language of his grandparents. She told her mother about Waitkus—she referred to him as "Eddie"—speaking as if he were a boyfriend. Me and Eddie this. Me and Eddie that. At some point, she began talking about the wedding. "Me and Eddie are gonna get married."

Waitkus had been traded in 1949—not his fault, but she blamed him anyway. He was not leaving the Cubs. He was leaving her: the marriage, the life they would live together. She cried for days. She said, *Eddie, Eddie, Eddie. Oh, Eddie.* She told her parents she was moving to an apartment in the city to be closer to Eddie. She worked as a secretary downtown, but her real life was all about Eddie. She built a shrine to him in her apartment, pictures lit by candles, headlines and scorecards, pennants, stubs from the more than fifty games she'd attended for Eddie. If that's not love, what is? The way she spoke of him was chilling. It was like John Hinckley talking about Jodie Foster. Love at its purest is insanity. "I used to go to all the ball games to watch him," Steinhagen said later. "We used to wait for them to get out of the clubhouse after the game, and all the time I was watching I was building in my mind the idea of killing him."

She purchased a used rifle and bullets, found out when the Phillies were coming to town and where they'd be staying, and got a room in the same hotel. She ordered drinks from room service—two whiskey sours and a daiquiri—then drank them to quiet her mind. "As time went on, I just became nuttier and nuttier about the guy," she admitted. "I knew I would never get to know him in a normal way, so I kept thinking I will never get him, and if I can't have him, nobody else can. Then I decided I would kill him."

She came out of the closet with the gun. Waitkus held up his hands with a half smile, saying, "What goes on here? Is this some kind of joke? What have I done?"

"When I turned around, there she was with this rifle," he said. "She had the coldest looking face I ever saw. No expression at all. She wasn't happy; she wasn't anything. She said, 'You're not going to bother me any more.' Before I could say anything, whammy!"

"For a minute I didn't think I shot him, because he just stood there," she said, "and then he crashed against the wall. I just looked at him. He kept saying, 'Baby, why did you do that?' And then I said, 'I don't believe I shot you.' . . . I asked him where he'd been shot—I couldn't see a bullet hole or blood or anything. He said I shot him in the guts, and I was convinced he was shot. I don't know why. I thought, well now it's time to shoot myself, and I told him. Then I tried to find the bullets, but I couldn't find them, and I lost my nerve."

Waitkus had been shot in the chest. A .22 caliber bullet pierced his lung and lodged near his spine. She stood there, looking at him. Then got down and hugged him, staring into his eyes. "I've dreamt and dreamt about killing him," she said, "and there I was holding him in my arms. Don't you see all my dreams had come true?"

Waitkus said, "Please, baby, I need help."

She ran into the hall and screamed, "Eddie Waitkus, the ball-player, has been shot!"

She shouted again: "I shot Eddie Waitkus!"

"I was burning because nobody was coming out," she said. "Nobody seemed to want me much. I could have walked right out of the place and nobody would have come after me."

Waitkus was rushed to the hospital, operated on and operated on again. He recovered and was back on the field in 1950. He'd play five major league seasons after the shooting, but was never the same. Haunted, sickly, scared. He had trouble keeping weight on. He retired early, died young.

Steinhagen was put in the Kankakee State Hospital. In a hearing, asked what she'd do if she got out, she said she'd finish what she started. "Eddie is the only one worth killing," she explained. She left the hospital in 1952, then moved into a house on the North Side, where she lived quietly the rest of her life. When she died in 2012, it took the newspapers months to notice.

The shooting resonated. It touched on the strangeness of celebrity and the fear every player has of fans. More than a cautionary tale, it was a parable. It said something fundamental about the game: the road trips and hotels, the strange women in the lobby bars, the music and booze and temptations and fear. It was a Chicago story, a blood-soaked chapter in the book of Cubs fandom.

It was reworked and woven into the lore, most famously by

Bernard Malamud, who, in *The Natural*, turned it into a kind of myth: There's a ballplayer from beyond the farthest city light, who, at fifteen, can already do everything. All the clichés apply: runs like the wind, hits like a hammer, throws like a cannon. Before he even gets started, though, he's summoned to a strange room in a strange Chicago hotel.

> Through the white-curtained window the sight of the endless dark lake sent a shiver down his spine.
>
> Then he saw her standing shyly in the far corner of the room, naked under the gossamer thing she wore . . .
>
> As he shut the door she reached into the hat box which lay open next to a vase of white roses on the table and fitted the black feathered hat on her head. A thick veil fell to her breasts. In her hand she held a squat, shining pistol.
>
> He was greatly confused and thought she was kidding but a grating lump formed in his throat and his blood shed ice. He cried out in a gruff voice, "What's wrong here?" . . .
>
> The bullet cut a silver line across the water. He sought with his bare hands to catch it, but it eluded him and, to his horror, bounced into his gut.

In class, they tell you that this disaster, which befalls the hero right at the start, stands for the end of innocence. To me, it's about the loss of potential. For the rest of his life, the kid would focus not on how good he became but on how good he might have been had he not been unlucky. *The Natural* took the sleaze of baseball, the whoring and drinking and racist hayseeds who were some of its biggest stars, and turned it into mythology. So many of the real-life events of the game turn up in its pages. The Babe is in it, only as the Whammer, a big, arrogant snap-brim-cap-wearing slugger who calls his shot. The gamblers who fixed the 1919 World Series are there too. Roy Hobbs, the Natural, confessing his dream of being the best ever, is Ted Williams, who early in his career said, "All I want out of life, is that when I walk down the street folks will say, 'There goes the greatest hitter that ever lived.'" It means that the game is better, cleaner and more true, than its players. The fantasy is beauty. The reality is booze. That's why Hobbs is shot down, why Baseball Annie is *right* to shoot him down—his pride must be bled so it can be replaced by something more worthy of the game.

Hobbs has an exchange with the shooter the night before the shooting. It's akin to the test given to knights who want to join in King Arthur's quest for the Holy Grail. She talks about David and Goliath, Sir Percy and Sir Maldemer. She talks about Homer, then asks, "What will you hope to accomplish, Roy?"

He had already told her but after a minute remarked, "Sometimes when I walk down the street I bet people will say there goes Roy Hobbs, the best there ever was in this game."

She gazed at him with touched and troubled eyes. "Is that all?"

He tried to penetrate her question. Twice he had answered it and she was unsatisfied. He couldn't be sure what she expected him to say. "Is that all?" he repeated. "What more is there?"

"Don't you know?" she said kindly.

Then he had an idea. "You mean the bucks? I'll get them too."

She slowly shook her head. "Isn't there something over and above earthly things—some more glorious meaning to one's life and activities?"

"In baseball?"

"Yes."

He racked his brain—

Eddie Waitkus never got a test—he was shot for no reason at all. Its meaning was in having no meaning. It was chaos, insanity, how fame can drive a person mad. Of course, it was not entirely meaningless for Cubs fans. To them, it suggested a deep truth: It had become weird and terrible to love this team.

The Cubs story is early excellence followed by biblical drought, an endless trek across the wilderness. In the first part of this trek, which ran from 1909 to 1945, the team did not win a World Series but was often good, sometimes very good. In the second part, from 1945 to 2015, the team was almost never good and often a disgrace. Between 1947 and 1966, the Cubs did not finish above fifth place. In 1956, they lost 94 games. In 1960, they lost 94 games again. In 1962, they lost 103 games. Between 1960 and 1966, when there were ten teams in the National League, their standings read like this: 7, 7, 9, 7, 8, 8, 10. When I talked to Tom Ricketts, the current owner of the franchise, about the long-suffering Cubs fans, we spoke of them as a breed, the way you might speak of the Mexican hairless. He said, "The fans who really deserve credit, the purest example of the type, are those who kept coming out to Wrigley Field in the '50s and '60s. Go back and look at how consistently awful those teams were—I dare you! From 1946 to 1983, they never even made the playoffs. That's really something. The 1969 team was an outlier, genuinely good. And there were a couple of years in the '70s when they looked all right at the All-Star break, but it always ended the same way."

■ ■ ■

It's a question we ask at Sunday school: Why?

Why were the Cubs so bad for so long? Why did it happen and what did it mean? How can a team continue losing like that, season after season after season? If you don't blame a literal curse—I do believe there was a psychological phenomenon at work—and focus on worldly reasons instead, you keep coming up with the same answer: Phil Wrigley, also known as P.K. It was all his fault.

Phil Wrigley took over the franchise in 1934, a few years after his father died. He did not love baseball—that was the big problem. It was a secondhand passion, thrust on him by inheritance. Worn stiffly, sullenly. In 1958, he told *Sports Illustrated*, "I don't think I've ever done anything I've wanted to do, or ever will." Buttoned-up, sober faced, dark hair slicked back. He said his favorite sport was "dice throwing." As for baseball, it seemed his main concern was the corporate balance book. "There are a great many stockholders in the Wrigley Gum Company who would be the first to complain if any of their money was used in baseball," he said. "So none of it ever has been used for that purpose, or ever will." He shortchanged the team in all kinds of ways that would hurt them for years. He did not develop young talent, sign quality veterans, bring in good coaches, or reward star players in ways that made them want to produce. Probably his biggest mistake was deciding not to build a farm system. Branch Rickey, general manager of the Cardinals and the Dodgers, devised the first network of minor league teams, in which prospects are matured and promoted, creating a steady pipeline of talent. Most other clubs followed. But Wrigley stuck with the cheap traditional

way—scout and sign. By the time the Cubs finally did put together a farm system, they were years behind.

The result was predictable: dreary play, mediocre athletes, defeats. But Phil Wrigley was a master marketer. He knew he had to
give fans some reason to pay for tickets. Instead of a winning
team, he decided to sell the experience of the ballpark. P.K.'s deal
with the devil was that he traded excellence for beauty, victory for
aesthetics. A perfect day in the glorious stadium—that's what we
got instead of good baseball. Forget the standings—just enjoy
Wrigley Field. "Our idea in advertising the game, and the fun,
and the healthfulness of it, the sunshine and the relaxation, is to
get the public to see ballgames, win or lose."

The defining moment came in 1937, when P. K. Wrigley told
Bill Veeck, Jr.—Veeck's father had died in 1933; the son was working for the team as a kind of special assistant—to plant the ivy. It
would complete the project. We'd get garden greenery, and all
we'd have to do was give up hope. It was Veeck's idea, but he'd
only been working out Wrigley's scheme. "A team that isn't winning a pennant has to sell something in addition to its won-and-
lost record," Veeck writes. "[The boss's] solution was to sell
'Beautiful Wrigley Field'; that is, to make the park itself so great
an attraction that it would be thought of as a place to take the
whole family for a delightful day."

Veeck nicked the idea from Perry Stadium in Indianapolis,
where the Indianapolis Indians had been playing in front of ivy
since the early 1930s. Planting ivy at Wrigley Field was a way to
realize a woodsy theme P.K. had in mind. Veeck planted Chinese
elms, too, in the bleachers, but those died. The ivy was set down
along the outfield walls in the course of a single night in 1937. It
was in full vigor by the following summer. That's the real dawn

of the modern era. It softened the angles, deadened the sounds. It put us into a blissful slumber, made the park comfortable in a nearly fatal way. A shroud, the green blanket of summer. It made us care about the wrong things. It seduced us with its beauty and soon we forgot the true object of our mission. Once, on Michigan Avenue, I ran into an old friend. I told him I'd been living in New York, and this led to a discussion of Yankee Stadium. "I finally got there," he said, "and wow is it ugly. It made me appreciate what we have with Wrigley Field." What he could not understand—because he was deep in an ivy-covered dream—is that Yankee stadium, though unsightly, was made beautiful by winning, whereas Wrigley Field, though beautiful, was disfigured by loss.

But Wrigley Field was not the *ultimate* cause of failure. It was the racism—that's what the diehards will tell you. The old-time racism of Cap Anson, which marked the Cubs like Cain, but also the latter-day racism of P. K. Wrigley. He was not a bad man, but he was a product of his time, a country-club discriminator who tended to champion players who looked like players he'd already known. In skipping black talent, he probably told himself he was merely giving fans what they wanted. It probably wasn't that he was a racist, but that he believed his customers were. In 1947, when Branch Rickey, then running the Brooklyn Dodgers, finally broke Cap Anson's color line in Brooklyn, the owners took a vote: Should Jackie Robinson be allowed to play? Phil Wrigley voted no, along with fifteen other owners.

It was not just that this was bad morality. It was also bad business.

The Cubs were lousy, a team without a farm system, a team with neither stars nor prospects, and here, in the Negro Leagues, was an untapped vein of world-class talent. The Yankees were questionable on race too—they did not sign a black player (Elston Howard) until 1955, but even so the Yankees were good and had been good. Good in 1947, still good in 1957. The Cubs had come up short for decades. If they had signed Negro League talent early, they could have improved fast—it was a huge opportunity missed. That's what the Dodgers did. Branch Rickey must have had winning games as much as civil rights in mind. Jackie Robinson was Rookie of the Year in 1947. Rickey then added several more Negro League standouts: Roy Campanella, Don Newcombe, Joe Black, Jim Gilliam. In 1953, when the Dodgers might have Robinson at first, Gilliam at second, and Campanella behind the plate, the Cubs had Eddie Miksis at second, Roy Smalley at short, and Warren Hacker on the mound. Brooklyn, which had often been just as woeful as Chicago, won six pennants between 1947 and 1958.

The Cubs did not find a genuine Negro League star until 1953, and even then it was a kind of happy accident. Gene Baker, a Kansas City Monarchs infielder, was the first black player signed by the franchise. A few weeks after P. K. Wrigley approved that contract, Cubs general manager Wid Matthews was back with another.

"Who is this?" asked Wrigley.

"Fellow named Ernie Banks."

"Gee whiz!" said Wrigley. "We're already bringing up a Negro player this year. Why did you go out and get another one?"

"Well," said Matthews, "we had to have a roommate for the one we've got."

■ ■ ■

I met Ernie Banks when I was a kid. In some way I still don't understand, he'd come to know my father. One day, I got home from school and there he was, sitting on our living room couch. It was like discovering Frank Sinatra in the car pool line, Harry Houdini at the supermarket. It made no sense. Banks had retired years before, but his legend still suffused Chicagoland—Mr. Cub, greatest of them all. I was a serious fan, so I knew all the numbers: 512 home runs; 2,583 hits; 2 MVPs. The ultimate shortstop, a first-ballot Hall of Famer. He was friendly and warm, charming when you saw him on TV, yet there was something enigmatic about him. You never knew what he was really thinking. He smiled when he could not possibly be happy. He seemed like a young man when I met him, though he must have been close to fifty. His eyes twinkled.

I said, "When I tell my friends, they'll never believe me."

He said, "What kind of friends are those?"

I said, "The only kind they've got at my school."

He turned to my father and said, "You should move to the South Side."

"What would a Cubs World Series mean to you?" he asked me.

"It'd mean my team is the best team in the world."

"What then?"

"I'd be happy."

"Good," he said, "remember that."

■ ■ ■

I met Banks again a few summers later. It was at an Old-Timers' Game in Washington, D.C., "the Cracker Jack." The rosters were riddled with Hall of Famers. My father had gotten us passes.

I met so many great players that day. Harmon Killebrew, Johnny Bench, Joe Torre. I saw Lou Brock leaning against the batting cage, laughing with Boog Powell, who was as substantial and grand as a long-haul trucker. I met Sandy Koufax, who grew up with my father in Brooklyn. (Spotting my father, Koufax said, "Hey, Herbie!") I saw the Orioles center fielder Paul Blair run from player to player getting autographs, as excited as I was. I shook hands with Bob Feller and Mickey Mantle. My father asked Bobby Richardson, the Yankee second baseman, if he remembered a particular at bat. "Sure," said Richardson. "He started me with a fast ball outside, but I knew that was bait. I was waiting on my pitch." I met Roger Maris. He was sitting in the dugout and seemed tired but was nice to me. We talked about Babe Ruth and the single-season home run record. There were deep black circles around his eyes. I later learned that he had cancer. He died the following December.

I saw Joe DiMaggio on a stool in front of his locker changing into his uniform. I've seen the great DiMaggio dressed as a Yankee. I've seen the great DiMaggio in a suit and tie. And I've seen the great DiMaggio nude. Reporters and photographers stood behind him. At some point, a flashbulb went off. DiMaggio blew his stack. "Goddamn you goddamn sons-of-bitches," he shouted. "Goddamn you cocksuckers. No more pictures today."

Later, on the field, my father, spotting DiMaggio, his favorite player, told me to go over so he could take a picture. "You heard him," I said. "Are you nuts?"

"Don't be a chicken," my father said. "He's an old man. What's he gonna do?"

We argued till it was decided I'd go over and stand *near* DiMaggio so my father could take a picture that had us both in the same frame; that's as much as I was willing to do. Then, as I stood there, smiling beside the Yankee Clipper's back, he turned and crashed right into me. Sheepish and scared, I said, "We just took a picture together, Mr. DiMaggio." He looked me over, said, "Let's do it the right way," then turned and smiled at the camera. That picture sat on my father's desk for years.

Banks came out of the clubhouse shortly before the first pitch. He was wearing his old Cubs uniform but it didn't fit like it did on the baseball cards—loose where it had been tight, tight where it had been loose. He talked to my father, then smiled at me and said, "Still waiting for that Wrigley Field World Series?" He gave me his glove, kneeled down, and showed me how to handle a grounder. I don't remember much about the game—only that Banks popped out and Bob Feller, who was sixty-five years old, still threw hard. An amazing moment came later, when the oldest player came to the plate—late seventies, older than my Grandpa Ben, stooped and gray, a living relic. But he stood in there, eyes on the pitch. His swing was ragged and elaborate and yet that old man hit the longest home run of the day. It just kept going. He hobbled around the bases. I didn't think he was going to make it.

■ ■ ■

By the time I met Ernie Banks again, thirty years had passed. I was middle-aged and half the people we'd seen in that Old-Timers' Game were dead. *Sports Illustrated* had sent me to interview Banks for the cover of the magazine's annual "Where Are They Now?" issue, though everyone knew exactly where Ernie Banks was—Chicago—and exactly what Ernie Banks was doing—being Mr. Cub.

We met between the towers of the Wrigley Building on Michigan Avenue on an early spring afternoon. We shook hands and spoke for a moment in the street, then went up to his office, two rooms, two desks, two views of water. I told him we'd met before. When I mentioned my father, he nodded like he knew him, but clearly didn't. He was still slim and elegant, but time had caught up with Banks. He was eighty-two years old. I asked questions that he did his best to answer, but we were having trouble connecting. Then I reminded him about that Old-Timers' Game. He lit up. He smiled. He threw his head back and laughed. He suddenly knew exactly who I was and where we'd met and even what we'd talked about. He said, "How is your father? I do miss him. And your mother, Ellen. What a wonderful woman. How is she?"

I told him that my mother had died.

He cursed and said, "No, no. That's terrible."

He was quiet for a moment, then reached out, squeezed my knee, and smiled.

"What about that game we both saw in Washington, D.C.? Do you remember when that old man hit that home run?"

"Of course I do."

"Who was that old man?" he asked.

I told him I could not remember.

"Me neither," he said. "Which is too bad. Because I think about it more than I should and I'd really like to know who I am thinking about. Do you still want that Wrigley Field World Series?" he asked.

"More than anything."

"And you'll be happy then?"

"Yes."

When I asked about the details of his life, when I asked him to tell me his story, which is all I'm ever really after in an interview, he answered with great specificity, animation. "I remember every day of it," he told me, "every hour of every day of it."

■ ■ ■

Ernie Banks was born in Dallas, Texas, in 1931. His father had been an amateur baseball player, a legend in the bush leagues, but was a broken man by the time Ernie was in school. He worked in cotton fields and now and then Ernie worked beside him, 6 a.m. till sundown. Ernie did not love baseball. Softball was his game, basketball too. He was offered a contract by the Harlem Globetrotters but instead signed with the Amarillo Colts, a semipro softball team—barnstorming, playing under the lights. He was noticed right away. Though slender as a string, he could hit with tremendous power. It's not just that some players do more of the same, but that what they do is different. The ball sounds different coming off their bat. Banks had a unique batting stance, unlike that of other power hitters. He didn't lean on his back leg or swing from his heels. He stood upright and squared off, like a man playing softball. He was calm as he waited, his urgency betrayed only by his fingers, which drummed on the handle of the bat. When he saw a pitch he wanted, he took a step toward the mound and swung. When I asked Banks how he achieved such power, he said, "With my belly. I hit the ball with my belly. My arms came around, my belly moved, and the ball went out."

He signed with the Kansas City Monarchs, a storied Negro League franchise, when he was nineteen years old, but was drafted before he could get going. He spent two years in the army, mostly playing baseball in Germany, and wasn't back till 1953.

Those were the sad waning days of the Negro leagues. Robinson had already been with the Dodgers six seasons; most of the teams had been picked clean of talent. Old men remained, and raw recruits, dead-enders, and those who'd never been good enough. Banks was mentored by great black stars. Satchel Paige, Elston Howard, Buck O'Neil. Banks hit .386 with twenty home runs for Kansas City in 1953. Chicago paid the Monarchs $20,000 for his contract.

He first stepped onto Wrigley Field on September 17, 1953. In the imagination of fans, the moment is dramatic, the young man dazzled by Euclidian symmetry, lake winds, and ivy. Banks spread that story himself. It was Ernie who dubbed Wrigley Field the "Friendly Confines."

The reality was different. Wrigley was a dump in 1953. Thirty-nine years old, which made it tired but not historic—just another run-down ballpark, no better than Shibe Park in Philadelphia or Ebbets Field in Brooklyn. Americans were not feeling terribly nostalgic just then. New—that's what people wanted. Spotless and clean. Wrigley was dirty, run-down. "I was shocked when I first walked onto the field," Banks told me. "I was expecting the big-time major leagues, a gleaming castle, seats up to the sky, but the place was falling apart, half empty, shoddy, and I thought . . . Is this all there is?"

From the start, it was clear that Banks could play. His biggest challenges came off the field—the culture shock. "During my half-month stay with the Cubs in September," he said, "I met more white people than I'd known in all my twenty-two years." Then there was the team itself, which was terrible. The Cubs lost eighty-nine games in 1953. Banks was said to have been called "up," but it felt more like a step down after the Monarchs. "I went from playing with the best to playing with some of the worst," he told me. And the Cubs were old. The finest player on that team was Hank Sauer. He was thirty-six. Dutch Leonard, a forty-four-year-old bullpen pitcher, had broken in with the Brooklyn Dodgers in 1933, when he played with Lefty O'Doul, who'd played with Carl Mays, who, having killed Ray Chapman, ushered in the modern era. That's the brevity of baseball time.

Banks stood out in 1950s Chicago, a flash of lightning in an inky sky. Check out pictures taken of him in 1953, 1954. We remember Ernie as an old man, but he was once as young as anyone has ever been—high cheeked, always smiling. In 1955, he hit .295 with forty-four home runs while playing shortstop, which was unusual. The shortstop had most often been a little guy, a defensive wizard, a lead-off hitter expected to bunt, certainly not to hit for power. One of the most famous shortstops of the era was known as "Pee Wee." Another as "Scooter." The Dodgers' Pee Wee Reese (5′10″, 160) never hit more than sixteen home runs in a season. The Yankees' "Scooter" Rizzuto (5′6″, 150) never hit more than seven in a season. At 6′1″, 180, Banks was in another class: forty-seven home runs in 1958; forty-five in 1959. He broke the mold. Not only the first black Cubs star, but also the prototypical power-hitting shortstop, a precursor to Cal Ripken, Jr., and Alex Rodriguez.

From 1955 to 1960, Banks was arguably the best hitter in baseball. He hit more home runs than Mickey Mantle, Hank Aaron, or Willie Mays. He was MVP in 1958 and again in 1959. That award is given to the player who has proved most valuable to his team. It usually goes to a player on a top club. Which is what makes Banks's back-to-back MVPs so remarkable. With Banks at shortstop, the 1958 Cubs finished in fifth place. How would they have done without him?

It was not just his production that made him a hero in Chicago. It was the way he played—the obvious joy, how he never seemed to forget he was one of the few people in the world doing exactly what he wanted to do. That's why Ernie Banks was Mr. Cub. That's why he was bigger than baseball. Because he loved it and we loved him for loving it. Ernie was the perfect Cub, ideally suited for the role of a great player on a terrible team. He never lost hope, never got down, never stopped trying. He gave people something to admire in even the most pathetic seasons. He happily shared the fate of the common fan—to be always going and never arriving, to spend an entire lifetime in the wilderness. His task was paramount. He was a shepherd. He led us across Sinai. His importance is captured in his famous phrase, spoken on a hot summer day, when everyone else wanted to retreat to the cool of the clubhouse: "Let's play two."

There have been many unbreakable records in the history of baseball, most of which were eventually broken. Pete Rose broke Ty Cobb's unbreakable career hit record. Cal Ripken broke Lou Gehrig's unbreakable consecutive games played record. Lou Brock broke Ty Cobb's other unbreakable record—career stolen bases—which was then broken by Rickey Henderson. The only record that really is unbreakable is the one that makes Banks the personification of the Cubs: 2,528 games played without appearing in the postseason.

He hugged me at the door at the end of the interview, then told me not to worry. He was positive the Cubs would soon win the World Series.

"Why are you positive?" I asked.

"Because of Theo," he said, "and because that's my choice—you always have a choice. I choose to be hopeful."

I spoke to Banks one more time. It came out of the blue. My phone ringing on a weekday afternoon. He started talking before I'd even said hello.

"Luke Appling!"

"What?"

"It was Luke Appling that hit that home run," he said. "He was seventy-seven years old. I'm sure he thought about that every day from then until he died. It just shows: Sometimes even an old guy can get some good wood on the ball."

CHAPTER | NO.
THE CHEMO COACH | 07

While working on a book about the 1985 Chicago Bears, the greatest team in the history of the NFL, a team that brought me back to life after the 1984 Cubs killed me, I heard a term that still lingers in my mind: "chemo coach." This came from Doug Plank, the Bears' safety, the so-called Human Missile and namesake of the 46 Defense. He was explaining the historical function of Mike Ditka, who coached that Bears team. "There are three kind of coaches," Plank explained. "First, there's the aspirin coach. He's the guy that comes in and feeds you a bunch of baloney and makes you feel better initially, but nothing changes. Then there's the penicillin coach. He comes in and fixes *almost* everything. The problems, the illnesses. But there's one thing he can't fix and that's cancer on a team. What's cancer? Guys don't like each other, the offense versus the defense, huge attitudes. You need the third kind of coach for that: the chemo coach. Bill Parcells, Mike Ditka. The chemo coach comes in, man, he's the new sheriff in town. He's so powerful by the way he looks, his presence, his actions; if you got a bad attitude, you don't buy into his system? He doesn't care who you are—you're gone."

Leo Durocher was the Cubs' chemo coach. P. K. Wrigley hired him after the 1965 season to turn around the franchise. He arrived in the wake of a management disaster. The hierarchy of pro baseball had been established with the ascension of Cap Anson in the late 1800s. Wrigley was the first owner to change that in seventy years. Instead of a manager, his mid-60s Cubs teams were run by an eight-person committee, with a new head man every few weeks. This was P.K.'s much derided "College of Coaches," a tangle of diffuse leadership and snarled command chains: The buck stopped here, or here, or maybe over here. Not only did those teams lose, they became a joke. Durocher, the man known for the expression "Nice guys finish last," was to be the antidote, the chemo. "There's only one boss on this team," he said when he arrived.

■ ■ ■

He certainly had the biography for it—his whole life had been about sticking it to the other guy. He grew up in West Springfield, Massachusetts. Alleys and vacant lots, some filled with broken bottles and rusty nails, some shaped like diamonds. His early passion was pool. He was a feared hustler in neon-lit halls. That was the way he played baseball too—like a hustler, full of feints, bluffs, and tantrums. He was discovered by a Yankee scout—Paul Krichell, who'd found Lou Gehrig not long before—while playing shortstop for the local electric company. Durocher was like the Indian on the buffalo nickel. Each feature cut in steel—sharp chin and bright eyes. He was small, filled with fury. He believed his size gave him the right to fight dirty. Dirty was the only way it was going to be fair. When he arrived at Yankee Stadium, where, for a few years, he'd be a tiny cog in a great machine, manager Miller Huggins nodded approvingly. *Yes, yes, a little guy. Little guys can help us win.* Durocher was a shortstop of the old school, all glove and no bat. He debuted with the Yankees in 1925, when he was nineteen. His first full season came in 1928. As a rookie, he famously checked Ty Cobb on the base paths, knocking him to the ground. In the lore, Cobb threatened Durocher, who then called Cobb, depending on the version, either "old goat" or "Grandpa," as in, "Get back to your nursing home, Grandpa."

In his book, Cobb denied it. After calling bullshit on one legend, Cobb adds, "Same goes for the much-circulated account of how Leo Durocher knocked me sprawling when I rounded second base. As it's peddled, Durocher said, 'That'll hold you, you old goat!' Leo gets all kinds of credit for having slyly slammed a hip into me and put me flat on my face. He never saw the day he could do it."

In New York, Durocher picked up nicknames like lint. "Leo the Lip" is the one that stuck. Because he talked all the time. The trash that came out of his mouth made even his own teammates blush. He had a knack for getting under your skin. He roomed with Babe Ruth on the road. It's a funny thing when you read about the Babe: He's a figure from the past, yet jumps off every page. Apparently, in addition to being the best player, he was a great guy. Everyone loved him, and he loved everybody. Except Durocher. The Babe hated Leo the Lip. He called him the All American Out. Because that's all he did. Ground out, strike out, hit into rally-killing double plays. Ruth gave him another nickname too—Leo the Thief. It was whispered wherever Durocher went: That's the guy who stole Babe Ruth's watch. Durocher could not stay in New York. Yet even after he left, it clung to him, that Yankee thing. It was part of the mystique he carried from town to town.

Durocher played seventeen major league seasons, but his real success came as a skipper. He started as a player-manager with Brooklyn in 1939, where he turned around what had been a mediocre team. The Dodgers finished below .500 the year before he took over. In 1941, he led them to their first pennant in twenty seasons. They won 104 games in 1942. He did it in the way of the chemo coach—screaming and threatening, squeezing every drop of blood from the sponge. It was a hard way to win, a nearly impossible way to live. It worked but could not be sustained. Always in high gear, always angry, a little man bouncing like a dashboard needle in and out of the red.

His players would work for him and work for him, until one day, overwhelmed, they quit. It was a pattern repeated everywhere he went—results, revolts. You see it in the statistics. His teams did best three or four years after his arrival. He had his people in place by then, everyone pulling in the same direction. Then, five or six years out, the wheels came off. By then, the rookies had become veterans, and, as veterans, they'd had enough. The team would flag, fail. Durocher would move on.

According to Doug Plank, this is the downside of the chemo

coach. He kills the cancer, but what does he do after the disease has been driven into submission? Keeps blasting away with chemo, because he's a chemo machine. In this way, he starts to kill healthy tissue. The result is often incidents of the spectacular tabloid variety. In Brooklyn, players signed a petition saying they'd stop performing if Durocher didn't lay off. During batting practice, Dodger outfielder Dixie Walker would wing balls into the dugout, hoping to bean Durocher. In 1945, Leo beat up a fan beneath the Ebbets Field bleachers. He said Brooklyn general manager Larry MacPhail fired and rehired him at least sixty times, "but I was there when he left."

He ran with a fast crowd in New York. This was the other Leo, the off-the-field, cologne-soaked nighthawk—always good for a line in the gossips, hanging out with starlets and crooners, a knock-around guy orbiting Sinatra, which meant mobsters and gamblers, fixers of just the sort that corrupted Shoeless Joe Jackson and Eddie Cicotte in 1919. He got in trouble. Bounced checks, borrowed money from the wrong people. "He had drawn headlines," *The New York Times* reported, "with his marriage to the actress Laraine Day, whose former husband charged that Durocher had stolen her away from him while posing as a family friend."

It all led to an investigation by baseball commissioner Happy Chandler. Usually, when a player or an executive is suspended from the game, it's for a specific reason. Failing a drug test, taking a job as a greeter at a casino. According to the report, Durocher was suspended in 1947 for "the accumulation of unpleasant incidents." That is, for being an all-around pain in the ass. He came back as manager of the New York Giants, where, with Willie Mays in center field, he won two National League pennants. He was the skipper in the 1951 postseason series that ended with Bobby

Thomson's famous Dodger-killing home run, "the shot heard 'round the world." That sealed Durocher's image—he was a headache but also a winner. By bringing him to Chicago, Phil Wrigley was making a statement. You don't bring in that madman unless you want to succeed. "Not everyone liked Leo," Cubs third baseman Ron Santo wrote later. "Yet, from the first day with Leo as manager, we didn't feel like losers anymore."

■ ■ ■

Ernie Banks was exactly the sort of player Durocher would have built a team around in 1954—the young Ernie with good knees and fast bat. But Banks was breaking down by 1965. Stiff ligaments. Bad everything. Hanging on. Durocher told Phil Wrigley that he wanted to trade Banks—now, while we can still get something for him. Wrigley would let Durocher do anything—that's what it means to hire a chemo coach—except that. You don't trade Mr. Cub. "He was a great player in his time," Durocher explained. "Unfortunately, his time wasn't my time . . . He couldn't run, he couldn't field; toward the end, he couldn't even hit. There are some players who instinctively do the right thing on the base paths. Ernie had an unfailing instinct for doing the wrong thing. But I had to play him. Had to play the man or there would have been a revolution in the street."

In other words, Durocher was stuck with a franchise player he did not want. Over time, he came to resent Banks—"He was jealous of the tremendous popularity and following Ernie had built with Cubs fans," wrote Santo—and Banks came to resent being resented. What seemed like it might have been a good relationship—Durocher had always handled stars well—turned cold, mean. It was the feeling beneath everything Durocher built in Chicago. Leo believed Ernie's popularity was a detriment, that it stood in the way of winning. It was like the argument I had with my friend on Michigan Avenue. Do we love Ernie Banks because he's a great player, or do we think he's still a great player because we love him? In Chicago, people are filled with sentiment. That's what it means to be cursed.

"Ernie never remembered a sign or forgot a newspaperman's name," Durocher said later. "All he knew was, 'Ho, let's go. Ho, babydoobedoobedoo. It's a wonderful day for a game in Chicago. Let's play twooo.' We'd get on the bus and he'd sit across from the writers. 'A beauoooootiful day for twoooo.' It could be snowing outside. 'Let's play three.'"

If you were going to make a movie about the '69 Cubs, you would center it around these two men and their relationship. The win-at-all-costs manager and the aging black star who believes he has more to contribute. Banks was still talking about it when I spoke to him decades later. Leo had been dead twenty years and Ernie would soon follow, yet it bugged him. "That man hated me," Banks said. "I never understood that. So what did I do? Did I challenge him? Did I take him on? No. He was the manager, the boss. He was allowed to hate me. My response was the same as it always has been—put my head down and play the game. That's all you got. The game. That's how a player is judged. How did he play the game? That for me was dignity—the fact that I went out there and played as well as I could every day."

Durocher did Banks a great service. He was indeed tailing off, in decline. Leo's disdain drove him back toward excellence—nothing motivates like disrespect. Durocher managed the Cubs for seven seasons. Every spring, he brought in another player to displace Banks. In 1967, it was Clarence Jones. In 1968, it was Dick Nen, tagged "the first baseman of the future." Banks went head-to-head each time and prevailed. Because he was better. His belly moved and the ball went out.

■ ■ ■

Durocher's Cubs followed the classic chemo pattern: 59 and 103 his first year with the club—tenth place; 87 and 74 his second year—third place. By 1969, they were poised, with a roster of great players and a lineup that will be remembered for as long as Cubs fans wander the earth.

Don Kessinger, who'd make six All-Star teams, at shortstop. Glenn Beckert—he took over from former Rookie of the Year Ken Hubbs, who, paralyzed by a fear of flying, learned, at the urging of a psychiatrist, to pilot a plane, then died in a plane crash—at second base. Billy Williams, a future Hall of Famer and one of the best pure left-handed hitters ever to play for the franchise, in left field. Jim Hickman, a thirty-two-year-old who was good in the pinch, in right field. Don Young, a twenty-three-year-old emotionally fragile rookie and the obvious weak link, in center. Randy Hundley, possibly the first major league catcher to catch the ball with one hand, behind the plate. Banks at first—he'd play 155 games and hit 23 home runs with 106 RBIs that summer. The pitching staff was strong, with four quality starters, including Kenny Holtzman, who, because he was a left-handed Jew, was touted as the next Koufax, and the future Hall of Famer Ferguson Jenkins. Fergie, who grew up in Canada, a descendant of a runaway slave, was six foot five, 205 pounds. He started forty games in 1968, tying a team record set by Grover Cleveland Alexander. He'd strike out 273 hitters in 1969 and win twenty-one games.

The team was led by its captain, twenty-nine-year-old third baseman Ron Santo. He grew up in the Italian section of Seattle known as "Garlic Gulch," which I mention only because he did, all the time. His parents divorced when he was seven. He used to wait with his suitcase on the corner for his father, who had weekends. "One day," Santo wrote, "he just didn't show up. I didn't see him again for twelve years." It ruined Santo and made Santo great. It gave him the intensity that fueled his game and the intensity that could make him hard to be around.

Santo was heavily recruited when he was still in high school. He was offered deals by half a dozen clubs but signed with the Cubs *because* they were terrible. He knew that if he signed with Chicago, he was likely to make it to the major leagues fast. At his first minor league clinic, he was instructed and appraised by Rogers Hornsby. After a few days in the cage, Hornsby gathered together fifty or so prospects, then, in the way of a fortune teller, told each his fate. "You'll never hit big league pitching," he told this one. "You'll never figure out the curve," he told that one. When he got to Billy Williams, he said, "You will be able to hit big league pitching." When he got to Santo, he said, "You can hit big league pitching now."

Santo was good at everything, but was unlucky and suffered. A few weeks before his first spring training, he learned, in the course of a routine physical, that he had juvenile diabetes. He took the news quietly, then ran to the library to look up the facts. "I can still remember the feeling I had when I read the description," he told the *Chicago Sun-Times* in 1990. "Life expectancy of a juvenile insulin-dependent diabetic: 25 years. It also stated that it would cause blindness, kidney failure and hardening of the arteries. At that point, I said to myself, 'I am going to fight this thing and beat it.' That's how badly I wanted to live and be a big league player."

Because he was afraid the Cubs would cut him if they knew, he kept it a secret. He vowed to tell the team only after he'd become an All-Star. How can they cut an All-Star? He eventually confided in a few other players—in case he needed help. His biggest fear was going into diabetic shock during a game. His doctor told him to watch for certain symptoms: light-headedness, ennui, double vision. In such a case, get sugar fast. Grover Cleveland Alexander stashed bottles of whiskey around the clubhouse. Ron Santo stashed candy bars.

It finally happened at Wrigley Field in 1967. The Cubs were trailing the Dodgers 1–0 in the bottom of the ninth. Santo was on deck—watching Billy Williams work the pitcher—when he felt a subtle change, like a drop in the barometric pressure. "I looked at the scoreboard and had to look again," he told me later, "because, my God! There were *three* scoreboards out there!" He stayed calm, tried to bluff his way through. "I was praying for Billy to strike out so I could get to my candy bar," he said, "but he kept fouling off"—the ball sailing into the upper deck, hitting the screen, bouncing off the dugout. It went on, and as it went on whiteness appeared at the edge of Santo's vision. "Then, son of a bitch, Billy drew a walk!"

Santo stood at the plate, staring out at three pitchers. "I decided to swing and miss and get it over with," he said. "Three balls coming at me—I chopped away and *boom*! It went over the wall, grand slam. It won the game for us. But now I had to circle the bases, and I wasn't even sure where the bases were. I figured, the only way to survive is to run like hell. I came up behind Billy, who was jogging, and I shouted, 'Go faster! Go faster!' I thought for sure I was going to pass out. Somehow I made it, but my vision was going blue. The whole team jumped on me. Beckert knew right away. My face was white. I could hardly talk. I was numb. He hurried me back to our dugout, where I got my emergency candy bar and wolfed it down and just sat there."

Santo had already played on five All-Star teams by 1969. He'd make it again that year, along with the entire infield. He hit .289 with twenty-nine home runs, but his personality was more important than his bat. He had an edge and could be as harsh as Durocher. To teammates, to reporters. Some people tell you that's why it took him so long to reach the Hall of Fame. Though he clearly belonged there, he was not inducted until 2012—two years after he died.

Following a comeback win early in the season, Santo, running along the left-field line, jumped up and clicked his heels. This gesture would become a '69 trademark, a symbol of the team in ascendance. "It was out of jubilation," Santo wrote. "One click of the heels from an emotional Italian . . . Leo approached me about it. I thought he was going to yell at me for showboating. Instead he told me to keep doing it. It'd become the Cubs thing."

The team got off to a jackrabbit start. They were 16–7 on April 30; 31–16 on May 30; 50–27 on June 30. At that point, they held first place in the NL East by seven and a half games. Euphoria swept through Cubs nation. This had to be the year. In the middle of the summer, several players sang on an album called *Cub Power*, which sits on my desk. It includes the song "Hey Hey Holy Mackerel." "Hey, hey, holy mackerel, no doubt about it, the Cubs are on their way!" We hear it now and cringe. Because we know what will happen, and they don't. It's impossible to tell whether this record heralded the disaster, was a symptom of the disaster, or caused the disaster.

On June 19, 1969, as the season was heating up, Leo Durocher married the socialite Lynne Walker Goldblatt, the widowed heiress of the Goldblatt department store fortune. The wedding was held at the Ambassador West on North State Street, *the* place for weddings and bar mitzvahs. (I won a disco contest there in 1977.) Durocher invited every member of the team, as well as Frank, Dino, Sammy, Peter, and Joey—the entire Rat Pack! All the Cubs showed—Banks, Santo, Holtzman, and Beckert in stiff suits, trapped in another sort of friendly confine. None of the Rat Pack did. Durocher kept walking to the door and asking, checking his watch and cursing, more unhappy about those who did not show than glad about those who did.

This wedding is the key to understanding what happened in 1969. Everything good and everything bad was on display that night. The dedication of the players, the omnipresence of the press, society as personified by the debutante who'd married first a Jew and then a lunatic jock, the fans who stood in the street. You saw the snobbery of Durocher, how he preferred celebrities to the men who played for him. The hypocrisy, too, how he demanded loyalty from his players but offered little in return. None of which mattered when the team was winning. When a team is winning, there are no problems. It's when things get tough that the cracks appear.

What had been implicit at the Ambassador West in June became explicit at Shea Stadium in July. "It all came down to that one series, and not just that, but to one game in that series, and, even more, to one inning in that one game," Banks told me. "When we left for New York, we were four and a half games ahead of the Mets in the division. I called all the guys together and said, 'Look, there'll be more media in New York, more reporters, than you've ever seen in your life. They'll be on the field, in the dugout, even in the clubhouse. Remember that and be careful about what you say—if you're not sure, then say nothing. And stick together. We have to stand up for each other in New York.' But did they listen to me? Did Santo even hear me? You ever hear that expression, 'It takes one bad apple to ruin an entire barrel'? Well, I saw that happen in New York."

The Mets had finished the previous season in ninth place— this was an expansion team, in just its eighth year of existence. They were better in '69, but still seemingly second-rate, no match, hitter for hitter, for the Cubs. But they did have pitching, powerful young arms at the start of great careers: Tom Seaver, twenty-four; Tug McGraw, twenty-four; Nolan Ryan, twenty-two. Asked by the *Daily News* writer Dick Young about the Mets before the start of the series, Santo scoffed, saying, "Are you trying to compare the Mets to the Cubs? Man for man, there's no comparison, Dick, none."

Shea Stadium sold out the first night—forty-five thousand fans, spillover in the aisles, standing along the fences. Fergie Jenkins started for Chicago. He had a quick, decisive delivery—it almost looked like he was playing catch. He did not give up a hit until the fifth, but that was a home run, a solo shot by Ed Kranepool. Banks and Hickman homered for Chicago, which led 3–1 going into the bottom of the ninth. First game of the big summer series—these are exactly the ones that good teams have to win.

Ken Boswell led off for New York—a half swing, a looper to

center field. Don Young, who'd been iffy all day, looked into the sun and lost the ball. It should have been an easy play, but fell in for a single instead. No outs, man on first. The tension started to build, hands drumming on seat backs. Tommie Agee popped out. Donn Clendenon came in to pinch-hit. Jenkins stepped off the mound and looked out to center field, trying to get Young's attention. Jenkins waved him back—back, back, back. Young did not move. Santo later said it was not the first time that day Young had either not understood or ignored instructions. Historical echoes—baseball is always recurrence, return. To me, Fergie Jenkins waving Don Young back at this key moment and Don Young staying put is Christy Mathewson waving back Giants center fielder Cy Seymour in 1908—Seymour similarly stayed put and ended the day weeping in the clubhouse. "Clendenon hit the ball exactly where Young should have been," Santo told me. It looked like an easy play anyway. In the footage, you see Young camped under it, gazing into the sky. Then, just as he's about to make the catch, the ball hits the top of his glove and caroms away, sending the runners into motion and the crowd into ecstasy.

The next batter, Cleon Jones, doubled—the only legitimate hit of the rally, according to old Cubs. Art Shamsky, a dark-haired, beetle-browed, unremarkable utility infielder who, in his commonness, stands for a thousand players who had been great in high school and in the minors but mediocre in the majors, drew a walk. Wayne Garrett, a twenty-one-year-old third baseman, grounded out, but the runners advanced. That brought Ed Kranepool into the pinch—men on second and third, two outs. He singled. Cleon Jones scored. Mets 4, Cubs 3. Game over.

A baseball season is 162 games. One game should not matter that much. At the end of this game, the Cubs still had a three-and-a-half-game lead in the NL East with 76 left to play. On paper, they still had a better team. And yet a season is like an afternoon—there's often a single moment when everything is decided. Either you seize that moment or you fade away. Every member of the 1969 Cubs I have spoken to cites this game, played on July 8, as the pinch. History is a garden of forking paths. If Don Young makes those plays, we take this path into sunlight. But he failed, so we took that path into undergrowth and gloom.

"So was it Don Young's fault?" I asked Banks.

"No, it was not Don Young's fault," he told me. "All of us have made big errors. The question is: Do your teammates pick you up? 'Cause it's really about the group, not the guy."

The Cubs sat in front of their lockers after the game—the press waited just outside. No one spoke, or even looked up. Only one person could be heard. Leo Durocher hollering as if he were in a pool hall back in West Springfield. Several reporters wrote down and published what he said: "Let me tell you something. It's tough to win when your center fielder can't catch a fucking fly ball. Jenkins pitched his heart out. But when one man can't catch a fly ball, it's a disgrace!"

After Hack Wilson made two errors in Game 4 of the 1929 World Series, manager Joe McCarthy had said, "He lost the ball in the sun, and he didn't put the sun there." After Don Young made his errors, Durocher said, "My son could have caught those balls! My fucking three-year-old son could have caught those balls."

Santo showered, got dressed, then stopped to talk to reporters. Asked about the errors, he thought a moment, then began with a phrase that should come as a warning to any speaker. "I know I should not say anything, but . . ." If you hear those words coming out of your mouth, shut up and leave. Santo did not shut up and did not leave, but stuck around long enough to trash Don Young. "He was thinking of himself, not the team," said Santo. "He had a bad day at the plate, and he's got his head down. Don's a major leaguer because of his glove. When he hits, he's a dividend, but when he fails on defense, he's lost—and today he took us down with him. He put his head between his legs."

If Kessinger or Beckert had said it, fine. But this was not Kessinger or Beckert. It was the captain. It was Santo's job to lead, and he failed just as surely as Don Young had failed. Santo realized his mistake early the next morning, when his phone started to ring. It was a huge story in Chicago, covered in the way of a scandal. Santo apologized to Young, then called a meeting and apologized to the team, but it was too late. The pressure and attention, the intense focus on a few mistakes, upset the players and ruined Don Young. This is what Ernie Banks meant by a bad apple—because, in a sense, as soon as Ron Santo had given that quote, the Cubs were finished. "It was never the same," Banks told me. "We just stopped being a team."

It was a long, weird summer in Chicago—'69, the summer of the collapse. Violence on the South Side, the Manson murders in L.A., the Vietnam War on television. On July 18, the Cubs beat the Phillies 9–5 and Ted Kennedy went off the bridge at Chappaquiddick. On July 20, the Cubs beat the Phillies 1–0 and *Apollo 11* landed on the moon. On July 24, the Cubs beat the Dodgers 5–3 and Muhammad Ali was convicted of draft dodging. The ground crew ripped the grass out of Comiskey Park and replaced it with AstroTurf in 1969, like a lady plucking her eyebrows then painting them back on. Eddie Cicotte, the White Sox knuckleball ace and ringleader of the 1919 World Series fix, died that May. Pat Piper was still working the PA at Wrigley Field, as he'd been doing since 1916. In the early years, he called the starting lineups through a megaphone. Rogers Hornsby, Hack Wilson, Andy Pafko, Ernie Banks—he'd announced them all. Joe Tinker at the beginning, Rick Reuschel at the end.

The Cubs were still in first on September 1st, but the gauge needles were spinning, warning lights flashing. The last good chance to arrest the fall came on September 8 and 9, when the team went back to Shea for a quick series. I won't go into detail, but suffice to say it was in the middle of the first game, with Chicago leading, that the black cat appeared. I had always assumed it was a feral cat that randomly wandered from the bowels of the stadium—the world was going to hell in 1969, wild animals taking over—and only later learned it was a stunt, the black cat sent out to spook the Cubs. "I was in the on-deck circle waiting to face Koosman," Santo wrote in his memoir. "I was studying Billy Williams at the plate when all of a sudden, a black cat jumped out of the third base stands! He ran in front of me, stopped to stare and headed toward our dugout, where he glared at Leo, who was on the front step of the dugout. Then headed back into the stands. I don't walk under ladders; I throw salt over my shoulder and I don't light three cigarettes on one match. I especially don't like black cats in my path."

The Cubs were swept in that series and the rout was on. How bad was it? The '69 Cubs were in first place in the National League East from early April till the second week in September, when they lost to the Phillies and dropped a half game behind the Mets. When I spoke to Santo, he said it was not that Chicago collapsed, but that New York surged. "We were not that bad in September," he said, "but the Mets went on a historic winning streak."

This is revisionist history, argued against facts. It's true that the Mets were terrific down the stretch—21–10 in August; 23–7 in September—otherwise they never would have caught the Cubs. But Chicago had such a big lead, they only had to be mediocre to clinch. If they'd played .500 baseball in September. If they'd played .450. Instead, saving the worst for last, they played .320, going 8–17 in September. Lost to good teams, lost to bad teams, lost to everyone. As if terrified of success. As if cursed. Santo denies it because no one wants his life reduced to a few woeful weeks. I understand. It happened when I was less than a year old. It happened forty-seven seasons ago. It happened in a city so different that it might as well be a different city and in a country so different that it might as well be a different country, yet it still hurts.

For as long as I can remember, people have been trying to understand the collapse and why it happened. Some say the players were tired and ran out of gas. By the 1960s, every stadium other than Wrigley Field had lights and every team other than the Cubs played most of their games at night. Phil Wrigley had planned to install lights before World War II interfered, then delayed, then kept on delaying till delay became a point of pride. Possibly without meaning to, the Cubs cast themselves as the last true baseball conservatives, playing the game as it had been played by the patriarchs. Real grass, manual scoreboard, trough system in the men's bathroom, day baseball. It was akin to a religious principle, like conducting the Mass in Latin. It's one of the many aspects, along with giving up on the corrupting concept of excellence, that made us the most faithful followers of the creed. Lights were not installed until 1988. It was a great event for some, a spiritual crisis for others. A night game at Wrigley Field even now takes me by surprise. But it was only after '69 that people began speaking of the lack of lights as a disadvantage. All those games under the summer sun, the pitchers out there inning after inning, while the Mets worked in the cool of nighttime Queens— it had to take a toll.

To others, it was not the heat but the booze. A major league game typically ends around 10 or 11 p.m., leaving a player just enough time to shower, change, go home. In Wrigley Field, with its 1:20 starts, a player is often done working by 5 p.m., leaving him far too many hours to goof off and carouse. It's a tradition that goes back to Grover Cleveland Alexander. After the game, you buy your favorite player a drink in the tavern. That too was said to take a toll. A ballplayer, according to this reasoning, must be scheduled as tightly as a toddler. Left to his own devices, he will find mischief.

To some, it was not the day games or the free nights that wore out the Cubs. It was Leo Durocher. He never laid off, never gave anyone a break. He kept his starting pitchers on the mound for far too many innings, pushed his position players past the limit, exhausted everyone in July and August so that, in September, when the Mets made their kick, the Cubs had nothing left. Just look at the numbers. Ernie Banks, at thirty-eight years old, played 155 games. Billy Williams, at thirty-one, played 162 games. Ron Santo, a twenty-nine-year-old diabetic, played 160 games. Whereas the Mets' starting pitchers combined for 969 innings in 1969, the Cubs' starters played 1,163. Randy Hundley, the Cubs' twenty-seven-year-old catcher, is the prime example. Catcher is the most mentally and physically grueling position in the game. The catcher has to devise a strategy for every hitter and work the pitcher while spending most of the day squatting and ruining his knees, getting pegged by wild pitches, clipped by wild bats, concussed by foul balls. In the course of a season, catchers have been known to lose fifteen or twenty pounds just by doing the job. Most managers give the catcher every fifth or sixth game off. An average starting catcher will play around 130 games in a season. In 1968, Hundley played 160 games—a record. In 1969, he played 151 more. That's how Durocher handled his players—squeeze 'em till there's nothing left. "If a man had a slight injury or was just plain tired, Leo didn't want to hear about it," Jenkins said. "He just rubbed a man's nose in the dirt and sent him back out there. You played until you dropped."

When Durocher was old and retired, a white belt holding up his blue pants, he admitted this and took responsibility for the collapse. He apologized to the team at a reunion shortly before he died. It was not just the way he worked the players but also his style, the harshness of his judgments, and how he imposed two sets of rules: one for the players, another for himself. One weekend in 1969, as his team was going hard, he vanished. Not in the dugout, not in the clubhouse. A doctor told reporters that Durocher had gastritis—characterized in the newspapers as "a powerful bellyache"—and would be out a few days. But the following afternoon, when he was supposed to be home in bed, Durocher was spotted at Camp Ojibwa in Eagle River, Wisconsin. Parents' weekend. He was visiting the twelve-year-old son of Lynne Walker Goldblatt Durocher. Another parent recognized the manager and called the scoop in to a friend, Jim Enright, a *Chicago Tribune* columnist who'd been feuding with the Lip.

Or maybe it's simpler than all that. Maybe the '69 Cubs just weren't good enough. Maybe Durocher *had* to overwork his players because the team lacked depth. Its center fielder wasn't big-time. Its captain wasn't much of a leader. It's greatest player was near the end of his career. I first considered this possibility while watching the 2016 Cubs. It hit me like an epiphany: Oh, so *this* is how good you have to be!

Then again, the 1969 Cubs really were a great team. Five future Hall of Famers, if you include Durocher—his Cooperstown plaque reads: COLORFUL, CONTROVERSIAL MANAGER FOR 24 SEASONS, WINNING 2,008 GAMES, 7TH ON ALL-TIME LIST. COMBATIVE, SWASHBUCKLING STYLE A CARRY-OVER FROM 17 YEARS AS STRONG FIELDING SHORTSTOP FOR MURDERERS ROW YANKS, GASHOUSE GANG CARDS, REDS AND DODGERS. MANAGED CLUBS TO PENNANTS IN 1941 AND 1951 AND TO WORLD SERIES WIN IN 1954. 3-TIME SPORTING NEWS MANAGER OF THE YEAR. Ten players on the '69 Cubs made at least one All-Star team. Which leads to the penultimate explanation of the collapse, the only one that incorporates and makes sense of all the others: There *really* is a curse. If not as metaphysical phenomenon, then as mind-set, internal weather, cumulative inertia that thickens as the team approaches victory. During a road trip in September 1969, Ernie Banks invited Kenny Holtzman into his hotel room. After a few cocktails, Banks turned thoughtful. "We had a nine-game lead," he said, "and we're not going to win it."

Holtzman asked why.

"Because we've got a manager and three or four players who are out there waiting to get beat," said Banks.

"I'll never forget it," Holtzman said later. "It was the most serious and sober statement I'd ever heard from Ernie Banks. And you know what? He was right."

"A lot of people say we blew it because we did not get enough rest," Banks told me. "They talk about Leo and how he pushed us, bad luck, the surging Mets, the black cat, but don't believe any of it. It was us, only us. The curse is not voodoo. It's just fear. When you have never won and your team has never won, not for decades, it works on you and gets into your head and you go out there waiting to see how you will fall apart, expecting something to go wrong, and when you look for it, you find it. That's something I've learned in life: Whatever you look for, you find. If you look for a curse, you'll be cursed. That's why it was so hard for us. Even our best players were waiting to see how it would fall apart. Winning was an unknown thing, not part of our routine, our habit. It surprised us. We did not know how to handle it. We did not know what it would do to us. We did not know how challenging it can be—even tougher than losing. We looked it right in the face and we blinked. That's what happened in 1969."

Because God has a sense of humor, the Cubs ended 1969 with a two-game home stand against the Mets, who'd already clinched the National League East. New York took the first—their seventh straight victory. The Cubs took the second 5–3. Banks tripled and hit a home run. As soon as the final out was made, fans dropped from the bleachers onto the field. They swarmed. To be in first place through acts one and two only to fall apart in the middle of act three—it was almost too much to endure. It demanded a demonstration, a breaking of boundaries, a stumbling dash across the grass. It was later described as a miniriot, the anger and frustration generated by the team's collapse bubbling over. That's why the organization installed the wire basket that runs along the top of the outfield wall: to keep drunken fans and their beers and trash off the field. When you see that basket, you are seeing the physical residue of the collapse and the madness that followed.

Some of the Mets stayed on the field, watching the bleacher bums, reveling in their anger. According to the *Chicago Tribune,*

Mets right fielder Ron Swoboda mocked one of the rioters. "It's hard to admit you were not good enough, isn't it?" Swoboda said. "You were good, but not good enough."

In *Sports Illustrated*, Robert Jones condemned not merely the fans but also the city. "Chicago appears in its true colors," he wrote. "A loser. Not even the Second City anymore, but the one city that has to blow it. For the stale smell of defeat lingers in every dark corner of Chicago, and not even the coarse, cold wind off Lake Michigan can scour it clean."

The key year in Cubs history is 1969 because it established a pattern and formed a sensibility. It created the expectation of defeat my father had in mind when he tried to steer me away from the team. The curse had been humorous lore. It did not seem so funny after 1969. No sane person could study what had happened and come away entirely dismissive. It was only after the collapse that people began to take the curse sort of seriously. This is when being a Cubs fan became different from being the fan of any other team.

■ ■ ■

What happens to a great team when that team fails? When it gets close, then chokes? When the players reveal their timid hearts? A near miss can bring a team together and push them over the top. Or it can destroy. The Cubs played decently in 1970 and 1971, but their moment had passed, their window had closed. Banks retired after the 1971 season. He hit three home runs that year. You can see the last one in the archive. It's Wrigley Field as it existed in my childhood, redbrick gloom, Jack Brickhouse doing play-by-play. It's filmed with the same stock used for Bozo's Circus. Banks is thick at the waist, getting old, but his fingers still drum along the bat handle. The pitch hangs, the belly moves, the ball goes out. He ambles around the bases with head down, a man who knows he's going away. Billy Williams and Kenny Holtzman left for Oakland. Santo was traded in 1973. The Cubs wanted to send him to Anaheim, but he refused to go. Chicago was his home. He'd accept only one trade: to the White Sox. South Side fans hung a banner at Comiskey to mark his arrival: RON SANTO, WELCOME TO THE MAJOR LEAGUES.

But the moment that really marked the beginning of the end came by way of acquisition. Here I sing the epic of the free-spending, toupee-wearing Brooklyn-born first baseman Joe Pepitone—his name itself partly accounts for his fame, the way, like "Lolita," you can't say it without becoming aware of the trip your tongue takes from the roof of your mouth to the back of your teeth. Pep-i-tone! He'd broken in with the Yankees, where he made three All-Star teams and appeared in a World Series. He was a good fielder and hitter, but most of us know him for what came later: his stint in Japan, how he took all that money to play for the Yakult Atoms and then basically blew them off—in Japan, his name is still a pejorative. If you do something half-ass, if you fail to deliver on a promise, you're a "Pepitone." His stint with the New Jersey Statesmen of the American Slow Pitch Softball League. His memoir, *"Joe, You Coulda Made Us Proud."* His nude spread in *Foxylady* magazine. His hitch in Rikers in the late 1980s. You run a red light in Brooklyn and next thing you know you're in cuffs as police comb through your car, coming away with cocaine, quaaludes, a gun. A camera caught him saying to the cops, "I didn't know cocaine was illegal." He was arrested for fighting in a bar in upstate New York in 1992. It started when another patron called him a has-been.

He already had the look of a spent shell when Durocher picked him up in 1970. He was not yet thirty years old. He was especially endangered by day games—out every night, in velvet and ermine, dancing. He'd drag himself in an hour before the game, bleary and suffering. Banks would smile and say, "Hey, Pepi! You ready to play baseball?" Pepitone would answer, "Yeah, Ernie. It's a great day for two—two more hours of fucking sleep."

He was vain—that's what Jim Bouton said about Pepitone in his book *Ball Four*. He was in front of the mirror for hours after every game, dousing, massaging, applying. He traveled with several pieces of luggage, one just for hair products. He had multiple toupees, a piece for casual times, a piece for the dance floor, a piece worn under his ball cap, which he called his "game piece."

Durocher hoped Pepitone would make people forget Banks at first base. When Pepitone failed to meet those expectations, Durocher came to hate him. One day in 1972, a year in which Pepitone appeared in just sixty-six games, Durocher saw something in the parking lot that infuriated him: a shiny red motorcycle, gleaming and new.

He asked around.

"Whose bike is that?"

"Pepitone's."

Durocher stared at the motorcycle, stewing. There it is, in physical form, the reason this team can't win. Where's the focus? The priorities? He called in Hundley—the catcher had always been Leo's favorite. He asked Hundley if he'd seen the motorcycle. He had. He asked if he knew whom it belonged to. He did. "No wonder the fucking guy can't hit a fucking baseball," said Durocher. "He's out all night riding that fucking motorcycle and his fucking hands are tired."

Durocher told Hundley to get the team together—time for a meeting. Hundley told Pepitone what was going on and also told him to sit through it and say nothing. "Let Leo have his say. He's just trying to shake things up."

The team gathered beneath the left-field bleachers. Durocher talked and talked. He started with the motorcycle, then went into a general diatribe. He spoke of effort and pride, the old-time Yankees, Pepitone's hangovers, Santo's hitting slump, the failings of the pitcher Milt Pappas. When he was finished, he said, "Any of you guys got anything to say?"

"Pepi had been warned not to talk," said Hundley.

"I do have something to say," Pepitone told Durocher, "but you're not going to like it."

"Don't think of me as your manager," said Durocher. "Think of me as another player—talk to me that way."

"Well, for one," said Pepitone, "why are you always blaming people? Pappas didn't mean to throw that pitch. Santo doesn't want to be in a slump. All you ever do is criticize."

Pepitone mentioned Ralph Houk, his manager in New York. No one likes being compared to a successful contemporary. "When I played for Ralph Houk, he stuck up for his players," said Pepitone. "That's why we won pennants. But all you do is criticize."

Durocher waited patiently as Pepitone went on, then asked, "Are you through?"

Pepitone nodded, and that's when Durocher blew up.

"What are you?" Durocher screamed. "A fucking clubhouse lawyer?"

"I knew I should have kept my mouth shut," said Pepitone.

"You had your say," said Durocher. "Now I'll have mine. Who

the fuck do you think you are? The only fucking reason you're on this club is because of ME! You were out of the fucking game! If it weren't for me, you'd be in the fucking gutter, asshole!"

Leo went into every aspect of Pepitone's character, picking it apart. It got so bad that the other Cubs started to defend their teammate, which further enraged Durocher, who turned on them, one by one. Finally, he went after the captain, Ron Santo. The Cubs were organizing a Ron Santo Day and Durocher said they were doing it only because Santo had asked them to do it, which Santo considered a terrible insult. Santo ended up with his hands around Durocher's neck. "Go ahead," yelled Durocher. "If you want to hit me, hit me."

Santo squeezed until Durocher's face turned purple. Breaking away, Durocher shouted, "That's it! I'm done." He stripped off his uniform—jersey, socks, and pants stood in a pile on the floor. He stomped on the pile, shouting, *Done, done, done, done, done, done!* He was talked back into his clothes, but it really was the end. He was fired in the middle of the '73 season. "You know, when I first knew Durocher he was one of the sharpest riverboat gamblers I ever saw in my life . . ." Jack Brickhouse said. "In those early days, he was a son of a bitch, but he was a sharp son of a bitch. But by the time he was finished in Chicago, he was just an old son of a bitch."

When I was thirteen, I began going to Cubs games on my own. This was my first taste of adulthood. I've associated Wrigley Field with freedom ever since. I'd catch the bus at the end of my street and ride it into Evanston, where I transferred to the El, the Red Line carrying me like a magic carpet above the rooftops all the way to West Addison Street, where it was ballpark ambience and peanut shells the moment you stepped off the train.

Five dollars got you into the bleachers. You followed ramps. Up top you made a choice: left-field bleachers or right-field bleachers. Like choosing a political party. Though you might have gone this way instead of that by whim, the decision became your destiny. I chose left field. Over time, I came to hate the right-field bleacher bums. I cursed them in chants that were never more elaborate than "Right field sucks." The left-field bums were sunnier and saner than the bums in right, whom I feared. To this day, when almost every other distinction has been erased from my life, I still feel like I'm being disloyal if I sit in right field.

For me, the seasons were defined by what was going on at Wrigley Field. Early spring meant bare ivy and players in long sleeves, a center fielder exhaling plumes. Late spring was new growth and freshly cut grass and hecklers, irrational hope, the queasy sound of a shattered bat. Summer was lush greenery, the rumble of a passing train, the trees along Waveland Avenue tossed by the wind and filling up like sails, and then the dog days of August when the ivy withered and the team drifted to the bottom of the standings. Because the Cubs never made it to the postseason, autumn was storm shutters pulled over outfield gates.

Best were weekday games that started at 1:05, games that had no meaning other than the meaning shared by every other unimportant thing. Seeing a game like that in the spring—and now I was older, sixteen—meant ditching school after fourth period, waiting for the bus on Green Bay Road. Familiar faces in the bleachers, my baseball family. To sit out there when everyone else was in class, to see the players playing the game without any effort to schedule it for a time when most of the world could watch, let me know that life was still going on even when I was trapped in school. One August, I took a picture. I was right behind the catcher, five rows up, using a disposable camera. I got the shot off a moment before an usher asked to see my ticket. I still have that photo. The pitcher—I think it's Rick Sutcliffe but it's impossible to say—has just released the ball. His body is still falling toward the hitter, who is already swinging. You see the bend of the batter's back leg, his hips following his eyes toward the point of contact. You see the ball suspended between pitcher and hitter. The infielders are moving, anticipating. You can't see the sun, but it's there in the shadows. Nor can you feel the wind, but it's there too, in the flags on the poles and wandering bits of trash. Nor can I be seen, though it's through my eyes. And the summer is there—going full blast, as if it will never end.

■ ■ ■

The 1979 Cubs are the first team I followed and the first team I loved.

It was a ragtag crew:

Pitcher Rick Reuschel is whom you noticed first because he seemed nothing like an athlete. Big and soft, a farm boy from the western part of the state. He looked less like a pro ballplayer than like a guy who teaches woodshop. But he was one of the best players on the Cubs. He threw pitches that looked as fat and wobbly as the man himself, the sort you imagined hammering into every part of Wrigley Field, yet few hitters could catch them clean. That was the Reuschel magic. He was already thirty years old in 1979 and still went on and on and on. Nineteen seasons in the majors. Every time I happened to see him—now pitching for the Cubs, now pitching for the Giants, now pitching for the Yankees or the Pirates—I was at a different stage in my life. A long career serves a time-marking purpose for a fan. It can carry you from childhood to adulthood, shoehorn you into grown-up life. It's a function of baseball, which is all about length—long games played over long seasons, which accumulate into long careers. A career

like Rick Reuschel's runs beside your life, allowing you to measure your progress. I was five and stumbling across the green
fields of Libertyville, Illinois, when he won thirteen games for the
Cubs in 1974. I was twenty-two and writing stories for *The New
Yorker* when he lost his last game for the Giants. I grew up in
between, in the shadow of that large man. And it was not just
Rick, but also his older brother, Paul. The brothers were on the
same roster for three seasons in Chicago. Rick was good, Paul not
so good. Rick looked sad, Paul looked even sadder. The baseball
card that features them side by side over the phrase BIG LEAGUE
BROTHERS has a prized place in any collection. I used to wave it
before my own brother, saying, "Maybe we're not good enough
to play pro baseball, but can we at least try to behave like big
league brothers?"

Ivan DeJesus was at shortstop in 1979. We spent much of our
time struggling with his name. Did it mean "of Jesus" or "from
Jesus"? He must've been religious, because he often crossed
himself between pitches, the bottom of the crucifix being his
crotch, which he adjusted as he stepped into the batter's box.
Steve Ontiveros was at third. Barry Foote was behind the plate.
There was a rotating cast of outfielders: Mike Vail, Jerry Martin,
and, most unforgettably, Dave Kingman.

It's strange how a player who hit so many home runs, and not
just regular home runs but God balls—so high they go all the way
up to heaven—can leave such a bad taste in your mouth. It was
his body and countenance, that mustache and those cold, angry
eyes, the mean way he carried himself not just in Chicago but
everywhere he played. Kingman, a lumpy six foot six, was a par-
ody of the haughty ballplayer, the anti-Banks, the man who
seemingly stays in the game not because he loves it but because

nothing else pays as well. He'd exaggerated the Babe Ruth swing to the outer limits, starting at his heels, swinging for the moon. It was feast or famine, monster shot or strikeout. The nicknames that attached to him suggest the dichotomy. He was known as King Kong and also as Ding Dong. You can never win with a guy like that. For one, he looked miserable out there, having no fun at all. Of course, you can't discount all those home runs entirely. It's on account of them that Bill James listed Kingman as the ninety-eighth best left fielder of all time. James writes that "77% of Kingman's career value is his home runs, the highest percentage of any player in history." (Cecil Fielder is next on that list; Sammy Sosa is ninth.) But as a fan you got a bad feeling from Kingman—like he hated you, not in general but in particular. Knew you and hated you. He'd hit thirty-seven home runs for the Mets in 1976 but they traded him the following June. Which tells you. He could not stay in a single city more than four years. By then, too much ill will had accrued. 1979 was his best season. He hit forty-eight home runs and—amazing for him—batted .288. He also struck out 130 times.

Kingman was with the Cubs just three seasons but it felt like forever. Speak his name to any fan between the ages of forty-two and ninety-five and watch the physical reaction—grimace, groan. Ding Dong. Like Nixon and Trump, he warred with the press. It began when the *Sun-Times* put him on its list of worst-dressed Chicagoans. He told his teammates to never again speak his name to the media. He sent a rat to one reporter and dumped a bucket of ice water over the head of another—Don Friske of the *Arlington Heights Daily Herald*. Kingman called it "a prank." In an attempt to monetize all that bad energy, the *Tribune* gave Kingman a column. He said he was not entirely comfortable with the gig, as "it's an insult to be called a writer." Asked if he used a tape recorder for interviews, he said, "Nah, I make it up like everyone else." Some of his columns ran. Some were killed, including one in which he suggested trading newspapermen like baseball players. He wanted to swap Mike Royko for Red Smith. In a profile, Kingman named his hobbies, a 1970s bachelor potpourri: hunting, fishing, woodwork, photography, "my dog." "After every game, Kingman takes to his boat to collect his thoughts and a few fish for dinner," according to the story. "During the season, he likes to be alone. 'When you're around a lot of people,' he complained, 'they always get around to talking about baseball.'" Asked to characterize Kingman, Bill Buckner said, "He's a teammate."

This meant something coming from Buckner, as Buckner was the greatest Cub of that fallen era. He was twenty-seven when he arrived in Chicago. His big shoulders and thick mustache, his serious way of approaching the game, seemed at once old-fashioned and brand-new. He would have looked comfortable playing beside Cap Anson or Kris Bryant. He was a first baseman and a .300 hitter, with an easy swing that sent screamers into the power allies. He was more than just a good player—he was a steadying presence among a team of incompetents. He filled that classic Cubs role—great player on a bad team. An All-Star, National League batting champion in 1980, our connection to first class, what we had instead of winning. Buckner carried the burden in those bleak years. He was *our* Mr. Cub.

I got to meet him when I was ten years old. It was like encountering a historical figure. It was like meeting John F. Kennedy. My father had become friendly with Dodger manager Tommy Lasorda. One spring, when that team came to town, we got passes.

We talked to Lasorda in his locker room office. He was wearing a ribbed undershirt, baseball pants, turf shoes. His pants were unbuttoned and his big belly hung down. Every Italian restaurant in the city had sent over its signature dish. Tins were scattered across the desk and Lasorda picked at them as we talked.

My father and I were in the midst of a fight, and Lasorda somehow sensed this. He kept asking what it was about. Finally, I told him. My father had made me remove my Cubs hat outside the locker room. He said wearing a Cubs hat in the Dodgers clubhouse would be disrespectful. Lasorda thought for a moment, looked at me, looked at my father, then said, "I like you, Herbie. You are a nice man, but I have to tell the truth: In this case, you're dead wrong! Dead wrong! What kind of kid do you want for a kid? A kid who changes colors depending on the company he keeps? 'Cause to me, that sounds like a rat. Your boy is loyal to his team. God bless him!"

Lasorda came around the desk and hugged me, took the Cubs hat from my pocket and put it on my head, then walked us through the tunnel and onto the field, where he waved over Buckner, whom Lasorda had once managed. Lasorda told Buckner about the fight. ("He made him take off his hat?" Buckner asked incredulously.) Buckner shook my hand. He was big and handsome and nothing unlucky had happened to him yet. We talked about the Cubs and we talked about the game. Then we turned and smiled and took the picture.

For the most part, being a Cubs fan has not meant 2016 or 1908. It's meant 1979. That's the real deal, the typical experience. The standout game that season—the part that represents the whole—was played at Wrigley Field on a blustery afternoon in May. The jet stream had settled fifty feet above the park. Any ball hit into the air was picked up and carried away. The Phillies hit four home runs in the first four innings and were quickly leading the Cubs 17 to 6. The Cubs tied the game at 22 in the eighth. Kingman hit three home runs, one of which is considered among the longest ever hit at Wrigley Field. It cleared the bleachers, landing, according to the announcer, "on the front porch of the third house across Waveland Avenue." Of course, it would not be a classic Cubs game without a classic Cubs finish: Mike Schmidt homered in the tenth to beat Chicago 23–22.

According to George Will, in *A Nice Little Place on the North Side*, Mike Vail made a throw from Wrigley's deep right field one afternoon that season. He hoped to nail the runner at home, but the throw sailed and beaned the batboy instead. There he lay, stretched out like a corpse. I've not been able to verify this story, but repeat it anyway because, even if it did not happen, it might as well have, as it captures exactly what it felt like to be a Cubs fan in 1979. We were all that batboy, wrongly believing we were watching from a safe distance.

■ ■ ■

Baseball is feudal. Change comes with the death of powerful men. What really mattered in 1977? That the Cubs traded Bill Madlock and Rob Sperring for Bobby Murcer and Steve Ontiveros? Or that, in the first weeks of the season, Phil Wrigley fell ill while watching the game on TV in Wisconsin? He began to hemorrhage, then died. He was eighty-two and had not been to Wrigley Field in over two decades. He left everything, including the team, to his son William, who, in 1981, to raise money to pay taxes, sold the franchise to the Tribune Company for just over

$20 million. It made sense. The Tribune Company owned WGN TV and WGN—it stands for "World's Greatest Newspaper"—broadcast the Cubs. The company had a programming interest in fielding a winner. What's more, if there was actually a curse, if the goat was indeed responsible, there was little reason to believe it would transfer to the new owners.

The Tribune made two great moves right at the start. The first had zero to do with on-field performance but would make our lives immeasurably more fun. In November 1981, after the retirement of announcer Jack Brickhouse, they hired Harry Caray to call the Cubs games on TV. Caray was just as colorful as any of the old-time greats, with a childhood straight out of a Hack Wilson biography. His parents died before he was nine years old. He was raised by relatives, educated in alleys and vacant lots. As far as I know, no baby pictures of him exist. If they do, I don't want to see them, as Harry has always been an adult in my mind, red faced with grand waxy white hair, besotted smile, stammer, rubbery lips, thick glasses, and slurry voice.

The only thing we know for sure about Harry Caray is that his name wasn't Harry Caray. It was Harry Carabina, which he changed for radio around 1940. He paid his dues at tiny stations across the Midwest. In 1945, he was hired to call the Cardinals games. He was part of a classic two-person crew: the play-by-play man describing, re-creating, even inventing; the color commentator, usually a retired athlete, analyzing. Play-by-play tells you what's happening; color tells you what it means. In his first years, Harry worked beside Gabby Street, who once caught games for Walter "Big Train" Johnson. If you listen to those early Cardinals broadcasts, you might be surprised by how conventional Caray sounds. His voice is youthful and clear, even high, and he works fast, so unlike the broadcaster we know from his baroque period. Yet even here you catch hints of what will make him a legend: how he loses himself in a game, is never far removed from his own memories. He was already using the phrase "Holy cow."

The Cardinals were purchased by the beer baron Gussie Busch in 1953. He had deep pockets, big plans, and what was described as a "trophy wife." There were rumors—someone said the wife had been stepping out. A private dick was hired. Harry Caray would find himself out of a job. Asked if he'd been having an affair with Mrs. Busch, Caray said, "I've never raped anyone in my life."

Caray was eventually hired by Bill Veeck, Jr., who then owned the White Sox. Caray worked those games with Jimmy Piersall, who'd been a good player but was most famous for the mental breakdown that put him in the booby hatch. He used to get into uniform at 2 a.m., head to the park, take his position, and play an entire game in his head. Anthony Perkins played Piersall in the movie *Fear Strikes Out*.

Caray would tease Piersall, saying, "You're crazy, Jimmy."

"Oh, yeah," Piersall would answer. "I've got a piece of paper says I'm sane. Do you?"

One night, during the seventh-inning stretch, Bill Veeck happened by the booth, where he spotted Harry, big head and big hair silhouetted against a half-empty stadium, singing "Take Me Out to the Ball Game"—off-key, to himself, but overflowing with love. The next night, Veeck had Caray's mic fed through the PA system. Caray later said it took him by surprise. He did not know he'd been singing to the stadium till his voice echoed back. This was Bill Veeck's genius—not getting Harry to sing "Take Me Out to the Ball Game" but hearing it and recognizing its greatness, then broadcasting it to the masses. It was a piece of found art.

Authenticity is what made it beautiful—it would exist even without an audience. Veeck merely hung it on the wall. That song, as sung by Caray, and later by the many people who have tried to fill the hole left by Caray's death in 1998, or by Harry himself on video, would become a staple tradition at Wrigley Field.

Caray and Piersall were replaced when Bill Veeck sold the Sox, but the real end came earlier. I won't go into tremendous detail, but it went something like this: Piersall had been trashing White Sox players on the air. He called it being honest. The wives of some of the players complained. It was arranged for Piersall and Caray to apologize on *Live at Five*. Caray did. When Piersall's turn came, he called the wives "horny broads." A moment later, Piersall was off the air and Harry was being hired by the Tribune Company.

It was among the greatest signings in Cubs history. Caray became the glue, the ribbon that held us together. He made even bad teams fun to watch. Now and then, between the action, in the dead space that he filled with his own eccentricity, you'd catch a glimpse of his backstory. You heard it one afternoon, when, interspersed with his play-by-play—this was his method—he wandered into a sort of Stanislavski monologue. "I don't know what the big deal about Cracker Jack is. Did you ever go buy a box of Cracker Jack thinking you were going to get a prize and find no prize in the box—HERE'S THE PITCH—that might not sound important to some people, but when you're a little kid, especially from a humble origin, and they cheat you out of a prize—THERE'S A BOUNCING BALL, THE SECOND BASEMAN HAS IT, OVER TO FIRST—it's hard to think in laudatory terms of the product."

Steve Stone, color commentator: "I think there was an occasional box of Cracker Jacks that found no prize for the little Harry Caray many years ago."

Harry Caray: "You got that right. And boy, when a box of Cracker Jack to me meant a lot of money—HERE'S THE PITCH, BOUNCED FOUL. That's the most asinine marketing I've ever heard of. ONE BALL, ONE STRIKE. And these guys say, 'Well, you sing about Cracker Jack.' And I said I only sing it 'cause it's in the song. THERE'S A PITCH, FOULED BACK. And I wouldn't be a bit surprised if even to this day some youngsters buy a box of Cracker Jack don't find a prize in the box. ONE BALL, TWO STRIKES, TWO OUTS. If you're gonna talk about a congressman being crooked—THERE'S A PITCH, FOULED OUT OF PLAY—why not talk about commercial products that don't do what they represent to do?"

The older Caray got, the more eccentric his broadcast became. At times, it seemed nearly deconstructionist. What you saw on the field had little relation to what was being described. Caray occasionally told us about something that was not happening at all. It was not information we wanted from him—it was personality. We anticipated his trademark phrases, his turns of mind. If a ball was fouled straight back toward the booth, he'd say, "Come out, Steve, I'll protect you." If a player was slumping, he'd say, "He's been hitting 'em hard, just at people." He created his own statistic, replacing batting average with what a player *should* be hitting because "he's been hitting 'em hard, just at people." He was optimistic. In his world, bad hitters were good hitters who were overdue, and terrifying foul balls that missed being home runs by a foot were "long strikes." At the end of each victory, he'd shout, "Cubs win! Cubs win! Cubs win!" It became a catchphrase along with "Holy cow," which is funny, because though immediate results might vary, the big picture remained the same: Cubs lose! Cubs lose! Cubs lose!

Caray hardly ever spoke about the curse. He was old-fashioned enough to steer clear of jinx talk. After the last game of the 1991 season, though, he did seem to foresee the coming of a new age. "Well, a lot of things happened today," he said. "And they were all great. And they were all thrilling. And they were all dramatic. Too bad we couldn't have had a victory that meant a pennant. But that will come. Sure as God made green apples, someday the Chicago Cubs are going to be in the World Series."

I met Harry Caray when I was twenty years old, though "met" is probably too strong a verb. "Witnessed" is more accurate. A friend and I snuck into the press section hours before a game. We went out onto the catwalk that led to the broadcast booths. Caray was alone at a desk, empty field below. We stopped and stared, dumbfounded. *My God, there he is!* I called out, "Hey, Harry!" It was as if I'd dropped a coin into an animatronic display—mechanical Abe Lincoln standing to recite the Gettysburg Address. His body—just the torso—turned slowly, slowly. I could almost hear gears, the straining wires. His face was fleshy and impassive as it moved. Then his eyes, finding my eyes, lit up and a smile appeared and his voice boomed, "Hello, Cubs fan!" Then he went slack as his body turned slowly back toward the field. Grabbing my friend, I said, "Remember this always—speak of it never."

■ ■ ■

The Tribune's Second Big Move?

Soon after hiring Harry Caray, they signed Dallas Green as the Cubs' general manager. Green, who'd been a mediocre big league pitcher, was the hot front-office exec of the moment. Working as a bench manager, he'd led the Philadelphia Phillies to their first championship in 1980. He was seen as a hex killer. At his introductory press conference, he spoke of creating a new culture in Chicago. He seemed to regard the curse as a psychosis, a mental block, a losing attitude that spread like a virus from player to player. He wanted to cut all links to the past, start new. He distanced the team from all the old-time Cubs—even Ernie Banks. Because they carried the disease.

In his first few months, he robbed his old team and its farm system, picked the Phillies clean. Several players who would define the Cubs—Gary Matthews, Bob Dernier—came from Philadelphia. In one of the best trades ever, Green sent Ivan DeJesus to the Phillies for veteran shortstop Larry Bowa, with a no-name thrown in. The no-name turned out to be Ryne Sandberg. Green had been keeping an eye on Sandberg since his first days in the minors. Sandberg could field and hit, and looked like a movie star. He'd later learn to hit for power, an adjustment that made him the best second baseman of his era. A lot of us copied Sandberg's stance. It was textbook, like a player on a logo, elbow up, feet at shoulder width. A lot of us wore our hat the way he did and fielded grounders the way he did too. He was the opposite of flashy, even somewhat boring, which we admired—he was so dedicated to the craft he became invisible. There had been Bill Buckner. Now there was Ryne Sandberg.

The Dallas Green team bottomed out on April 29, 1983. Keith Moreland, the right fielder, had gone into the bleachers to tangle with fans who doused him with beer. Asked about it after, Cubs manager Lee Elia performed a soon-to-be-famous soliloquy—it's right out of Shakespeare: "Fuck those fuckin' fans who come out here and say they're Cub fans that are supposed to be behind you rippin' every fuckin' thing you do. I'll tell you one fuckin' thing, I hope we get fuckin' hotter than shit, just to stuff it up them 3,000 fuckin' people that show up every fuckin' day, because if they're the real Chicago fuckin' fans, they can kiss my fuckin' ass right downtown, and PRINT IT. They're really, really behind you around here . . . my fuckin' ass! What the fuck am I supposed to do, go out there and let my fuckin' players get destroyed every day and be quiet about it? For the fuckin' nickel-dime people who turn up? The motherfuckers don't even work! That's why they're out at the fuckin' game. They oughta go out and get a fuckin' job and find out what it's like to go out and earn a fuckin' living. Eighty-five percent of the fuckin' world is working. The other fifteen percent come out here! A fuckin' playground for the cocksuckers."

By 1984, Lee Elia was gone and Dallas Green had built a great team. I'd never cared about any club in any sport the way I cared about that team, and never would again. It was April in Paris in my love affair with the Cubs. I watched them come together and waited for them to win. Which they had to. Because they were so good. Harry Caray called it the "all-animal infield." Leon "Bull" Durham at first, "Ryno" Sandberg at second, Larry Bowa at short, Ron "the Penguin" Cey at third. Not only the best infield in the game, said Caray, but the best-*looking* infield . . . Durham? Strong, powerful, handsome. Sandberg? Classical good looks. Keith Moreland, the burly redhead, was in right. Bob Dernier, with Harpo Marx curls, in center. Gary Matthews, skinny in his early days but getting fat, the team leader, in left. The other players called him "Sarge."

A few weeks into the season, Green completed the team by bringing in, via trade, two great pitchers—Dennis Eckersley from

Boston and Rick Sutcliffe from Cleveland. Sutcliffe. "The Red Baron." Huge and barrel-chested, he hid the ball through his windup, masking it behind his leg—shadowing. He was perfect for Wrigley, because he threw sliders that resulted in ground balls. He'd go 16–1 with a 2.69 ERA for the Cubs that season. For long stretches, he seemed unhittable. He did not lose a game after June.

Until he did.

The trade that brought in Dennis Eckersley was more problematic. It was one of those moves that test a fan. There was a sadness around the rise of the Dallas Green Cubs. Because, as the team got better, there was less and less room for Buckner. For starters, it seemed like Green did not want him—because he'd been the face of the Cubs in the 1970s, hence a carrier of the disease. Because there was no good spot for him on the field. He'd played first base and Durham played right, but when Moreland came in, Durham was pushed to first, leaving Buckner in the dugout, where you'd see him peering from the shadows. Bad knees made him a defensive liability. In 1984, he was used mostly as a pinch hitter. It seemed unfair. He'd carried the team when the team was bad. Now that the team was good, they didn't want him. That's why it did not bother me when he was traded to the Red Sox. Boston had the designated hitter, the ideal spot for a hobbled infielder who could still hit. The Cubs got Eckersley, who rounded out a pitching staff that included Sutcliffe, Steve Trout, Scott Sanderson, and closer Lee Smith. Of course, Bill Buckner would never stop being a Cub. In fact, when the bad thing happened, we felt closer to him than ever.

■ ■ ■

TOP: The original jewel box, the West Side Grounds, on August 30, 1908, in the home stretch of the last championship season of the twentieth century. It may have been the model for Oz's Emerald City.
(Library of Congress)

ABOVE: Tinker, Evers, Chance—the Cubs' great double-play combination as seen on their 1911 baseball cards. They came in packs of cigarettes.
(Library of Congress)

RIGHT: Cubs second baseman Johnny Evers was five foot nine but weighed next to nothing. Some teammates at first refused to play with him, afraid he might be killed in a collision.
(Library of Congress)

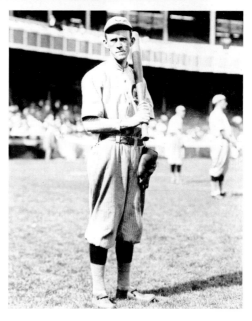

LEFT: Frank Chance, Cubs first baseman and manager from 1905 to 1912, was beaned dozens of times. He collapsed on the field on July 1, 1911, and was dead at forty-eight. (Library of Congress)

BELOW: Grover Cleveland Alexander (left), the great ace pitcher, in 1915, a few years before he signed with the Cubs. He was different when he came back from the war. (Library of Congress)

ABOVE: Even if they don't know it, modern pitchers are copying grips Mordecai Brown mastered by necessity. A childhood accident mangled his hand and earned him the nickname "Three Finger."
(Library of Congress)

RIGHT: The pitching hand of Three Finger Brown as it looked in 1915. Ty Cobb called Brown's curveball "the most deceiving, most devastating pitch I ever faced."
(Chicago History Museum / Getty Images)

ABOVE: Wrigley Field, July 27, 1929. Before the bleachers were built,
before the billy goat was kicked out, before the drought became intolerable
(Library of Congress)

BELOW: William Wrigley, Jr., April 1930. He had the most essential qualities for
an owner: he loved baseball and wanted to win.
(Library of Congress)

Hack Wilson at spring training on Catalina Island, California, February 1931, a few months after his record-setting season. He had an eighteen-inch neck and wore a size six shoe. (Associated Press)

ABOVE: Hall of Fame catcher Gabby Hartnett signing a ball for Sonny Capone as his father, Al, talks Cubs baseball (Bettmann / Getty Images)

LEFT: All-Star first baseman Eddie Waitkus on June 21, 1949, a few weeks after he'd been shot by his biggest fan (Associated Press)

RIGHT: Ernie Banks (right) and Ron Santo at Wrigley Field in the summer of 1965
(David Durochik /Associated Press)

BELOW: Shea Stadium, Queens, New York, September 9, 1969. The black cat walked by Santo, stared down Durocher, and the collapse was on.
(David Pickoff /Associated Press)

LEFT: Me and Bill Buckner in the summer of 1978—not sure why I'm not wearing my Cubs hat
(Courtesy of the author)

BELOW: Harry Caray on November 16, 1981, talking to the press about the deal he'd signed to call the Cubs games. He made it fun to watch on even hopeless days.
(Knoblock / Associated Press)

RIGHT: Ernie Banks showing me how to use my body to block a ground ball, summer 1982
(Courtesy of the author)

BELOW: Leon "Bull" Durham going long against the Cardinals on August 11, 1983. He was the bedrock of the "all animal infield."
(John Swart / Associated Press)

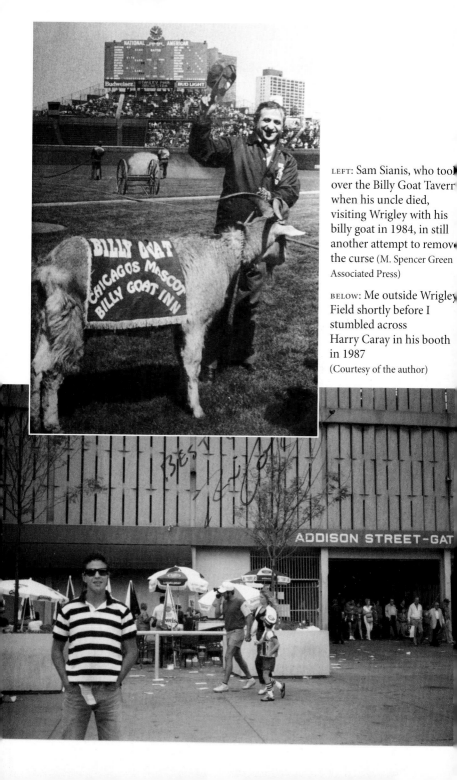

LEFT: Sam Sianis, who took over the Billy Goat Tavern when his uncle died, visiting Wrigley with his billy goat in 1984, in still another attempt to remove the curse (M. Spencer Green / Associated Press)

BELOW: Me outside Wrigley Field shortly before I stumbled across Harry Caray in his booth in 1987
(Courtesy of the author)

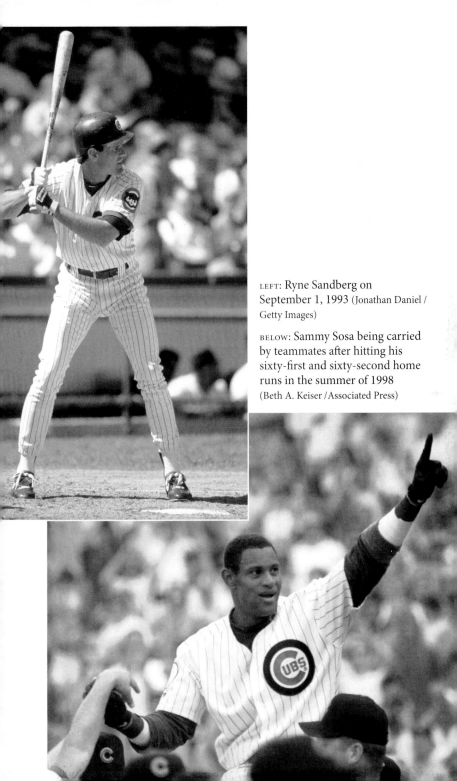

LEFT: Ryne Sandberg on September 1, 1993 (Jonathan Daniel / Getty Images)

BELOW: Sammy Sosa being carried by teammates after hitting his sixty-first and sixty-second home runs in the summer of 1998 (Beth A. Keiser / Associated Press)

October 14, 2003. Steve Bartman reaching for a foul ball and setting in motion a series of events that we are still trying to live down (Morry Gash /Associated Press)

Javier Báez watching his own home run at spring training, 2013. He has played just about every position for the Cubs. (Chris Carlson /Associated Press)

TOP: Dexter Fowler before Game 6 of the 2016 NLCS, doing what many of us dream of doing (Jaime Squire / Getty Images)

BOVE: Anthony Rizzo after completing the double play that sent the Cubs to their first World Series in seventy-one years. He cranked the *Rocky* soundtrack in the clubhouse. (Robin Alam /Associated Press)

Kyle Schwarber flying out in Game 3 of the 2016 World Series
(David J. Phillip /Associated Press)

Aroldis Chapman in Game 5 of the 2016 World Series. He throws
105 miles per hour. (Nam Y. Huh /Associated Press)

Kris Bryant running the bases in May 2017. He's like me on laughing gas—smiling all the time. (Jack Dempsey / Associated Press)

Theo Epstein and Joe Maddon in April 2017, waiting to present World Series rings to a few 2016 Cubs who had already moved on. Even the best team can't stay completely intact for more than a season. (Daniel Bartel / Associated Press)

The Cubs showing off their World Series rings, April 12, 2017
(Jonathan Daniel / Getty Images)

Bill Buckner played 114 games for the Red Sox in 1984, hitting .278 with eleven home runs. It was a comeback. That's baseball. You die over here and are born again over there. And he looked terrific in that uniform, the thick mustache, the intelligent eyes. He would play five seasons for Boston, was there, off and on, from age thirty-four to forty. He grew up at Wrigley Field but got old at Fenway Park. He'd end his career, after twenty-two seasons, with 2,715 hits. That's not the sort of stat that puts you in the Hall of Fame, but it will get you close. All of which is beside the point, because anyone who knows a little but not a lot about baseball knows Bill Buckner for just one play.

October 25, 1986. Shea Stadium, New York. World Series, Game 6. The Red Sox were leading the Mets by two runs in the bottom of the tenth, just one out away from their first championship since 1918. Mookie Wilson was up at bat, desperately trying to avoid a terrible fate—being the last out of the season. He picked up two strikes, then started fouling off—staying alive, staying alive, staying alive. A wild pitch brought in the tying run, taking pressure off Mookie and putting him in a good position to win the game. He hit a grounder to Buckner at first. Should've been an easy play. Should've been the third out. Should've been the Red Sox heading into the eleventh. But the ball went through Buckner's legs. As if it knew exactly what it was doing. As if it had a sensibility. Buckner stood there dumbfounded, watching. And that was it. The Mets won the game, then the World Series. Buckner went from being a symbol of steadfast dependability—excellence amid mediocrity—to being the clumsy butterfingered buffoon who'd blown it. In that moment, we knew that Bill Buckner, no matter what jersey he happened to be wearing, was acting as a Chicago Cub.

The ball that went through Buckner's legs—the "Buckner Ball"—was picked up by right-field umpire Ed Montague, who gave it to Mets executive Arthur Richman, who carried it to Mookie Wilson, who was celebrating in the clubhouse. Mookie wrote on the ball: "To Arthur, the ball won it for us, Mookie Wilson, 10/25/86," then passed it around. Lenny Dykstra kissed the ball, leaving a tobacco stain. Then it vanished—only to reappear in 1992 at Sotheby's in New York, up for auction.

I was twenty-three, working as a *New Yorker* messenger and writing "Talk of the Town" stories. I knew I had to write about that ball. To many, it represented the Mets in their moment of triumph. To me, it represented the futility of the Cubs. It held the mystery of the curse. I stood before it in the auction house, trying to feel the holy emanations. It does not glow, but everyone who has seen it speaks of the patina. Dirt brown, stained with Dykstra's tobacco spit. I called Mookie Wilson. He talked about those foul balls, then the error. "I worked for that error," he said. Then I called Buckner. He'd been out of the game only a few years, but he sounded old. He told me he was angry—about the selling of the ball, which struck him as a put-down. "How is it that you play hard for twenty years and are remembered for one bad moment? That's not right." When I tried to talk about what sort of people might bid at the auction, he cut me off, saying, "It's not the same ball."

"What?"

"It's not the same ball. I don't know what they're selling, but the ball that got by me that night, I have it. I've always had it. So somebody is being conned."

"So how did . . ."

"Look, I've already told you. It's not the same ball."

Then he hung up.

I thought of the picture I'd taken with Buckner when I was a kid. Wrigley Field, the summer of 1977.

The ball was purchased by the actor Charlie Sheen for $93,000. It has since been sold again and again, most recently in 2012 for $418,250.

In the years that followed, Bill Buckner seemed to unravel. In 1993, while working as a minor league hitting instructor for the Toronto Blue Jays, he was stopped by a kid and asked to sign a baseball card. As he reached for a pen, an eighteen-year-old heckler shouted, *Hey Buckner, make sure it doesn't go through your legs.* According to Robert Lipsyte of *The New York Times*, "Buckner walked to his truck, deposited his gear bag, then returned to pick up the 18-year-old by the shirt front. 'I got his attention,' reported Buckner, in his usual laconic style."

Buckner had gone back to college to get his degree while he was still in the majors. Lipsyte tracked down his English teacher, who gave a glimpse into the first baseman's state of mind. "He was quieter than most in class, but I could tell from the condition of the spines of his books . . . that he was doing the reading," the teacher said. "I wanted to make the point that literature can connect you to the species, and I was using the concepts of grace under pressure and playing hurt from 'The Old Man and the Sea' . . . Hemingway opened up Buckner. He talked about that last scene of the old man lying face down in the sand, the skeleton of the fish beside him, and how it reminded him of the last day of the 1980 season. He was with the Chicago Cubs and they were playing in Pittsburgh and if he got a hit on his last at bat he'd win the batting title. If he didn't get a hit, someone else would win the title. Well, he got a hit, and at the moment of triumph he looked up and the stands were empty and the sky was dark. In his moment of glory he felt terribly alone. I was stunned. We stayed friends after that and I found him a good and perceptive man, but we rarely talked about the error. The fans made him a scapegoat. What else was there to say?"

■ ■ ■

The Cubs won the NL East by six and a half games in 1984. They were cruising at the finish. The only possible warning sign was the song "Men in Blue," released that summer, on which Rick Sutcliffe, Jody Davis, Keith Moreland, Gary Woods, and Leon Durham sang, "As sure as there's ivy on the center field wall / the men in blue are gonna win it all." It was vainglorious and seemed to repeat the error of 1969—Stupid! Stupid! Stupid!—but who could beat us? In the National League Championship Series, we'd play the San Diego Padres, a mediocre team—one great player (Tony Gwynn) surrounded by former greats (Steve Garvey, Graig Nettles, Goose Gossage).

I went into the series with my own backstory: My sister was then at the University of San Diego Law School and dating a fellow student named Jerry Schmelter, a local kid, a surfer and a Padres fanatic. He and his friends were always talking about the Padres: Kevin McReynolds, Tony Gwynn, Garry Templeton. I needed the Cubs to beat them down and shut him up. In my mind, as he talked, I said, "Soon you'll be talking out the other side of your face."

I got two tickets to Game 1. Missing school was acceptable to my teachers. I didn't even need a note; a stub was sufficient. The game started midafternoon. We got there early. The sky was filled with fair-weather cumulus, warm with a suggestion of autumn, a stiff lake wind. In dreams, the wind at Wrigley Field is always blowing out.

The Padres had Eric Show on the mound. I'd feel differently about him later—because he was tortured—but I despised him in 1984. He was said to be a racist, a member of the John Birch Society. He won fifteen games that year but was no match for the Cubs. Bob Dernier led off with a home run, then Gary Matthews homered. Rick Sutcliffe homered in the third, a monster shot by the pitcher using Ryne Sandberg's bat. Matthews homered again later, then Ron Cey hit one. It was a phantasmagoria of extra bases. Show had been driven from the game after four innings, his pitching line just as ugly as the Birch Society. Four innings, five hits, five runs, ERA 11.23. I screamed through it all. It was a release, the filling of a biological need. I'd been nervous my entire life but realized it only now. I put my arm around everyone and said, "Did you see that!" I did not drink but was drunk. Sutcliffe gave up two hits in seven innings and struck out eight. We talked over every play on the train home, the Red Line bursting with fans. At school the next day, I was greeted as a hero, as if I myself had done something, which I felt I had.

I experienced Game 2 secondhand—on the televisions set up everywhere in school, rolled into place by the AV team. It was not quite the drubbing of Game 1, but it was good enough. Cey doubled, Sandberg doubled, Steve Trout pitched eight and a third, and we won.

The NLCS moved to San Diego, where the Cubs had to win only one out of three games to advance to the World Series. To me, it seemed like a simple mop-up operation. I explained this to my sister's boyfriend. I gloated. In other words, I stood exactly where so many Cubs fans had stood before me: on the precipice of what seemed certain victory, waiting to party. There was a sad, amused look in the faces of old fans I spoke to during the travel day. They could have warned me but chose not to. Why tell the condemned that the governor has not called and the reprieve will not come? Let the boy enjoy his last meal—he'll learn soon enough.

The Cubs were blown out in Game 3—so bad we forgot about it the moment it was over. We watched Game 4 in the living room on a TV with the sound turned down so we could listen to Harry Caray's WGN radio broadcast. Sandberg later said it was one of the most exciting playoff games ever. The lead changed hands five times. In the top of the eighth, Cubs catcher Jody Davis tied the score with a double off Goose Gossage. At that point, we figured we'd win and the train would continue on down the track. Instead, in the bottom of the ninth, with reliever Lee Smith on the mound, Steve Garvey, as square jawed as Clark Kent, hit a home run that ended the game—Padres 7, Cubs 5—and killed a part of me forever. The footage that followed—Garvey rounding first with a fist in the air, the stadium delirious, the cheers causing the camera itself to vibrate, the Cubs walking off—summed up all the unfairness of the world.

Game 5: The Cubs got on the board right away, with Bull Durham—his goatee and thick glasses gave him a scholarly aspect—hitting a two-run homer in the first. Jody Davis followed in the second. Cubs 3, Padres 0. That lead was chipped at. Going into the bottom of the seventh, the Cubs were just one run ahead, the abyss yawning below.

Sandberg knocked over a cooler in the dugout before the game, soaking Durham's glove with Gatorade. "Leon tried everything possible to dry it off, including using towels and a hair dryer," Sandberg writes in *Second to Home*. "It was all sticky when the game began, so he asked [coach Don Zimmer] if he thought he should still use the glove. 'Go ahead and use it,' Zim said [speaking like a superstitious old baseball hand]. 'It might bring you good luck.'"

It might bring him *good* luck?

Did Don Zimmer realize what team he was coaching?

In the end, it would be the condition of that glove, and, by association, Sandberg, that Durham blamed for his disaster.

One out, a runner on second, Sutcliffe cruising, the Cubs seven outs away from the World Series, so close that some of us, the stupid young, had begun to count them off, make check marks beside each successful play.

Tim Flannery came to the plate for the Padres. He was a familiar figure in Cubs history, the nondescript journeyman who appears just long enough to shank us, then slink away. The agent of inevitability. Each generation will see the goat in a different guise.

Flannery grounded to first. It should have been a routine play, but it went through Durham's legs instead. On TV, they showed it again and again: Durham getting in position, the ball skipping through; Durham getting in position, the ball skipping through; Durham getting in position, the ball skipping through. Because the Gatorade made his glove funky and weird, he said later. "Durham dropped down to one knee, but suddenly the ball hit the lip of the infield and never came up for him," Sandberg wrote. "He saw a bouncing ball and he lifted his glove a tad off the ground to meet it, but the ball stayed flat on the ground and it went right under his glove." In other words, Zim had been right. It did bring luck—just the wrong kind.

One run had scored, the game was tied at 3. At that point, a team that has not been cursed will go after the next hitter, end the inning, win the game. The Cubs fell apart. Go back and watch the film. You see it in the eyes of every player. They had been thinking about the World Series. Now they seemed to be thinking: *My God, the curse is real!*

Alan Wiggins singled to left. Men on first and second, one out. Tony Gwynn at the plate. He was hitting close to .370 in the series. He grounded sharply to the right side of second base. "My first thought was, it's a one-hop, double-play ball," Sandberg wrote. "It's a do-or-die play, and I had one shot at it, but just as I was about to stab it, it took a big hop and almost ripped my face off as it went past me. I turned around and the ball seemed to roll forever. That's what I remember most about that series. I turned around and that ball wouldn't stop rolling. It was torture. It rolled and rolled and rolled into right-center before Keith Moreland cut it off. Two runs scored on that play and another before the inning was over, and it was 6–3 after seven innings."

That's the demise of the 1984 Cubs in a phrase: "The ball seemed to roll forever." In it, you catch a suggestion of the metaphysical, objects following laws other than those of nature. In Sandberg's mind, something else came onto the field that night, a greater force. That phrase gives Ryno away—he too carried the disease.

■ ■ ■

I was on the living room couch in Glencoe, surrounded by my family, but sitting in silence. If I had helped the Cubs win, it seemed I must now take some part of the blame for the loss. I had failed but was not sure how. I knew only that I was still counting outs but no longer wanted to get to zero. My father tried to console me, then gave up, saying, "I told you not to follow this team. I told you what would happen." By the time the Cubs' last hitter came to the plate—Jody Davis, who grounded out—the fans at Jack Murphy Stadium in San Diego were swinging stuffed Cubbie Bears on nooses and chanting, "Forty more years." I was wild, looking everywhere for relief. I noticed my sister in the hallway on the phone.

"Is that him?" I shouted.

"What's your problem?" she said.

I stormed over. If I had been in a bar, I would have insulted a man twice my size. I would have picked a fight I could not possibly win in hope that the beating I took would ease my pain. I ripped the phone out of her hand and shouted into the receiver: "Listen to me, Jerry, and listen good!"

I was sixteen years old and heard something worse than laughter—a person trying to repress laughter, muffle it, the son of a bitch. I could also hear the room behind him, cheers and backslaps. I could hear high fives. I could hear tops being popped off beer bottles.

"Don't worry, pal," Jerry said. "You'll get 'em next year."

"Fuck next year," I screamed, "and fuck you too."

"What?"

"Listen good," I said again. "You are celebrating but you should be mourning. Your team will be a poor representative of the National League. The Tigers will kill your team because your team sucks."

"Hey, calm down."

"You are celebrating," I said again, "but there is nothing to be happy about. The better team lost."

Then I hung up. I mean, I really hung up, in the old emphatic exclamation-point way. It's one of the big things we lost with the coming of the cell phone—the ability to make a point by slamming down the receiver.

I ran out of the house seeing red, seeing jagged lines, flashing lights. I sat on the front steps and looked at the trees. The leaves were already turning yellow. Winter was coming. In the Chicago of my childhood, winter was endless and miserable, less a season than a color, the gray of the slush that lined the roads. I cried because all at once I realized that life is not fair and that things do not work out and that there might be justice in the world but not for me. I became a man in that moment, cynical and experienced. When I went back into the house, I had the same name and clothes and parents, but I was not the same person.

NO.

09

A s I got older, I became fixated on a single question: Why can't the Cubs win?

Years had gone by and I had grown up and moved away and Cubs teams had formed and dissolved and still the result was the same. I decided that if I really wanted to figure it out, I'd have to go see for myself. In the summer of 2000, I pitched the idea to *Harper's Magazine*. Let me travel with the team, hang out in the clubhouses and around the batting cages, talk to the players and coaches and executives—maybe I can solve the greatest riddle in professional sports.

Two weeks later, I had credentials and was walking into Wrigley Field. It was mid-July and the team was already more than a dozen games out. They'd go on to lose ninety-seven that season. The clubhouse was cramped, not much better than a high school locker room. The Cubs lingered in front of lockers, jerseys on hangers, bats and cleats, gloves and supplements on the shelf above. They sat taping their ankles and knees as their radios played. I wandered from athlete to athlete, asking my question in all three tenses: Why didn't you win? Why aren't you winning? Why won't you win?

I talked to Mark Grace, the classic Cub of the 1990s, slim and blond, with eye black and chew and sneaky charisma. You loved him because he was old-time—no batting gloves, no weight room, just a beer with the fans at Murphy's after the last out. He was thirty-six years old and had spent a dozen seasons with Chicago. He was a great baseball player. When I asked him why the Cubs did not win, he gave me a Little Rascals double take, laughed, then said, "Expectations. No one here expects us to win, so we don't. They're happy if we finish above .500, so sometimes we do."

I talked to Joe Girardi. He started his career as a Cub in 1989, then came back as a thirty-five-year-old catcher. He grew up in Peoria, Illinois. "When I was in third grade, I wrote an essay about how I would play for the Cubs," he told me. "Ten times a summer, I drove with my father from Peoria just to see the games. When I left the Cubs the first time, I was crushed. I had always wanted to be a Cubbie." Between 1996 and 1999, Girardi played for the Yankees, where his team won three World Series in four seasons. It made him uniquely qualified to answer my question: Why don't the Cubs win?

"In New York, you go into spring training expecting to get to the World Series," he said. "You feel it when you walk in the clubhouse. The pictures of all those Yankee greats, the monuments. There is something special about putting on the pinstripes. In Chicago, they hope for a good season, maybe the playoffs."

"But they have pictures here at Wrigley Field," I said. "The Cubs' greats. Hack Wilson, Kiki Cuyler."

"Yeah, but think about those pictures," Girard told me. "Still shots, each player by himself. In Yankee Stadium, it's group shots, the team celebrating on the mound, in the clubhouse, the champagne, winning it all. Here you won't see that."

I spoke to Kevin Tapani, a thirty-six-year-old pitcher. I don't remember what he looked like, but I do remember what he told me. I've been thinking about it ever since. "No one on this team felt like a lovable loser when he got to here," he said. "Probably everyone here was the best player on his Little League team and high school team—won at every level. Then they get here and put on the Cubs hat and people start telling them they're a lovable loser—'cause of the black cat, 'cause of the billy goat, whatever. And you know what? Pretty soon, you start to feel that way. You catch it like you catch a cold."

Sammy Sosa was the star of the 2000 Cubs. He was thirty-one years old, exuberant, difficult, full of life. He lived for home runs. Feast or famine. When he did hit one, he skipped out of the batter's box: the stutter step, the trademark hop. He banged his chest, then pointed at the sky, letting the world know that this particular home run was neither for his personal glory, nor for the glory of the Cubs. It was for the glory of God, whose throne is buried in touchdowns, dingers, and dunks. Sosa hit sixty-six home runs in 1998, the year that he and Mark McGwire chased Roger Maris's single-season home run record. Sosa was almost as prolific in 2000, with fifty home runs and a .320 batting average.

But his focus seemed individual in just the way Girardi had in mind. Sosa was all about Sosa. Mark Grace would choke up on the bat with two strikes, determined to put the ball in play. When I asked Sosa if he changed his style for the situation, he smirked and said, "What are you talking 'bout? I always hit it as hard as I can."

It was easy to see how Sosa's personality affected other players. They bristled when he came into the clubhouse. He had a few friends on the team, two or three guys—everyone else was out. It was like a high school clique. Woe to him who accidentally sat at Sosa's lunchroom table! He turned up later than everyone else, plugged in his radio and cranked his music, drowning out whatever had been playing.

As I waited to talk to him one afternoon, I overheard a conversation between Sosa and a local reporter. She'd written a story in which several Cubs described Sosa as an asshole. He told the reporter she was wrong.

"My teammates love me."

"Sammy, I just wrote down what they told me."

"Do you want me to get you five teammates that will say they love me?"

"Do you want me to get you ten who will say you're an asshole?"

"Fuck my teammates."

Each era has had its Mr. Cub, a player who stood for the team. The quality of a particular Mr. Cub will determine the nature of a particular team. In the 1950s and '60s, it was Ernie Banks. In the 1970s and '80s, it was Bill Buckner. It the 1980s and '90s, it was Ryne Sandberg. From 1998 to 2003, it was Sammy Sosa, a jacked-up, pudge-faced slugger from the Dominican Republic who lost his soul to the long ball. He'd come from the White Sox, who'd gotten him from the Texas Rangers. When listing the charges against George W. Bush, people used to include Sammy Sosa. Bush had been managing general partner of the Rangers when Sosa was traded.

Sosa soured the locker room. Whatever space he entered became his space. When he was in a game, it became his game, his statistics. The players on the 2000 Cubs seemed angry and irritated. Sosa seemed to pull rank constantly, as if that, as much as the home runs, was the point. Like Sonny Barger, he had to let everyone know he was the primo leader. One day, when I was in the dugout talking to Billy Williams, then working as a Cubs hitting instructor—"There is no such thing as *Harper's*," Williams was saying. "Harper is a man, not a magazine. You've made it up for free tickets!"—Sosa burst out of the tunnel shouting, "I just took a big shit. It feels good when you take your big shit."

I hung around Wrigley Field for a week. It was the same routine every day: clubhouse to field, field to press box for the game, press box back to clubhouse for comments on the game. The beat writers seemed to hate me—because I'd parachuted in to make sport of their pain—so I hung out with a kid.

"The only friend I made among the press was a kid entirely untouched by the stinking heartbreak of history," I wrote in the piece. His name was Nick, and he was on summer break from Drake University in Iowa. He had landed a part-time job writing about the Cubs for his hometown newspaper in Oak Park. A few times a week Nick went to the clubhouse and, without the least hesitation, pulled aside his favorite players. Before this game, he had talked to some of the Cardinals, even to Will Clark, rumored to be the crankiest man in the league.

Nick said, "Can I ask you some questions, Mr. Clark?"

Mr. Clark said, "Get the fuck away from me, kid."

Nick told me that Mr. Clark had stunk of beer.

I followed the Cubs to Houston, then Arizona. The stadiums were like terrariums. Same routine with hotel added. You could slip into it as you slip into a bath, forget your life and worries. You were always doing exactly what you were supposed to be doing. It was easy to see how you could set off for a season and not look up till ten years had gone by.

I had come here to learn about loss—to gather evidence and plumb the mystery and solve the riddle. Had the Cubs gone on a winning streak, I would have been presented with a challenge. I would have been in an editorial fix. But that's not what happened. In fact, as the days went by, I found myself thinking of lines from a poem we memorized in high school, "After Apple-Picking" by Robert Frost: "I am overtired / Of the great harvest I myself desired." And then: "Magnified apples appear and disappear, / Stem end and blossom end, / And every fleck of russet showing clear." It was like that for me on the road with the Cubs, only instead of apples, it was games—defeat after defeat after defeat, all of them russet colored.

The longest losing streak in baseball history was twenty-six games—the Louisville Colonels, 1889. The longest losing streak in the modern era was twenty-one—the Baltimore Orioles, 1988. The Cubs lost sixteen straight in a streak that began at the end of 1996 and continued into the spring of 1997. The number of games I saw them drop in succession was therefore not historic, but did feel endless. Seven in a row, every loss its own bleak drama. After each defeat, I followed the beat writers down to the clubhouse, where Don Baylor, the Cubs' manager, tried to explain what had happened. The mood turned grim as the days went by. Players averted their eyes, spoke in whispers. If a player was questioned about a botched play, he'd answer, but his eyes would ask, *Really, dude?* Each day, the mood turned darker, heavier. I started to dread going to the clubhouse. It was like visiting the hospital room of a terminally ill friend. So here it is, I thought. The place for which I had been searching, the heart of Cubs history. It was a black hole, dark and quiet. I had not experienced such a depressing room since early childhood. Though Cubs tradition is cumulative, each moment must be borne by a handful of guys, most of whom will soon be forgotten and who only wanted to play ball. After each loss, the reporters stood around Sosa, who spoke energetically of his most recent home run.

■ ■ ■

After the seventh straight loss, I said to myself, "I can't take this anymore," went to the airport, got on a plane, and flew back to Chicago. I wanted to talk to the Cubs' general manager, Andy MacPhail. He was forty-seven years old, a member of one of the sport's first families. His father had been president of the American League. His grandfather had worked for half a dozen teams, including the Cincinnati Reds, where he introduced night baseball. Andy MacPhail had been with the Houston Astros and the Minnesota Twins, where he won two World Series. He was another in the line of messiahs brought to Chicago to kill the curse.

We met in his office at Wrigley Field. Strange being in the stadium when the team is on the road. Like your grade school on a weekend. MacPhail—boyish and bespectacled, short blond hair—knew everything about the franchise, all the history, the ups and downs. I questioned him as you might question an elder.

He told me how he was working to improve the roster, that there were tremendous prospects in the minors, in the pipeline. "I can see it even if the fans can't," he said. "It's coming."

"Will we win?"

"Yes."

"You promise?"

"No one can make such a promise," he said, "especially after ninety-two years, but I feel good."

"Very good?"

"Pretty good."

In other words, he seemed enthusiastic, but not incredibly. Maybe it was the losing streak, maybe the man had problems of his own.

"Why is it that the Twins can win, and the Blue Jays can win, and the Marlins can win, but not the Cubs?" I asked. "You spend money, get good players, hire the best managers and general managers, and still it never happens. I don't get it. Why?"

He looked at me and looked at me, then said, "You want the truth?"

"Yes."

"You can handle the truth?"

"Yes."

"That's what Cubs fans always think," he told me, "till they actually hear the truth, then they curse me. Are you going to curse me here today?"

"No, never. I need to know."

"It's Wrigley Field," he said.

"What?"

"You heard me."

"What do you mean?"

"Think about it," he said. "The Cubs were the best team in baseball before they moved into Wrigley Field. They won six of the first eleven National League pennants, moved into Wrigley Field in 1916, and haven't won a championship since. Figure out why that is, you'll answer your own question."

I pressed MacPhail. We went back and forth. He gave me statistics and historical examples. In the end, his argument came down to this: Wrigley Field is schizophrenic. You cannot build a team with its particulars in mind because it has no particulars. On paper, it looks like a hitter's park. And is. When the wind blows out. On such days, no pitcher in the world can keep the ball from going over the fence. That's why you get scores like Phillies 23, Cubs 22. But on days when the wind blows in, it's a pitcher's park, and would-be home runs become easy outs. In Boston, a general manager can fashion a team for Fenway, loading up on right-handed hitters who can bang the ball off that big green monster. At Yankee Stadium, it's the close right-field fence, the "short porch," which turns good left-handed hitters into sluggers. "Wrigley has nothing like that," MacPhail told me. "There is no home-field advantage. To win you need to be an all-around good team—pitching and hitting, everything. It takes a long time to build a team like that."

My story ran in *Harper's* the following summer. I was happy with it but felt I had not dealt fully with the core problem—possibly because I was scared of the wrath of fellow fans. Phil Wrigley exchanged on-field excellence for the beauty of the park, the aesthetic of the experience. The stadium became more important than the team that played there. It became a kind of temple. Criticizing or blaming it would be seen as sacrilege. But not reporting what I had learned felt like cowardice. It took me years of brooding and losing, but I finally got up the courage. The story ran in *The Wall Street Journal* in May 2012 under the headline "Why Wrigley Field Must Be Destroyed."

1. The Park is schizo. A few years ago, when I was traveling with the Cubs for a story, I had a long talk with Andy MacPhail, then the team's general manager. MacPhail had just come from Minnesota, where he won two World Series. In Chicago, he told me, the big challenge was building a team that could win in Wrigley, a stadium that suffers multiple-personality disorder. In Minnesota, he'd been able to fashion a roster designed to win in the Metrodome, where the Twins played, as the Yankees were long able to design a team for their stadium, where left-handed power hitters take advantage of the so-called short porch. But Wrigley has no such peculiarity. It looks like a home-run hitter's park, and, when the wind blows out, it is. But when the wind screams off the lake, the park turns nasty. Even balls headed for the seats are knocked in to routine flies. For the Cubs, MacPhail said, every game might as well be away. Which means the front office has to build a kind of All-Star team, perfectly rounded for every kind of park. And that's impossible.

2. Wrigley is too damn nice. Going to the Park is so pleasant, the game itself has become secondary. The sunshine, the lake air, the red brick—that's what draws the crowds. The bleachers are filled even when the team is terrible, which takes pressure off of the owners. Cubs fans are the Buddhists of the game, free from the wheel of profit and loss, happy to live in the now of Wrigley. There's a conspiracy theory: Following the death of William Wrigley, Jr., the chewing gum tycoon who bought the

franchise, his successors, not really caring about the game, made a decision to substitute the park for the team, turning the experience into the attraction. This is when Bill Veeck, Jr., the great baseball man, planted the ivy, and people began lauding Wrigley as the greatest space in the national game. My view on this changed when I moved to New York from Chicago and took the Yankee perspective: It's not ivy that makes a place beautiful. It's winning. Conversely, a century of stinking renders even the loveliest of parks a monstrosity.

3. Losing some of the time makes you want to win; losing all the time makes you a loser. They call it a curse, and it is, but not the kind summoned by Greek tavern owners (the curse of the billy goat). It's the kind known as a complex . . . what a hundred years of losing does to your psyche.

My prescription was intended to shock, as it takes a shock to wake the sleeper from the dream: "The struts and concessions, the catwalk, the bases, ivy, wooden seats and bleachers, the towering center field scoreboard—all of it must be ripped out and carried away like the holy artifacts were carried out of the Temple in Jerusalem, heaped in a pile and burned. Then the ground itself must be salted, made barren, covered with a housing project, say, a Stalinist monolith, so never again will a shrine arise on that haunted block. As it was with Moses, the followers and fans, though they search, shall never find its bones."

When this piece was published, I was called a traitor and a fool, vilified, cut up, handed out, eaten and digested. It hurt, because I love Wrigley Field and the team, but the prophet must tell what he knows even if the people drive him into exile. At one point, I sat in a TV studio, staring at a black screen, listening on headphones as six guys in another studio called me an idiot. Which I am. I'd only suggest that everyone else is an idiot too. We're all idiots. The onslaught ended that June when a reporter asked Kerry Wood, the great Cubs pitcher, why the team had not won and he in essence said, Wrigley Field.

■ ■ ■

I spent the late 1990s and early 2000s watching Sammy Sosa blossom, then fade. To me, he represented a bloated period in Cubs history. It was not just his style—it was his body. He was a perfect example of baseball in the age of steroids. He had that look. Blown up, inflated. He could stand for just about every power hitter of the era. Players who'd always hit twenty home runs were suddenly hitting fifty. Dugouts were filled with behemoths, guys with giant forearms and giant necks, with monstrous thighs straining the fabric of monstrous pants, stiffly swinging bats that looked like toothpicks. It ruined the aesthetics. Ted Williams's fluid elegance had been turned into something muscular, mean. It separated players from fans—these guys looked like members of a different species. A game between the Cubs and the Cardinals—Sosa versus McGwire—seemed like a match between Schwarzenegger and Stallone. The numbers that connected disparate eras of the game were distorted to the breaking point. You could see it in the arc of Sosa's statistics. He hit 36 home runs in 1997, a big year for anyone. Then he hit 66, 63, 50, 64. Sosa denies using drugs, though he failed a test. The belief that he juiced has probably kept him out of the Hall of Fame. A number—609 home runs—that would have guaranteed his entry at any other time instead seems phony, as does that whole era. In this, too, baseball served its function. It mirrored society. America was supersized in the 1990s. Big cars and cluster bombs, an economic boom seemingly without end. Escalades and giant sodas, mammoth players blasting gargantuan home runs.

It was a decadent time that culminated on October 14, 2003. The Cubs had gone 88–74, winning the National League Central. It was one of those not great winning teams you remember only if you happened to be ten years old that summer. Sosa was thirty-four and showing signs of decline. He was covered in watches—time was all over him. Pitching is what made that team, strong young arms. Mark Prior, Carlos Zambrano, Kerry Wood. Dusty Baker managed the team. It was his first season in Chicago. He said he did not believe in curses. Your eyes went to him whenever things got weird. You wanted to ask, "What about now?"

The Cubs were leading the Florida Marlins 3 games to 2 in the eighth inning of the NLCS. Game 6, Wrigley Field, stupid young fans counting down—just five outs away from the World Series. Luis Castillo was at the plate for Florida. Mark Prior was pitching for Chicago with a 3–0 lead. He was twenty-two years old, dark and lean. Castillo popped the ball down the line. Cubs left fielder Moisés Alou gave chase. The ball was coming down a row or two into the stands. If Alou made the catch, it'd be the second out of the inning—just four away from the World Series.

It would turn out to be a famous play. I see it in dreams, reduced to three elements: player, ball, fan. Alou drifts to the barrier, jumps. As he reaches out for the ball, a fan does the same, interfering. The ball slips away. There's been a lot of debate: Was that ball playable, or was it too far into the stands? To me, it seems clear it was playable and could have been caught, but that misses the larger point. The ball was in the seats and in the seats you've got fans who crave and interfere with foul balls. It's a known hazard, like a sand trap on a golf course. You just have to accept it and deal with it. Which is not what Alou did. He screamed and stomped and cursed. Alou blamed the fan, so a lot of other people did too.

The fact that the underlying situation had not changed—the Cubs were still winning 3–0, still just five outs away—did not seem to matter. It was as if the fans and players had been waiting for something they knew had to happen and had been curious only about the details, about what form the billy goat would take, and now they saw it was a man-child in a Cubs hat with wire-frame glasses and headphones. That was the pinch—not the interference but how the team reacted, how they suddenly seemed to lose focus. The batter drew a walk. The next singled. A run scored. Then a Marlin hit a ground ball to Cubs shortstop Álex González. It should have been an easy double play. The inning would have ended with the Cubs ahead 3–1, three outs away. But González mishandled the ball and everyone was safe. González, a Gold Glove infielder who'd turned that play dozens of times, should have been the goat, but the fans had already fixed on one of their own—on themselves. It was self-hate, psychosis: They expected to lose, even needed to lose to make sense of their suffering. Because we blamed ourselves, because deep down we knew we deserved it, we needed a fan to take the blame for all fans—a scapegoat. The Cubs gave up eight runs that inning. There'd still be a Game 7, but it didn't matter. It was all over. The camera found Dusty Baker in the dugout. From the look on his face, the expression, you knew exactly what he was thinking: *My God, it's true.*

Then the TV announcers noticed it. The weird energy, the bad mojo in the park. Something was happening in the seats where Alou almost made that catch. People were menacing the man-child who'd reached for the ball. You heard it on the broadcast. "Good job, asshole!" Fans started to chant. "Asshole! Asshole! Asshole!" "Fuck you! Fuck you! Fuck you!" It took them about two minutes to turn into a mob—that's our world. Curses gave way to threats. "Somebody hit the cocksucker!" The man-child was pelted with pizza, doused with beer. Some of these fans must have known it was wrong even as they were doing it, but could not help themselves. That's the meaning of psychosis. You don't want to do it but can't stop. The man-child was being turned into a martyr. He was paying for our sins. In my mind, he's painted by El Greco, among the clouds. Security had to disguise him as an usher to get him out of the park. He was brought to a nearby apartment that belonged to a Cubs executive, a kind of safe house. Late that night, he was checked in to a hotel. "I hope he made it home, but I'm angry at the guy," Governor Rod Blagojevich said. "Part of having home-field advantage is that on every single pitch and every single play, you do what you can, will what you can, to help the team win. In this case, that meant getting out of the way."

The next morning, the newspapers reported the location of the fan's seat: aisle 4, row 8, seat 114. One of them reported his name: Steve Bartman. That's when Game 6 came to be known as the Bartman Game, when the foul came to be known as the Bartman Ball, and when his career as a symbol began. Steve Bartman was twenty-six years old, a computer consultant from the Northern suburbs. He coached Little League, was slight and pale. He'd been wearing headphones so he could listen to the radio broadcast. Only the most serious fans, only the biggest nerds, only those so focused on the team they've given up any thought of being cool, do that. How strange it must have been for Bartman to realize, as he listened, that the announcers were no longer talking about the game—they were talking about him.

Bartman issued a statement to the press: "I had my eyes glued on the approaching ball the entire time and was so caught up in the moment that I did not even see Moisés Alou, much less that he may have had a play. Had I thought for one second that the ball was playable or had I seen Alou approaching, I would have done whatever I could to get out of the way and give Alou a chance to make the catch." Then he vanished. He "became such a figure of ignominy in Chicago," Ira Berkow wrote in *Wrigley Field: An Oral and Narrative History of the Home of the Chicago Cubs*, "that he would not again be seen in public, receiving death threats and inspiring rumors of having undergone a face-lift to disguise himself." To this day, many fans are ashamed of the incident. Bartman did not fail us—we failed him. When the Cubs made it to the World Series in 2016, there was talk of Bartman throwing out the first pitch. Theo Epstein invited him to the first home game, but nothing came of it.

He was finally coaxed back to Wrigley in the summer of 2017, where Cubs owner Tom Ricketts presented Bartman with his own 2016 World Series championship ring. "While no gesture can fully lift the public burden he has endured for more than a decade," the team said in a statement, "we felt it was important Steve knows he has been and continues to be fully embraced by this organization. After all he has sacrificed, we are proud to recognize Steve Bartman with this gift today."

Bartman didn't even get the ball—that's the punch line. It bounced around the seats until some other guy picked it up. It later sold at auction for over $100,000. In 2004, as part of a kind of exorcism, it was detonated in front of Harry Caray's restaurant on Kinzie Street.

■ ■ ■

Sammy Sosa was like a steam engine. He got smaller as he went away. Production faded: home runs less titanic, more infrequent. In June 2003, he was caught using a corked bat. He said he had no idea the bat had been doctored. ("When Sammy Sosa said he didn't know the bat was corked, the line had a resonance that sounded familiar," Ira Berkow wrote. "It was from a 1940s song, 'I Didn't Know the Gun Was Loaded.'") If Sosa had indeed been corking *and* juicing, you can at least say he left nothing untried. By October 2004, it seemed obvious that his time as a Cub was finished. The reporters who'd pumped him up tore him down. He took off during the first inning of the season's last game, violating an ancient code. He said he'd only left the dugout and was in the clubhouse, but a surveillance video showed him driving away. Before anyone could talk to him, he was back in the Dominican Republic. This man, who'd been blown up to monstrous proportions, simply deflated. To many, his entire career came to be seen as a kind of charade. No one talks much about Sammy Sosa anymore—he was a false messiah who led us astray. In 2016, as the Cubs made their World Series run, the franchise brought back all sorts of former players—to throw out first pitches, just to be around. Jenkins, Sandberg, Maddux. But no Sosa. Not there and little mention, as if he'd never happened. Asked by ESPN Deportes what he would do with his life, Sosa said he would "calmly wait" for his induction into the Hall of Fame.

And then I decided, "Fuck it." I'd been through Bartman. I'd been through Sosa. I'd been through 1993 and 1989 and 1984. I'd been through Dave Kingman. I'd been through everything and suffered heroically and was in the exact same place I'd been when I started. But I was old now, with my own children. I did not want them to suffer as I had. When I thought of the Cubs, I said to myself, "There is no one on this earth who was on this earth when the Cubs were champions." History had become too heavy. I wanted to live unencumbered, without the numbers and false hopes pressing on me. I'm not sure of the exact day, but at some point I said to myself, "I'm done." I stopped following the Cubs, then stopped caring. Buddhism for a Cubs fanatic. What causes suffering? Attachment to the team. What's the cure for that suffering? Give up that attachment. It was the only way off the wheel, the only way I could stop experiencing the same heartbreak again and again. I emptied myself of all desire for a championship. And it turned out to be the smartest thing I could have done. Because it was only when I was empty of that desire that it could finally be fulfilled.

I no longer live in Chicago. Not a day goes by when I do not wish I were there. But the fact is, if I'm being honest, I have to admit that I never really did live in Chicago. I lived in the suburbs. Though it felt like I was part of the big thing, Chicagoland, every now and then someone reminds me of my inauthenticity. I was living in New York on 9/11. I could see the World Trade Center from my window. A few days after the attack, I spotted a Chicago cop working traffic at the corner of Hudson and Perry Streets. I recognized the uniform and the manner—black leather coat and cap, big mustache, no nonsense. I was overwhelmed by the sight of this man. It was as if my hometown had come to help me in a time of need. I shook his hand and thanked him, and as I thanked him I welled up and as that happened I tried to explain. "It's because I'm from Chicago," I said.

"Where in Chicago are you from?" he asked.

"Glencoe."

"That's not Chicago," he said, and waved me away.

But when the Cubs started to look good in a way they'd never looked before, it was not Glencoe I longed for—it was Chicago. I wanted to get back to the bleachers and soak up the vibe. I wanted to watch and drink and be drunk, but mostly I wanted to know how they'd finally done it.

I stood in the reception area of a building off Roscoe Street, a few blocks from Wrigley. A tall, dark-haired man came out, shook my hand, and took me in to see a huge scale model of Wrigley Field. Not the park as it was but the park as it would be if all went according to plan. More seats, more luxury, more flags on poles, a plaza, a hotel across the street. He walked around the model as if it were a train set, showing off each feature he hoped to build. There's not been such gee-whiz energy around the franchise since the death of William Wrigley.

He continued talking as we walked through rooms filled with young people—men and women at screens, studying statistics— and back to an office, where we sat down and got into the Cubs. This was Tom Ricketts, who, along with his father and siblings, purchased the franchise in 2009. The Ricketts' money was made mostly on Ameritrade, the online brokerage firm founded by his father. Which is perfect. In each era, the Cubs have been controlled by a fortune indicative of the time. Luncheonettes in the aughts, chewing gum in the 1930s, media in the 1980s, cyber-commerce today. I thanked Ricketts for the World Series championship, then said, "but I'm not surprised. It was preordained." For a few months in 1937, when the bleachers were being rebuilt, a sign above left field proclaimed: EAT DOWN THE BEST. RICKETTS TROPHY BAR, 2727 N. CLARK. It was like one of the premonitions of Jesus that Christians spot all over the Old Testament. You're living in a fallen time, but portents of redemption can be seen everywhere.

He knew about the sign but laughed anyway. "I was a late convert to the Cubs," he told me. "I grew up in Omaha, Nebraska, in the 1970s. I knew all about the Big Red Machine and the Yankees, but the Royals were the team most people cheered. I did not fall for the Cubs until I was older. I'd come up here to attend the University of Chicago. It was summer and I was living above a tavern—the Sports Corner—at the corner of Sheffield and Addison, across from Wrigley. After a summer like that—the crowds and the noise and the fans—you're either going to hate a team, or love them forever. For me, it was love. It helped that this was the summer of 1984"—that is, the summer the Cubs won the NL East, the summer of Durham and Sutcliffe singing "Men in Blue."

"There are three kinds of Cubs fans," he continued. "First are the people who inherit it from their parents, grew up in Chicago, born Cubby blue—that's the biggest segment. Second are the people who grew up in different parts of the country but followed the Cubs on WGN. They didn't have a local team so took to the Cubs. Third are those who didn't have a strong affiliation with any team, moved to Chicago, and walked into Wrigley Field one day and *bang!* That's me. My brother too—he was here and we started going to games. We spent our twenties in the bleachers. I met my wife there, and, over time, became not just a fan but a nut."

Ricketts took his father to a Cubs game in 2006. "I wanted to share the experience," he told me. At some point, he turned to his father and said, "Why don't you buy this team?" He presented it as a business opportunity, akin to owning a "zero coupon bond." The value will only increase, he argued. In fact, the team is currently worth triple what the Ricketts family paid. It was more than an investment, of course. Tom Ricketts loved the Cubs. The fact that they had, at that point, not won a championship in ninety-eight years made them even more attractive. Ricketts knew that whoever broke the curse would go directly to heaven without the inconvenience of purgatory.

"One of the questions we had going through the process in '07, '08 was, do we still want to buy the team if they win the World Series?" Ricketts said. "I honestly don't know the answer. It just wouldn't have been the same. You want to be the one that gets the team through the drought and wins that first championship. That was big."

Tom Ricketts took over the Cubs in 2009. The first task was to restore Wrigley Field. It was a jewel but had been allowed to dilapidate. Players hated it—the locker rooms and other facilities were about what you'd expect from 1914. For fans, there were fears of falling beams and rodents. Ricketts had to fight the city. The big issue was the huge electronic scoreboards he wanted to install behind left and right fields. City officials worried the scoreboards would block the view from nearby rooftops. "The park is privately owned, the project is privately financed, the team delivers tens of millions of dollars every year to the city in taxes, hundreds of millions of dollars a year in economic activity, and you're telling me that I can't put up a video board because of the rooftop guys?" Ricketts said. "Insane. It got frustrating. We just wanted to put up video boards! If we couldn't do that, we were going to have to leave. The fact that it even had to get to that point was insane. But that's where it had to get."

Ricketts invested more than $300 million in the park. The bleachers were rebuilt and expanded, as were the clubhouses and facilities. The result is a new park that is still the old park—body remade, soul intact. And those video boards! They serve as tremendous buffers, taming the wind—Thorazine for Wrigley's schizophrenia. I asked Ricketts if the case I'd made in *The Wall Street Journal* influenced his planning.

"Sure, why not?" he said, laughing. "If that helps you, feel free to believe it."

"What about the team itself," I asked. "Did you come in knowing what you wanted to do?"

"My plan at the beginning was just to learn as much as I could," he said. "I think it would have been a mistake to make changes right away. You can read all the articles and books in the world, and it still won't help you understand what you have to do to make a team better. Nothing prepares you for doing it but doing it. So I came in with eyes open and tried to learn as much as I could in the first couple years."

"What about the curse?"

"What about it?"

"Do you believe in it?"

He paused, then said, "The people you'd want to ask are the players, because the only way the curse has any real meaning or impact is if the players felt pressure in a way that affected their performance on the field. I think objectively you have to say, 'There is no such thing as a curse.' The fact is, the Cubs, over time, have typically had pretty bad teams, and, when they have been good, they've had bad luck in the playoffs. That's been the real problem."

"Bad luck in the playoffs? That sounds like a curse."

"Well, not necessarily. If there's one thing I have learned in this job, it's this: You have to build a team that's not just good enough to get to the postseason but good enough to get there again and again. Because once you're in, it's luck. The ground ball through Durham's legs? The grand slam in the first inning in 1989? Something always went wrong. The fact is, when you go back and look, you'll see there's little correlation between how many games you win during a season and how far you go in the postseason. Almost zero. You build a team for that 162-game season. After that, it's like rolling dice. Statistically, you can prove this. The goal is to build a team that has a chance of winning the division and getting back to the playoffs, because once you're there, you have a one-in-eight shot at winning the World Series. If you look at what happened to the Cubs in the past, there was never a team, in our lifetime, with back-to-back playoff seasons. That's why they never won a championship. The odds were always working against them. Here's how the baseball guys describe it: You need a core of controllable young players to work around, then you fill in blanks every year to try to put the best 162-game team on the field. Then, at playoff time, you just hope you're healthy."

The Cubs finished in fifth place during Ricketts's first season. By the middle of his second, he'd seen enough. "It was time for a change," he told me. "We had one of the oldest lineups in the league. We had a lot of long-term contracts. We had an underperforming farm system without a lot of prospects. We needed to do something significant."

He wanted a new person to run the club, and he put together a list of ideal candidates. Theo Epstein, first name of that list, was considered unattainable. Epstein was the general manager of the Boston Red Sox—the team he'd grown up following—where he'd broken the curse of the Bambino, leading the team to two world championships. As it turned out, Epstein was not entirely happy in Boston. He'd been struggling with his boss, Larry Lucchino. It was disguised as a contract dispute but was probably about who should get credit for the team's success. Then, in September 2011, the Red Sox, who'd been cruising toward the playoffs, fell apart in a manner worthy of the '69 Cubs. Because Boston players, including future Cubs Jon Lester and John Lackey, were said to have been eating fried chicken and drinking beer in the clubhouse as the wheels came off, it was tagged "the chicken-and-beer collapse." As the press went into a blaming frenzy, Epstein dreamt of escape. "I hated that I was seen as running from the collapse," he told ESPN, "but I guess on some level, I was running from something."

"In August 2011, Theo made it public that he was *not* going to extend his contract with the Red Sox," Ricketts told me. "I called him the next morning, and we met that afternoon in New York. He flew in from Boston, I flew in from Chicago. We had dinner in my family's apartment. We talked for hours."

"What were you looking for at that meeting?" I asked.

"Theo—he's like Cher or Bono, he's got that profile," Ricketts said. "He's just Theo. But what kind of person is behind that? That's what I wanted to know. Is he the kind of guy who has a big ego? The kind of guy who doesn't treat people well? I wanted to know. 'Cause when you go into this kind of business partnership, you want to know who this person is as a person as well as their accomplishments. And the first thing he said was, 'I'm not who you think I am. Nobody does this by themselves. You need a whole organization. You have to bring in the right people for a bunch of different jobs, and they all have to work toward a common goal for years to build a good organization.' Which is what I wanted him to say. I wanted to hear it wasn't all about him. I wanted to know that he gave other people credit."

Ricketts asked Epstein to explain some of the moves he'd made in Boston—those that had worked and, more important, those that hadn't. "And he was not defensive at all," Ricketts told me. "He was very objective about his own decisions. I don't know a lot of GMs, but I imagine that he's more objective than other people. Number one, he doesn't have to be defensive because he's had such success. Number two is, if you know why you make a decision, you can know which assumption fell through if it goes wrong. You can say, 'This is what we assumed would happen, this is what actually happened.'"

Epstein's deal was announced in the winter of 2011. As the new president of the Cubs, he hired Jed Hoyer as GM. Epstein had worked with Hoyer in San Diego, when both were impossibly young baseball executives, under Larry Lucchino, then president of the Padres. In Chicago, news of Theo's arrival was greeted with excitement and fear. Excitement because we knew what he'd done in Boston. Fear because we'd stood in the street to welcome messiahs before. I'll never forget how I heard. I was in Scottsdale, Arizona, knocking on the door of Jim McMahon, the "punky QB" who infuriated Mike Ditka as he led the 1985 Chicago Bears to the Super Bowl. His lower lip was fat with Skoal when he answered, his T-shirt asked and answered a simple question: GOT MILK? GOT POT. "Hey, did you hear!" shouted McMahon, gripping my arm and pulling me inside. "Theo is coming! We're gonna win the fuckin' World Series!"

■ ■ ■

Theo Epstein grew up a short walk from Fenway Park. He could hear the crowd from his stoop on summer nights, that sweet ambient noise, the PA announcer going through the lineup. Wade Boggs and Jim Rice, Tony Armas and Carl Yastrzemski. Three events, occurring at around the same time, drove him into baseball. First his discovery of Bill James, the baseball historian, the man who invented the new stats that yielded the new understanding of the game. ("I remember reading the Abstract and thinking, God, after reading one book I've changed the way I look at the game on the field," Epstein told *The New Yorker* in 2003. "I never thought that could happen from reading a book.") Then computer baseball, the Apple IIe version released in 1985, general manager's edition. Not only could you choose the pitchers and pitches and set the lineups, you also could make trades and negotiate deals. It gave Epstein his first taste of the awesome power of the front office. Then the 1986 World Series, when the Red Sox came within a single out of a championship. Epstein was twelve when Mookie Wilson's grounder went through Buckner's legs. It created the sort of trauma you'll spend a lifetime trying to erase.

Epstein sent a letter to the Baltimore Orioles in 1991. He was a freshman at Yale, looking for a summer job. He started as an intern and continued up the ranks each summer and after graduation, working first for the Orioles, then for the Padres. In 2003, Red Sox president Larry Lucchino made Epstein, then twenty-eight years old, the youngest general manager in baseball history. I met him in a diner a few blocks from Wrigley Field shortly after the 2016 World Series. He's tall and handsome and neat, everything fixed and tucked, with short dark hair that accentuates sharp features. His face creases when he smiles, his eyes glitter. When thinking, he has the deep focus of a mathematician. For a Cubs devotee, the fact that it took a Red Sox fan to break the curse is a little unsettling. We're in a position not unlike that of the Parisians after World War II. We're happy to be free but slightly ashamed we couldn't do it ourselves.

When I asked Epstein about this, he looked down and laughed. He's a storyteller—that's how I see him. Maybe because I know that his father, Leslie, is a wonderful novelist—*King of the Jews*—and that his grandfather Julius and great-uncle Philip together wrote some of the classic American movies—*Casablanca, Arsenic and Old Lace*. It helps explain why Theo was able to defeat not one but two historic curses. Because what's a curse? It's a story. How do you change a story? You write a better one. That's why Epstein wanted the Cubs job. It was the only story even greater than that of the Red Sox, the only place he could put together a worthy sequel. If you win in Boston, then in Houston, who cares? But if you win in Boston, then Chicago, you've got *The Godfather* and *The Godfather II*.

Epstein told me he'd been only vaguely aware of the curse before he came to Chicago. "I'd once seen a picture of a bar owner trying to get a goat through a turnstile," he said. "It was no greater than that. The first time I thought about it more deeply was in 2003, my first year as GM in Boston. We were playing the Yankees in the ALCS and the Cubs were playing the Marlins in the NLCS. We lost Game 5 and flew to New York and got there in time to watch the NL Game 6 on TV. I watched the Bartman Game in my hotel. It was completely shocking. Of course, I didn't think about it as the Bartman Game at the time. I looked at it from a baseball standpoint—a blown lead. But over the next couple of days it trickled out about all the hostilities and the horrible shit going on in the stands."

"So was it the curse?" I asked.

"What?"

"The Bartman Game?"

"No, it was a blown lead, like I said."

"Do you believe in the curse at all?"

"No."

"Then how do you explain it?"

"Explain what?"

"All the terribleness, year after year."

"I can't speak about ancient history, but I can speak about recent history," he said. "The Cubs were not good because the organization focused on the wrong things. Not to quote Sarah Palin, but they were putting lipstick on the pig. They always wanted to make sure next year's team looked like it had a chance to win because the team was going to be up for sale at any moment. They needed them to be a competitive team—so what does that mean? Well, if it's 1988, it means making sure the 1989 team looks like it has a chance. And if it's 1989, you are busy making sure the 1990 team looks like *it* has a chance. It means lack of long-term planning, focus on the short term, focus on optics. The Red Sox were like that too: always focused on the next day's sports section. It's hard to execute any sort of plan when the focus is on everything except what defines a healthy baseball operation. What was the goal for the Tribune Company? Was it really to win the World Series, or was it to keep the sale price high and generate content for WGN? They needed the team to be interesting enough that people would watch. You can't do one year in baseball.

"That was the big question for me when I met Tom in New York," Epstein continued. "Was he willing to let the team get really bad? As bad as it's ever been? Was he ready for the pressure that would come from the fans and reporters when we got rid of their favorite players and lost a hundred games? Because that's how bad we'd have to get to get good."

The curse was not entirely unreal, Epstein added. It's just that it wasn't magic, nor imposed from the outside. It was a mental state. People expected to lose—that was the culture. Change the culture, kill the curse. That meant developing young players and acquiring others, bringing in coaches untouched by Cubs history. It meant no holdovers to tell the stories of '69 and '84. It meant starting anew, approaching the task in the way of an expansion team. Epstein said it would take five years, the same amount of time Stalin said he'd need to create a workers' paradise.

Finding the right sort of players would not be easy. Epstein had been one of the early utilizers of the new stats pioneered by Bill James, an early practitioner of what Michael Lewis dubbed "moneyball." The thinking goes like this: For over a hundred years, baseball executives relied on imprecise measurements. Batting average, home runs, RBIs—numbers that do not necessarily translate to wins. It takes twenty-seven outs to lose. You therefore want players who are tough to retire—hard outs. But old stats did not really focus on that—they focused on flash. The new stats were specifically designed to find players who have a gift for staying alive. OPS became the primary number of the new model:

on-base percentage plus slugging. Epstein and his cohorts found hidden gems this way, good players missed by an antiquated system. In those first years of moneyball, they were like buyout kings spotting hidden value everywhere. Of course, it works only as long as no one else knows how you're doing it.

"One day, in Boston, John Henry, the owner of the Red Sox, told me to meet with Michael Lewis and show him what we were doing," Epstein said. "I was like, 'Why? These are trade secrets.' Then, when Lewis started asking questions, again, I was like, 'Why would we ever tell you that? It's a secret. It's a competitive advantage.' And he says, 'Well, it's not going to be a secret for long. This is going to be a big book.' And it was. It was a *New York Times* bestseller. And you know who reads *New York Times* bestsellers? Rich old people on yachts who own baseball teams. They read it and started asking their GMs questions like, 'How are we making decisions? Do we have people who look at the game this way?' When I started in baseball, there were just a couple of teams that had statistical people on staff, and no one listened to them. Now it's just about everyone."

"Did that change the way you did the job in Chicago?"

"Completely," said Epstein. "I had to find my players and execute my plan in an entirely new way. But some cool things happened as a result. First you have to dig a lot deeper to find any kind of advantage. As it turns out, that's fun. We've done some really cool shit that's actually worked. Ninety-five percent of it doesn't work, but five percent does and you can use it to get a player in the draft you would've missed, or make a good trade you wouldn't have even seen."

I asked Epstein to share some of those secrets.

"All right," he said, smiling, "just one. We're studying players' brains. Neuroscanning. We developed it in Boston with a couple of neuroscientists who came up with a software program that's a lot like a video game you can give a player. One is a game with a ball coming in at ninety miles an hour. You have to hit the space bar as it crosses home plate. But if the ball turns red as it crosses, you're not allowed to hit the space bar. That measures their sense of timing and their inhibitory control: Can they stop when new information is introduced? It assesses the caliber of the neuropathway in the brain that goes into being a good hitter. We tested it on Red Sox for years. It's one of the reasons we took Mookie Betts—he aced that test. If a kid's brain functions the way the best major league hitters' brains function, we move him up on our draft board.

"With the secrets out, the pendulum swung back," Epstein continued. "The competitive edge is not going to be in reading a spreadsheet to figure out who can play, but in being able to look at the human being and figure out who that person is and how to put him in a position where he can succeed. I think that's what sets our organization apart: We do a great job of understanding the player as a person—whether it's doing thorough work gathering background and makeup information before the draft, or working with players so they're accountable in the minor leagues for their own development. We sit with each player and come up with an individualized development plan: How are you going to become a big leaguer? Now that there are all these objective tools to assess future performance, and it's hard to find a competitive advantage, the magic and separation occurs in getting the person to perform. 'Cause none of us is just the numbers on the back of our baseball cards. You're not just a writer from the North Shore. That's what it says on the back of your baseball card, but your essence, what we're going to tap into to get you to perform, is more elusive, and I can only figure it out by having a hundred of these conversations. That's how we're looking at players now: not just a six-foot-two, 185-pound shortstop from East Bumfuck, Oklahoma, but someone who grew up in this type of house, with these type of parents, this kind of education and personality, this adversity, these insecurities. We're going to surround you with teammates and give you a program and build you a system. We're investing in the people, not stats."

■ ■ ■

Epstein started by cutting deadwood. Compare the 2011 roster to 2012. So many of the old names are gone. Some traded, others let go. This included standouts from the last good Cubs team. Every star is a hero to some kid, meaning Epstein had to be remorseless. This is the man who brought David Ortiz to the Red Sox, but also the man who traded Nomar Garciaparra. John Henry called that "one of the bravest moves anyone could make in baseball. It shows how incredibly special and selfless Theo is . . ." Fans hated him for it—until the Red Sox won the World Series. Carlos Zambrano, who won eighteen games for the Cubs in 2007, Ryan Dempster, who won fifteen games for the Cubs in 2010, Aramis Ramirez, who hit .306 with twenty-six home runs for the Cubs in 2011—gone, gone, gone.

It accomplished at least two things. First, it changed the culture. If the curse was real, it existed in the players, who passed it from generation to generation. You get rid of the disease by getting rid of its carriers. Second, it shed wasteful contracts, freeing up money, putting Epstein in position to make deals. "We had to clean house," he told me. "I mean, what was even there? A big part of our job is understanding the other twenty-nine organizations. Who's on the big league club, who is in their minor league system, their good contracts, their bad contracts, their young talent. So we knew the Cubs and we knew it was not good. If you look at the big league roster when we came in, you had Starlin Castro—he was a legitimate, if you want to dehumanize it, asset. He was a twenty-one-year-old shortstop, already pretty good, looked like he was going to get better, which it turned out he didn't. You had pitcher Jeff Samardzija. He was in the bullpen. He turned out to be an asset, but was hidden. Then you look at the minor leagues—it was the oldest team in the division, the most expensive team in the division, and they weren't going anywhere. So we had to clean and acquire. We drafted a high school kid the first year, made a couple of deals. We traded for Travis Wood and Anthony Rizzo right off the bat. We traded Dempster at the deadline for Kyle Hendricks. But when we looked at the board, it still seemed like we were years away from any of these players making it to the big league team. [Albert] Almora—maybe he'd be up by '15 or '16. Javier Báez, maybe by '14 or '15. But to win, you need ten to twelve good players and half a dozen impact players. Where the fuck were they going to come from?"

When it came to trading, Epstein had one great advantage. He did not have to worry about the short term. In most cases, if you trade a star, fans expect you to get something immediate in return. But since Ricketts had given Epstein permission to let the big league team fail—this was a gut renovation—he could trade with only the long term in mind. Established players for prospects—present for distant future. Green bananas. "We never focused on whether we won or lost," he told me. "It was all about building a healthy operation. We wanted to make sure we were not just guessing when we evaluated players. That meant we needed to build a really effective scouting department. On the development side, we had to make sure we weren't just rolling bats and balls out and hoping players got better—we needed the right people, the systems that would make these kids better."

According to conventional wisdom, championship teams are built around pitching. You get four, five strong arms, add some hitting, you're in the World Series. Because baseball—I feel my father's hand on my sleeve, hear his voice in my ear—"is 90 percent pitching." But that's not what Epstein did in Chicago. Epstein built his team as you might build a softball team. Look for the best players and worry about the rest later.

"Why not start with pitching?" I asked.

"Because pitchers get hurt," he told me. "That's the main reason we've invested heavily in position players—less injury, more predictability of performance. Then, and just as important, in fact more important, they impact your team ethos more. A position player, a Kyle Schwarber or Anthony Rizzo, shows up in the lineup every day. Their personality shapes the feel of the club more than a starting pitcher who's only out there once every five days. I like building with position players for that reason."

"What about my father?" I asked.

"What about your father?"

"He says baseball is 90 percent pitching."

"Yeah, well, that is what people say," Epstein answered. " 'Baseball is 90 percent pitching, you can't win without great pitching, pitchers are more important than position players.' But I don't buy it. Look at it this way: Winning is a question of scoring more runs, right? Teams that create more runs, teams that allow fewer runs. Exactly 50 percent of the game is run creation, exactly 50 percent of the game is run prevention. And your run creation is some percent hitting and some percent base running. Correct? Forty-five and 5, 40 and 10, however you want to split up that 50 percent. Your position players are 100 percent responsible for that. So they get 50 percent of the run equation while being on offense. Now what about run prevention? It's some combination of pitching *and* defense. So what's the breakdown of that 50 percent? Maybe 35 percent pitching and 15 percent defense. So who impacts your defense? Your pitcher but also your position players. They're on both sides of the equation. So that comes out to something like 65 percent of the game being determined by position players, 35 percent by pitchers. I think the people who say pitching is 90 percent of the game have it exactly backward."

It's an answer that shows how his mind works: math and percentages, wheels within wheels. "So we needed position players," he explained. "We needed people to account for all those runs. Where would they come from?"

He started with Anthony Rizzo, a first baseman who would become a team leader. Epstein had known Rizzo since he was in high school. He'd brought him to Boston, then traded him to San Diego, reluctantly parting with a phrase like, *We'll meet again.*

Rizzo had had cancer in his teens. He fought through it and made it all the way back—in other words, he was just the sort of person suited for the Cubs. He was more than bat and glove. He was resilient. He beat cancer—do you think he'd go wobbly at the appearance of a billy goat? "His strength and character are incredible," Epstein told me. "Six months after he was diagnosed, he hit a double off a big league pitcher in an instructional-league game.

"We did it in phases," Epstein continued. "First tear down, then build. That means we had to transact, right? And there's only a few days a year when you get to transact in baseball. It's not like being a day trader, looking to improve your portfolio. You can't just wake up and make a thousand trades. In baseball you have the draft, one day a year, to bring in the best amateur talent. Then you have the trading deadline later in the season. That's when you can get other teams engaged. We had a real opportunity there because we weren't focused on standings. We could invest in long-term players and give them short-term players. Then there's the off-season, winter meetings. Those are the three times a year you have an opportunity to acquire. We stayed single-minded about it: We wanted young impact talent. The only way we could get it was draft and trade, so we knew we couldn't fuck those opportunities up. And we knew we didn't have forever—four or five years. And we knew, to get it done here, we had to be really good. And lucky. We had to hit on all these guys. Then slowly, as it became clear that Rizzo was going to be what we thought he'd be, we started to feel a little better. Some other guys we drafted started to look like they'd turn out. When we drafted Kris Bryant and he became a lead prospect, we felt even better. Then we drafted Schwarber and felt even better. The nucleus kept building. That was our focus each day: Who's our core? Who are these guys going to be? Do they have the talent? Do they have the personality? How do they fit together?"

Meanwhile, the big league team was going to pieces. 2012 was among the worst seasons in Cubs history. They lost 101 games, finishing in fifth place, 36 games behind the Cincinnati Reds. They were slightly better in 2013. The first of the Epstein era players began to arrive: Jake Arrieta, Travis Wood, Pedro Strop.

They still finished last, though, thirty-one games behind the Cardinals.

But here's the truth: The guys on those teams were not supposed to win; they were placeholders, burning innings while the actual team, the team that would break the curse, was coming of age in the minors. Did they know it? Did they sense it? Oh, to be a member of an in-between generation, to realize your function is to merely kill time. "We had unbelievable morale in our minor leagues," Epstein told me. "We had a shitload of talent down there, prospects that believed in themselves, in each other, proud to be Cubs. We showered them with attention and invested in making them better. That was juxtaposed with the morale at the big league level, which sucked. We had a hard time figuring out how to create the right environment for the kids when they became big league players, which is super important because, if you're basing the fate of your franchise on a half a dozen players who are all going to break in around the same time, you want to make sure the environment is right so they can make the adjustment quickly. We needed our guys to hit the ground running. And we managed that. That's why Addison Russell was able to take over as shortstop in the middle of a pennant race and succeed. That's why Kris Bryant looks like he's always been here. That's why Kyle Schwarber came up in the middle of the season and jumped right in."

"What about the curse mentality?" I asked.

"We defeated it in the minor leagues," Epstein said. "During '12, '13, '14 when nothing good was happening with the big league club, we had a terrific secret and it was the mood and energy in the minors. We were building a new tradition down there. Not to sound too much like a cult, but we called it 'the Cubs Way.' First thing we did when we got here was to get everyone together, all our scouts and player-development people, and have a four-day meeting. We tried to answer every question: What are the Cubs going to stand for? How do we want our players to play the game? How do we want to teach? What kind of people do we want? We wrote it all up in a big manual and it became the vision that united our organization. In '12, '13, and '14, if you had gone to the back fields in spring training and seen the minor leaguers, or to the instructional league in September and October in Arizona, you'd have seen an incredible spirit—it was just the opposite of what was happening with the big club. They started to throw around a new compliment in the minors—when someone made a great play or backed up a base or saved a run or picked up a teammate, you'd hear one of the kids say, 'Way to go, that's Cub.' First time I heard that I knew we were on to something good as far as vibe and morale. So I think these young guys, as they made their way, expected to win. It was a spirit. We could see it. We'd sit there, as our big league club was getting hammered, watching the minor leaguers on TV. We'd be shouting, 'Did you see that play Báez just made?' We'd be fired up in the box, excited about our future. When we went down to the Wrigley clubhouse to talk to the manager, we'd have to be sure to wipe that smile off our faces because our guys just got their asses kicked."

■ ■ ■

The project had entered a new phase by 2015. Players had spun off the belt, key pieces had been added. Pitcher Jon Lester, who won two championships in Boston, joined the Cubs, hoping to break the curse. Anthony Rizzo had come of age. Kris Bryant made his major league debut at third.

Baseball people had been buzzing about Bryant since he was in college. He's tall and lanky, a right-handed power hitter and a versatile infielder. His hair is dark, his eyes are blue. He plays with a smile on his face. In fact, he smiles so big and so often it makes you nervous. Bryant's father, a player who never made it out of the minors, had spent time with Ted Williams and made a bible of Williams's book *The Science of Hitting*, accumulating knowledge that he passed on to his son. In the weeks before he arrived at Wrigley, I asked my *Sports Illustrated* editor if Bryant lived up to the hype. "Oh, yeah," he said. "I saw him at spring training. The sound the ball makes off his bat is like nothing else I've ever heard."

Dexter Fowler came in to play center. Javier Báez made his first appearances at second. Shortstop Addison Russell came in a trade for pitchers Jeff Samardzija and Jason Hammel. That completed the infield. Then David Ross, who came to Chicago as Jon Lester's "personal catcher." Lester gave the team a bulldog presence on the mound. Ross gave them something else. He was thirty-eight years old when he arrived, goatee going gray, an assuring adult presence, a camp counselor—an especially important role for such a young team. How many times have you seen Rizzo, Báez, or Bryant talking to Ross after a big play? They called him Grandpa. "We didn't get Ross in for stats," Epstein told me. "He's one of those rare guys who isn't just a veteran but is a veteran who is truly invested in getting to know the young players, understand them, help them get better and understand the ingredients that go into winning. What does that mean? Support and advice, great night conversations in the hotel room when you're slumping, getting over a tough loss, going to dinner together on the road. It all matters."

I asked Epstein if he built this team with Wrigley Field in mind. "Did you tailor it for the park's eccentricities?"

He laughed. "That'd be like building it for a schizophrenic girlfriend you can't please no matter what you do," he said. "Fenway was pretty easy to build around. Fenway rewards good habits for left-handed hitters because they reach for the big wall, which means going the opposite way and using more field, and it encourages bad habits for right-handed hitters because you get guys who are going to sell out and pull to that wall. But Wrigley? Wrigley just plays two different ways. It's so schizophrenic, so you can't really build a club for Wrigley other than just trying to put together a team that's strong in all areas, that can beat you in a number of ways, that can hit a lot of home runs, but also win 2–1."

Kyle Schwarber—a rambling bear of a kid, surprisingly fast, with a short left-handed power swing—came up midseason in a game at Cleveland. He got four hits in his first major league start. He's big but not nearly as big as he looks on TV—six feet, 235 pounds. He played linebacker at Indiana University and was a star on the baseball team. It was the swing that excited the Chicago scouts, quick and compact. It seemed familiar. You'd seen it, but where? Then, one night, on NBC, Bob Costas showed footage of Schwarber swinging beside footage of Babe Ruth. *My God, it's the same swing!* It made you appreciate Schwarber, but also made you appreciate Ruth. He'd always seemed ancient, spectral. Seeing him beside Schwarber put him right back into the present tense. You suddenly understood just how good Ruth would still be today. He'd lead the league in everything. Schwarber looks like the Babe too. The same jowly face, pug nose, big shoulders, strong but not weight-room strong—throwing-bales-of-hay strong. He'd been a catcher in college but does not quite have a major league arm. He can play first, but you have Rizzo. He ended up in left, where he could seem lost.

Maybe the most important move came before the season, when Epstein hired Joe Maddon to manage. Maddon was born in 1954 in West Hazelton, Pennsylvania. He'd gone to Lafayette College on a football scholarship—another quarterback from Appalachia—but loved playing baseball. He was drafted by the California Angels and spent four years in the minors but was never good enough. If he's a great manager, it's probably partly because he was a mediocre player. Nothing came naturally. He had to learn each particular, which meant he could teach the same way. He spent thirty years in the Angels organization, first as a player, then as a coach. He worked his way from the minors up to the majors. He was part of the 2002 team that beat the Giants in the seventh game of the World Series.

In Tampa Bay, which hired him to manage in 2006, he took a team that had always finished near the bottom, a team with one of the lowest payrolls in the league, and led them to four straight playoffs. In 2008, he brought the Rays to the World Series, which they lost in five games to the Phillies. He has a gnomic quality that keeps players loose. If his team is slumping, he might surprise them with animals from a petting zoo or bring in a magician—anything to get them out of their heads. Nor does he look like other big league managers. He wears thick glasses with heavy frames. His face is dark and stubbly, full of mischief. Now and then, he drives to Wrigley Field in a 1976 Dodge van with a western landscape painted on the side. It's all tousled orange carpet inside—burnt orange and leather seats with ostrich trim. He calls it the "Shaggin' Wagon." He has a 1972 Chevelle with blue carpet in the trunk and the 1908 Cubs logo. He spends the off-season crossing the country in an RV called "Cousin Eddie" with his wife—because the only thing better than a house is a house on wheels. Epstein first met Maddon in the mid-2000s, when he was looking for someone to lead the Red Sox. He ended up hiring Terry Francona, but he never forgot Maddon. "I just saw how different he was than anyone else we ever interviewed—his offbeat sense of humor and use of language and the way his mind worked," Epstein said. "Everything about him was different than what you'd expect from a manager, and it was refreshing."

Maddon came to mind as soon as Epstein began looking for someone to lead the Cubs. He caught up with him in a campground. Even if Epstein did not hammer out the details beneath the tin awning of Maddon's RV, beside a mesquite fire, in the glow of a bug zapper, I am going to imagine he did. Maddon opted out of the last year of his Tampa Bay contract, joining the Cubs in the winter of 2014. He began his tenure by meeting reporters at the Cubby Bear Lounge. He called it "a shot and a beer press conference."

Maddon turned out to be a perfect leader for a young team—because he's fun and easy, not bogged down by tradition. He's like a young father with a young family, energetic and new to it himself. He moves players around with the abandon of a Little League coach, the sort who wants to give everyone a try everywhere. He started Kris Bryant at multiple positions in 2016—in the infield and in the outfield. Twenty-five percent of the time Bryant ended a game in a different place from where he started. Javier Báez played all over. In the so-called left-field game (June 2016), rather than remove a reliever, thereby losing him for the rest of the day, Maddon moved pitchers from left field to the mound and back, as needed. You'd see him on the top step of the dugout, waving in one pitcher, sending another back out.

He did not make the mistake of denying the curse, as every other Cubs manager had done. He embraced it. He faced it down with slogans that turned up on posters and T-shirts, where they could help fans as well as players. Because it's a societal problem. It took the entire community to make the curse and would take the entire community to break it too. Even if the slogans did not address the curse specifically, they were about it all the same. "Do Simple Better," "Try Not to Suck," "Embrace the Target."

■ ■ ■

As spring deepened to summer, I felt an overwhelming need to see that team for myself. I took my sons. We watched a four-game series with the Cardinals from the grandstand. I had my qualms. Especially when the Cubs were behind, or looked feeble. Why am I doing this? I asked myself. Why infect my children, why give them the disease, why hand the misery down to another generation? I worried it was a kind of abuse. I now know my children will live in a world far different from my own. In their world, the Cubs are the best team in baseball.

I went back to Wrigley Field by myself in August. I wanted to spend a week in the bleachers. I wanted to see if they had changed, and they had. I had been one of the youngest people out there in the 1980s. There had been drunk bums and sober bums, and I was often the object of their ridicule and counsel. Some had memories that went back to Rogers Hornsby and Hack Wilson. To me, these were the classic Cubs fans: melancholic and world-weary and wise. They expected to lose. If the team was winning, they were not joyful—they were cynical, waiting to see how it would fall apart. These fans lived in the three tenses: have lost, are losing, will lose. But the people I met in the bleachers in the summer of 2015 were young and hopeful, less interested in what had happened than in what was happening. They lived in one tense: the future, the five minutes from now. When the Cubs fell behind, they anticipated a comeback.

I learned the story of Moses and Exodus when I was a child. My father told us how Moses led the Hebrews out of Egypt and into the wilderness, how the tribes wandered in the desert for forty years before they entered Canaan. I never could understand that. Why did a walk that should have taken no more than a week consume four decades and entire lifetimes? I found the answer in the left-field bleachers. The tribes had to dwell in the desert till the slave generation had died off. It would take a new people, born free, to conquer the Promised Land. It would take a new mentality. It would take a people who expected to win. So that's what I am, I said to myself—a member of the slave generation. Born in Egypt, I spent my life crisscrossing Sinai, and while I was crisscrossing, a new generation was coming of age and that generation filled the benches all around me and I was not only old to them, my mentality was the product of a vanished world, inscrutable, distasteful. Then it hit me: I never will make it to the Promised Land. Even if the Cubs win, it's too late. My mentality has been formed. The wilderness is inside. I take it with me wherever I go.

The Cubs won ninety-seven games in 2015, enough to get them into a wild-card playoff—a one-game winner-take-all against the Pirates. Jake Arrieta, the broad-shouldered pitching ace, riding one of the great hot streaks in franchise history, all alone at center stage. He'd come from Baltimore as a reclamation project. His motion was considered unsound. Coaches changed it and he struggled. In Chicago, they let him throw his own way, and a string of dominance followed. He'd win the Cy Young Award in 2015 with twenty-two wins and a 1.77 ERA, but what I remember is that night in Pittsburgh, the big man in the spotlight, shouldering the Cubs deeper into the playoffs. Six foot four, 225 pounds, twenty-nine years old, from Plano, Texas, he looked like he'd just stepped from the Brawny paper towel label. He was a lumberjack with a black beard. He had felled a thousand trees and would fell a thousand more. He was weirdly flexible for such a big man, a devotee of Pilates and yoga. He stretched elaborately in the outfield before each start. Hands on the ground beside his feet, he walks his fingers along the grass—every muscle jumping— until his body is horizontal. He threw a complete game against the Pirates—no runs, five hits, eleven strikeouts. The Cubs won 4–0.

The Cubs played the Cardinals in the NLDS. Kyle Schwarber was the breakout star. He went five for ten at the plate in the series, walked twice and hit two home runs, including one that will never be forgotten. Wrigley Field, Game 4, bottom of the seventh inning. Kevin Siegrist was on the mound for St. Louis. Third pitch: Schwarber's swing was short and sharp and followed a rocket-science trajectory. The ball went up and up and up. On the broadcast, they diagrammed its path. It carried into the sky. Arcane stats were posted: exit velocity (112.5 mph), launch angle (35 degrees), max height (136 feet), projected hang time (6.7 seconds), projected distance (419 feet). But it seemed like a magic beyond numbers because, though fans waited on Sheffield and on rooftops across the street, the ball never came down. It was as if God had raptured it. The camera crew finally located it atop the right-field scoreboard, quickly dubbed the Schwarboard, where it was shown resting gently. It was not removed till late autumn. If the Cubs had won the 2015 World Series, it might have stayed up there forever, like footprints on the moon.

Anyone who watched those Cubs regularly knew their flaw. They were streaky. They hit a lot of long balls and scored a lot of runs, but every now and then the big bats just went silent. The stars would stop hitting all at once, as if not hitting were a contagion that could pass from bat to bat. Such periods, which could last two games or a week, fell upon the team like a drought. The ground itself seemed hard and mean, the ivy withered. You waited for some act of will, a clever hitter to break the spell. All it took was one blast, a single clap of thunder—then the skies opened and the rain came down. Maddon said it was because the team was so young. Many of the 2015 Cubs were twenty-two or twenty-three years old and had been in the big leagues less than a full season. They had yet to learn the little tricks and strategies that get you across the cactus land.

That's what happened in the 2015 NLCS, in which the Cubs were swept by the Mets. New York had strong pitching, but it felt more cyclical than that. After the feast of the St. Louis series, when the Cubs scored twenty runs and hit ten home runs, came the famine of New York, with the Cubs scoring just eight runs in four games. Bryant went 3 for 14. Báez went 1 for 10. Rizzo went 3 for 14. And the trouble came not just at the plate—they fell apart in the field too. Schwarber, who'd stood for fecundity in the division series, stood for futility now. He hit two home runs, but it's the fielding errors you remember. He seemed lost in the vastness of Citi Field, charged balls he should have let drop, missed and chased and rolled around, looked less like a major leaguer than like a big clumsy puppy still learning to use its legs. It somehow made you like him more.

It was a wipeout, and yet an interesting thing happened. Unlike the last game of 2003, 1989, and 1984, this loss did not make you self-pitying or sad. It did not wreck you. It was invigorating. You came away with hope because you realized how far this team had gotten and how close they had come. You knew they would neither quit nor be taken apart, but would mature, get better. They had to fail; they needed that experience. And they had failed well—you felt it. In the past, when we came up short, we knew we'd had our chance and blown it. Darkness rolled in. This was different.

CHAPTER

GO CUBS GO!

NO.
12

I did not watch every game the Cubs played in 1984, but I tried to. Day games were easier. I'd get home from school, cook SpaghettiOs, and turn on WGN. There's nothing like watching the same team every day. You come to know the players in the way of friends. For many years, I hardly watched the Cubs at all. Because I had been wounded and was saving myself. Because I was in the wrong time zone, wrong market, wrong frame of mind. When I did watch, it was like dropping in on a new family living in your old house. I rooted for them on the few occasions they reached the postseason, but I did not make a show of my rooting. I did not feel entitled to it. I had not put in the hours. But I'd come back in 2014 and had the MLB cable package by 2016 and was determined to watch every game. I was certain that this was the year. I'd put in the time so I could enjoy the party.

I decided to change my habits in hopes of helping the Cubs. For my entire life, I have carefully avoided the jinx. I'd never talk about playoffs or World Series, nor did I boast about the prospects of my team, believing this would bring down the ax. "Well, how has that worked out for you?" I asked myself that spring. "You've avoided the jinx for forty years and in every one of those forty years the Cubs lost." I decided to do the opposite of everything I had done. Not only did I not watch my words, I taunted the jinx. I told people I could make no plans for October as "I'll be in Chicago for the World Series." I booked tickets and made hotel reservations. When asked if I'd be coming in for business, I said, "Nope, to watch the Cubs win the championship."

■ ■ ■

"In 2012, we'd been in the building phase," Epstein told me. "By 2016, we'd reached the winning phase. That means trading for the short term, an entirely different mentality."

The pitching had been good in 2015, but once the team got deep into the playoffs, it was clear they were a few arms short. In December, they acquired John Lackey, a starting pitcher—he'd played for Epstein in Boston—from St. Louis. Two years, $32 million. This would both help Chicago and diminish a rival. Jason Heyward, also acquired from the Cardinals, ended up with the team's biggest contract: eight years, $184 million. Known to teammates as J-Hey, he played right field and was supposed to be a solid hitter in the middle of the lineup, but every time I turned on a game he was popping out or grounding into a double play.

Heyward's lack of production would become one of the season's only negative story lines. He'd hit .230 and strike out ninety-three times. "Players who sign big contracts and sink right away can get themselves in trouble," Epstein told me. "There's a momentum sending them into isolation, hiding. Some physically go away 'cause it's too much for them to take. Others get disconnected from their teammates or don't talk to the media or give up and say, 'I'll fix it in the off-season.' But Heyward stayed connected, which is hard when you're struggling more than any other player. He managed to help in all kinds of hard-to-define ways."

Dexter Fowler signed a one-year contract to return to center field. Starlin Castro, crowded out of the infield by young talent, was traded to the Yankees for pitcher Adam Warren. Then, in the middle of the season, catcher Willson Contreras came up from the minors—he homered in his first at bat. Pitcher Mike Montgomery arrived from Seattle.

Ben Zobrist was brought in specifically to solve the big problem—the streakiness, how, now and then, the bats went silent. He grew up in Eureka, Illinois, a thirty-five-year-old switch-hitter who knew how to get himself on base and get his team going. He played on Maddon's World Series team in Tampa and had been a crucial part of the Royals team that won the 2015 World Series. He was everywhere that October—an agitator, a maddening fly. Precisely the sort of spark plug the Cubs had been missing. He looks jumpy at the plate—sandy hair, sandy goatee, hands choked up, waving his bat around as he waits. He does not amass huge numbers, but stats don't tell the story. He always seems to be driving the ball into the gap. You see him rounding first, looking for more—a slap hitter of old, working every angle.

He'd played second base in Kansas City, but by midseason Báez was often at second, pushing Zobrist into left field, which would put Schwarber . . . where?

It seemed like a problem with the roster, like bad planning. Epstein wanted position players—now he had too many. Schwarber, Heyward, Fowler, Zobrist, Jorge Soler—that's five starting outfielders. Where would they play? When I asked Epstein, he laughed.

"Yeah, everyone was panicking," he acknowledged. "Not enough positions to go around, etc. But guys get hurt and the season is long and too many players means we can be flexible. It means we can rest guys, and means, each day, we can send out the best lineup based on our pitcher and their pitcher. If we know who is starting for the other team, if it's more of a four-seam guy than a two-seam guy," says Epstein, speaking of two different kinds of fastball, different grips resulting in varying trajectories, "then we put in hitters who pick up the four-seam fast ball. We also think about our pitcher and okay, let's say it's Jon Lester. He induces a lot of ground balls to third, so let's let Báez play third that day. If it's Kyle Hendricks on the mound, that means a shitload of balls to second, so let's put Javier at second and Zobrist in left. Having depth means we can give guys proper rest and custom design each day's lineup and can withstand injuries. I think it's one of the reasons we won last year."

Epstein was proved right the third game of the season. Kyle Schwarber, playing left and running for a ball in center, collided with Dexter Fowler, destroying his knee. Schwarber would require surgery and be out for the entire season. And yet, because of that depth, the Cubs did not miss a beat. Zobrist took over in left, the machine rolled on. The Cubs won twenty-five of their first thirty-one games. Hitting and defense—they executed like the 1908 Cubs—small ball, the extra base, guys caught napping off first. The entire infield made the All-Star team. There was the occasional concern: streakiness, the tendency of all bats to fail. Going into the midseason break, they dropped five straight games. Also relief pitching: The Cubs had no real closer, no pitcher to shut down the other side in the pinch. Epstein knew how to fix this, though he didn't really want to. It would mean making an unsound trade, long term for short term, which goes against his instinct. "Why'd I decide to do it?" he asked me. "Because of the way our team was playing—they deserved it."

A few weeks before the trading deadline, Epstein dealt one of the Cubs' most promising prospects—Gleyber Torres, a nineteen-year-old shortstop many consider a future star—for Aroldis Chapman, a twenty-eight-year-old Cuban closer with massive legs and massive arms and a mean scowl looking in. He might be the hardest thrower in baseball, occasionally touching 105 mph. A pitch going that fast moves as it approaches the plate, fooling and unsettling hitters.

This combination—speed and movement, a cocktail with a hint of danger—made Chapman a unique commodity, a four-time All-Star who'd saved more than thirty games five times. Such a player can help a team even when he's not playing. His mere presence makes the enemy despair. But Chapman was damaged goods in 2016. There'd been a domestic incident. He'd fought with his wife, gotten a gun, gone into his garage, and fired several bullets into the ceiling. He was not charged by police, but was suspended from the game. His own team lost interest—he'd become toxic. It seemed no one would take him. Then the Yankees did. He signed a one-year deal and performed brilliantly. Knowing they wouldn't make a playoff run, the Yankees swapped short term for long term. "There were a lot of reasons not to make that trade," Epstein told me. "And trust me, my life would have been easier if we didn't make it. But we felt like the other twenty-four players deserved it. We knew we were going to the postseason, we knew we were going to have a lot of close games in the postseason. And there was a real risk that our ball club wasn't quite good enough. We were missing that one more dominant guy. Chapman clearly was that guy. And yet the trade did not make sense on paper. Six and a half years of Gleyber Torres for a third of a season with Aroldis Chapman? But I would do it again. If you have a chance to win the World Series but don't take that final step because it doesn't add up, that's bullshit and not fair. If you don't make that investment, that can put dents in trust and wreck the culture that you've been so careful to build. We went around and asked a lot of our players. They all wanted to go for it."

When Epstein says, "And trust me, my life would have been easier if we didn't make it," I am almost certain he's referring to Chapman's off-field issues. The 2016 Cubs were likable and good—they smiled when they played. Fun was a part of the equation. Chapman could muck that up. When I close my eyes and think of Kris Bryant, he is blue-eyed and grinning as he hammers a ball over the ivy. When I close my eyes and think of Aroldis Chapman, he is emptying a chamber into the garage ceiling. There's a DJ at Wrigley Field. He plays a song chosen by each player as that player approaches the plate. It's a kind of theme that usually goofs on name or biography. It's called walk-up music. For Kris Bryant, he plays "Warm It Up" by Kris Kross. For Anthony Rizzo, he plays "Bad Blood" by Taylor Swift or "Good Vibrations" by Marky Mark. For Jason Heyward, he plays "Hype" by Drake.

For Ben Zobrist, he plays "Alive" sung by Ben's wife, the recording artist Julianna Zobrist. For David Ross, he plays "Young Forever" by Jay-Z. In August, as Chapman walked off the mound having pitched a scoreless ninth, the DJ went rogue, playing "Smack My Bitch Up" by The Prodigy. And was fired the next day.

■ ■ ■

When I was a kid, Wrigley Field was often desolate in September. Empty seats, meaningless games, first chill of autumn. In 2016, Wrigley did not seem fully alive *until* September, every seat filled, every fan flying because everyone was starting to believe. Best was postgame if the Cubs won. In most stadiums, even when a game is close, part of the crowd exits early. At Wrigley in September 2016, everyone stayed. They wanted to see the last pitch, they wanted to see the players swarm the mound, and mostly they wanted to sing "Go Cubs Go."

I think "Go Cubs Go" is the greatest sports anthem ever, precisely because it is not braggy, does not threaten to crush, maim, and kill. It's modest in its aims, not even promising a championship but merely making the case that, "They got the power, they got the speed, to be the best in the National League . . ." It was written in 1984 by Steve Goodman, a folksinger from Park Ridge, Illinois. Steve Goodman was short and wise and wrote classics, including "City of New Orleans" and "You Never Even Call Me by My Name." He turned his love for the Cubs into a handful of timeless tunes. "When the Cubs Go Marching In." "A Dying Cub Fan's Last Request." It's not just the words of these songs I find moving. It's Goodman's voice, which is the Chicago accent north of the city, the nasal flatness that peaks in Minnesota. It's exactly how people sounded when I was growing up. The spiritual gap between "Go Cubs Go" and Goodman's dirge, "A Dying Cub Fan's Last Request," is the distance every fan must travel—from hope to disillusion, from earnestness to dark comedy. As Auden said about Yeats, "Mad Ireland hurt you into poetry." Well, it was like that with Steve Goodman, only instead of Ireland it was the Cubs and instead of poetry it was this music. He died September 20, 1984, soon after the '84 team clinched. He was thirty-six years old. He did not live to see that team fall apart, but he knew it would happen.

In the song, he said he wanted his funeral held at Wrigley Field on a weekend afternoon—a day game. He wanted the groundskeepers to carry his coffin around the bases, umpires calling him out at each base "in all their holy wrath." Ernie Banks would be there, ditto Jack Brickhouse and Keith Moreland, who, in dreams, is forever dropping an easy fly ball. He wanted his casket burned at home plate in a huge bonfire made of Louisville Sluggers. Carried by a screaming northwest wind, his ashes would settle on Waveland Avenue.

In 1988, some of Goodman's ashes were indeed scattered above Wrigley Field, where I like to imagine them mixing with the previously scattered ashes of Bill Veeck, Jr.

The Cubs won 103 games in 2016, finishing seventeen and a half games ahead of their closest rival. They played San Francisco in the first round of the playoffs. It seemed fitting. The last time the Cubs won a World Series they got there by snatching the Merkle Game away from the Giants. Now we'd have to get past the Giants again. It was one of those series: all about the first game. Jon Lester was facing San Francisco right-hander Johnny Cueto. It was scoreless into the bottom of the eighth when Javier Báez, who, at twenty-two, was just emerging, tagged a fastball. He flipped his bat, then headed toward first, already celebrating. The wind caught the ball and brought it back, back, back, dropping it into the basket on the left wall—a home run, but barely. The Cubs took the game 1 to 0, the series 3 to 1.

I flew to Chicago for the first game of the NLCS—Cubs versus Dodgers—dropped my bags at the hotel, walked to the train. The Red Line was so jammed I had to wedge in—it's what I wanted, to dive into a sea of fanatics. The train started in a tunnel downtown, then climbed. It's a thrill even now: emerging into the daylight, cars weaving between redbrick apartment houses, wooden fire escapes, postage-stamp yards, little grills on balconies, bratwurst fires, billboards and chimneys and kitchen windows and neon signs and smokestacks. West Addison Street. As soon as I was down the stairs and through the turnstile, it might as well have been 1932. Organ music, peanut shells, the edifice of the ancient park.

I found a seat in the auxiliary press box, high above left field. The night was so blue it was velvet. The foul pole—I felt as if I could touch it. Lester started. He was the anchor of the pitching staff. When he was a free agent trying to pick a team, Epstein wrote him: "If you do decide to join us in Chicago, we look forward to taking care of your family, to great fun to be had together, and to the biggest celebration in the history of sports!"

He'd gone 19–5, with a 2.44 ERA in 2016. It seemed like he was always tapped for the statement games. He had the experience, the aura, was big and barrel-chested, gritty and mean—a sock full of marbles. He also had a damaged quality that made him interesting, for here was a man with the yips, a strange baseball disease that's a factor whenever he pitches.

What are the yips?

In the middle of a career, for no apparent reason, a player, often a good player, forgets how to throw a baseball. He tries, but it sticks in his hand. Or he does, but it sails. It's like psychosis: You forget how to do what you've always done automatically. The bang-bang plays—those you can handle. It's the easy throws, when you have time to think, that confound. Whenever your brain gets involved, you're in trouble. That's the yips. There have been famous cases. Chuck Knoblauch, the Yankees' second baseman who could not make the throw to first. Mackey Sasser, who caught for the Mets in the 1990s until he forgot how to get the ball back to the pitcher. It's terrifying because the analogy to everyday life is obvious. Players don't talk about it—if you talk about the yips, you might get the yips.

It did not affect Lester's pitching, though. He was still among the best, with an outside shot at the Hall of Fame. It was his defense. He could field his position but could not throw to first. He'd step out of the way of a grounder, let Bryant or Rizzo take it. If the ball did end up in his glove, he'd jog toward Rizzo, then toss underhand. If forced to make a play, he might throw his entire glove with the ball inside. The bigger problem came with men on base. In most cases, a pitcher keeps the runner from stealing or taking a huge lead by throwing to first. Lester did not like to do that and the runner knew it, which meant havoc whenever he was on the mound. The best solution was to keep the runners on the bench. Which is what he did most of that game, allowing only scattered singles into the fifth, when he gave up a solo home run to Andre Ethier. By then, the Cubs had scored three runs, one on a play I'd never seen in person. Javier Báez got caught off third. The Dodgers catcher threw behind him. With the ball in the air, Baez broke for home, sliding in a beat before the tag. I turned to the sportswriter next to me and asked, "Did he just steal home?"

That's the thing about the 2016 Cubs. You were constantly seeing something that you'd never seen before: the pitcher who can't throw to first, the second baseman who steals home.

Chapman came on in the eighth. Closers like to come in clean—it's something they talk about. No men on. My own canvas, don't have to straighten out another pitcher's mess. In this case, Chapman was taking over with bases loaded, no outs. "The 28-year-old Chapman throws a baseball harder than any man alive," Tom Verducci wrote in *Sports Illustrated*. "At 6′4″ and 215 pounds he is, in the words of his manager, Joe Maddon, a mass of 'wrapped steel.' " He struck out Corey Seager on four pitches, then struck out Yasiel Puig on four more. It looked like a mismatch, like hitters chasing gnats. But Adrián González managed to get his bat on the ball, sending a grounder through the infield. Two runs scored—the game was tied. And so the old feeling returned, the dismay bubbling up from the bottom of my Cubbie soul. Here's what I was thinking: That's the cruelty of the curse—it does not just defeat you; it teases and taunts, and then it defeats you; it takes you all the way to the NLCS, then drops you from the top of the stairs. I stared into the middle distance, laughing at my vanity: What made me believe this year would be different?

Then something happened, something I'm still trying to understand. The fans in the seats just below the press box, the multitudes along the left-field line, began to chant, first just a few, then thousands: "We don't quit! We don't quit! We don't quit!"

Once again, I turned to the sportswriter next to me. "Who are they talking about?" I asked.

"The Cubs."

"The Cubs?"

"Yes. The Cubs."

"You mean to tell me that they're saying the Cubs don't quit?"

"Yes."

It had become a slogan. "We Don't Quit." I'd started to see it on T-shirts and banners. We'd gone from THE CHICAGO CUBS, WORLD CHAMPIONS, 1908 to WE DON'T QUIT. What fools, I said to myself. Has history taught them nothing? Don't they know that we do quit? We're the Cubs. We're the team that quits. Maybe that's what it takes: ignorance. I expected the bats to fail and the Dodgers to score and the Cubs to go meekly. Because I'm damaged.

They expected the Cubs to win. Because they're healthy.

Zobrist led off the bottom of the eighth with a double. Addison Russell grounded out. Dave Roberts, the Dodgers' manager, then made a perplexing decision, intentionally walking two hitters to get to the light-hitting Cubs catcher Miguel Montero, who'd come in to pinch-hit. It was a move that had the stink of statistics, percentages. But when you intentionally load the bases to get to a batter, you challenge that batter's pride. You also put your pitcher—thirty-five-year-old Joe Blanton—in a corner. Two outs. Bases loaded. Everything must go perfectly. Montero is a stocky, pock-faced veteran. He'd signed with the Cubs though probably could've played a larger role elsewhere—he eventually became the team's third catcher—because he wanted to be part of the big thing. In other words, he'd signed on for just this moment.

Blanton got two quick strikes. But the third pitch, meant to break, didn't. It hung over the plate. The classic mistake. Montero, whose jersey was loose and a little sloppy, who is dark eyed and holds his hands low, hit the ball as if it were on a tee. Tagged it. And knew it was gone. A grand slam. It landed halfway up the right-field bleachers, with all those hands reaching out, all that color against all that black sky. A quick shot of the pitcher—because you always identify with the loser, the bad luckster, the man who will think about it for the rest of his life. Blanton looked dazed, pushed his hat away from his eyes and ran his fingers over his face.

Final score: Cubs 8, Dodgers 4.

The second game was all about pitching—a classic duel—tension and near miss. You're on pins and needles the whole time, waiting for something that will never happen. It's like watching a horror movie that consists entirely of false scares without the catharsis of a big kill. Kyle Hendricks was pitching for the Cubs. He allowed only three hits, but one was a home run. Clayton Kershaw started for the Dodgers. He gave up just two hits—singles by Báez and Contreras—and no runs. Some say Kershaw, who is tall with long blond hair, is the best pitcher in baseball, though he has struggled in the playoffs. To win the series, the Cubs would have to beat him at least once. It was like that in every round of the 2016 playoffs. A great ace that must be defeated before, in the way of a video game, you can move on to the next screen.

Final score: Dodgers 1, Cubs 0.

The real story of that game, to me, anyway, was Bill Murray, who'd become a fixture of the postseason, the celebrity who spoke for the fans in general—of curse and drought, of fear and trembling. He sang at the stretch, drank beer, smiled, cried, and was on camera constantly. I'm a Bill Murray fan, and believe he is honest and true, but I was starting to resent how a handful of celebrities—Bill Murray, Eddie Vedder, John Cusack—were being presented as stand-ins for the rest of us. It reduced a big moment of millions to a handful of representative faces—because if it's not happening to someone famous, it's not happening. Maybe this was just my fear. When you lose, there's more than enough for everyone. When you win, you have to fight for your share.

The Cubs were blown out in Game 3. Did not score, hardly hit—three singles and a double. By the eighth inning, you realized that, in the last two games, the bats had once again fallen silent. The characteristic flaw: streakiness, the machine gearing down. It was all the TV announcers talked about: 0 for this and 0 for that. Would the break ever come? At a certain point, when your team has stopped producing, it's hard to imagine them ever hitting again.

Final score: Dodgers 6, Cubs 0.

It did not happen till the middle of Game 4, by which time Chicago had gone twenty-one straight innings without a run. They were 0 for 10 at the plate that night when Zobrist led off the fourth. He'd been acquired for precisely this situation: to be the spark plug that, in one way or another, got the engine going. He was batting cleanup—traditionally the power spot—facing Julio Urías, a twenty-year-old rookie, the youngest pitcher to ever start in the playoffs. This was the pinch, the moment when the story could have gone this way or that. Statisticians say there is no such thing as a clutch hitter—that it all evens out. But anyone who watched Zobrist in the postseason knows that's not true. How do you break a curse? With players who have a gift for winning. Zobrist waved his bat like he was looking to power his team out of its funk, then, at the last moment, dropped a perfect bunt down the third-base line. He beat the throw to first. The clouds had been seeded, the rain came down. Báez singled. Russell hit a home run. Fowler doubled. More innings, more hits. What started with a bunt ended with a ten-run flood.

Final score: Cubs 10, Dodgers 2.

The flood continued into Game 5, with the Cubs scoring eight runs off thirteen hits and heading back to Wrigley Field a single victory—twenty-seven outs—from the World Series. They'd been this close before—in the Bartman Game, they were five outs away; in 1984, when the ball went through Leon Durham's legs, they were seven outs away. But this felt different. Because this team had been here in 2015 and had suffered and come back. Because this team seemed better than the others—stronger at almost every position. Because the present always looks better than the past.

The Cubs still had that riddle to solve: Kershaw. They'd yet to score a run off him in two games. Experts were already talking about a Game 7 . . . but . . . We don't quit!

The hitters got to Kershaw right away. Fowler led off with a ground rule double—a sharp bounder swallowed up by the ivy. Bryant drove in Fowler. Zobrist drove in Bryant. Then the crowd got going, and it was all over. Kershaw gave up four earned runs and was gone after five innings—chased from the game. Hendricks shut out the Dodgers: seven and a third innings, two hits, no runs. Chapman closed it. The party was on. The curse had not been killed, but it had suffered a serious blow. The Cubs had not won a World Series since 1908 but hadn't even been to a World Series since 1945. Never in my lifetime had they gotten this far. I wrote a story about this moment for *The New York Times* and was mocked for counting chickens and courting jinxes. "Hey, idiot, the Cubs haven't won anything yet. Idiot." To which I have two things to say: One, my active courting of the jinx is possibly what got the Cubs into the World Series in the first place, and two, just getting there was almost enough. When you love a team, you want to see that team win but also just want to see that team play—as much as possible. Getting this far could mean as many as seven extra games. In Chicago, where the winter starts as soon as baseball season ends, it also meant a reprieve from that cold dark night.

Fans lingered at Wrigley long after the game. They sang "Go Cubs Go" again and again. They could be heard from over a mile away.

It was a time of lists. People could just not stop setting down the many things that had happened since the Cubs last won the World Series. Communism had risen and fallen. Two world wars had been fought. The atomic bomb had been invented, dropped, and dropped again. The microchip had been built, turned into a calculator, then into a computer that, once wired to other computers, destroyed everything. Or they wrote about what life had been like when the flag was last raised over Wrigley Field. Only it wasn't Wrigley Field, because Wrigley Field had yet to be built. It was the West Side Grounds, home of dead ball and spitter and Tinker to Evers to Chance. There were no highways then. No credit cards, batting helmets, black major leaguers, designated hitters, airplanes. The tallest building in Chicago was 395 feet.

By making such lists, people were trying to express the enormity of what had happened—why it was a big deal, almost bigger than baseball, as big as anything else going on. Just think of all the Cubs fans who had been born and grown up and suffered and died and never seen this happen. Bill Murray got at the core of it in one of his interviews. He said something like, Yes, the lists, all true, but that's not the point. The point is: What is it like to wait for something all your life, to wait so long that you've made peace with the fact that it will never happen, then it does?

The Cubs would play the Cleveland Indians in the World Series, which made a good story, as the Indians were trying to overcome a funk of their own. They had not won a World Series since 1948—but they had been to the World Series and come up short. In other words, I felt bad for the Indians but much worse for us. What they had suffered was a drought—not a curse. A curse is supernatural, a different order of bad luck altogether.

The Indians had surprised people by reaching the World Series. They won ninety-four games, best in the AL Central, but had been a playoff underdog. They were led by still another ace, still another riddle the Cubs would have to solve, Corey Kluber. He'd been nearly untouchable in the postseason. There were also great relief pitchers, closer Cody Allen, who had thirty-two saves, and set-up man Andrew Miller, who'd come from the Yankees the same week Chapman went to the Cubs. The thinking was: If the Indians are ahead after six, they win the game. They had good hitters too—Francisco Lindor, José Ramírez, Mike Napoli—but their second baseman is worth special attention. Jason Kipnis grew up in Northbrook, Illinois, a product of Chicago's North suburbs. While considering whom the Indians might face in a World Series, he said to himself, *Anyone but the Cubs.* A great moment came before Game 3, the first World Series game at Wrigley in seventy-one years. Kipnis, looking like he'd stumbled through the wardrobe into Narnia, went out to right field and gently touched the ivy.

GAME 1

The 2016 World Series opened at Jacobs Field in Cleveland, which had been built as a kind of throwback, a new park made to look old, that is, a new park dressed up as Wrigley Field. Kluber was starting for the Indians. They called him Klubot because he was as effective and remorseless as a machine. He was drafted by the Padres, then traded to the Indians. He made his major league debut in 2011. He was a good pitcher who then got better. In 2014, he won the Cy Young Award. He pitched eleven and a third innings in the 2016 ALCS, yielding just two runs. The playoffs tend to be about pitching, which is why young teams like the Cubs can struggle. During the regular season, a big job of a pitching staff is merely to burn through all those innings, consume baseball time. Pitchers are left on the mound after they've tired, fattening offensive stats. The postseason can feel like a different sport. Every hitter studied and gamed, every pitch planned and calibrated. A hitter is lucky if he sees one fat pitch in nine innings, one out over the middle of the plate. The starter is yanked at the first sight of fatigue. Ditto the relievers. Some nights, a spectator spends what feels like hours just watching pitchers warm up. Many games are decided by a single mistake—a pitcher loses his grip, the ball hangs.

Kluber started by striking out Fowler, then Bryant. Both came as strikeouts looking—marked on the scorecard by a backward K. Meaning the batter had been fooled. Meaning late action on the breaking stuff. It looks like it's coming in there, then catches the edge of the strike zone. You stare at the ump as you walk away.

Jon Lester, who started for the Cubs, seemed shaky in the bottom of the first, as he often does in the early moments of a big series. He's like a kid who needs two or three weeks to get into the swing of school. He gave up a single to Francisco Lindor with two outs. Which meant a man on base. Which meant the yips. Lester held the ball in his glove, staring at the runner, who took a huge lead—it seemed like mockery—then took off with the pitch. Catcher David Ross had the ball and reared back, but it flew out of his hand before he could make a throw. Mike Napoli walked, so did Carlos Santana. Just like that: bases loaded. Lester stared in, stared in. He's six foot four and solid as a tree. He has a terrific poker face. The worse it gets, the calmer he looks.

José Ramírez came to the plate. When you watch a series like this, you start out knowing little about the players on the other team. By the end, if it's a good series, you hate them. Ramírez was a twenty-three-year-old Dominican infielder, small for the majors but fast with a good bat. He swung at Lester's second pitch, topped it, sending a dribbler toward third. It had the same effect as a bunt. Bryant charged, bare-handed the ball, and started to make the throw, but Ross, seeing that the runner was already nearing first, screamed, "Eat it." One run in, safe all around. Brandon Guyer was next up. Lester got two quick strikes, then hit Guyer on the leg—another run. Cleveland right fielder Lonnie

Chisenhall popped out to end the inning but, as Harry Caray used to say, "Not before the damage has been done."

Ben Zobrist led off the second with a double to center, bringing Kyle Schwarber to the plate—this was the surprise story of the World Series. Schwarber, a bear of a man who could kill you with one half-hearted blow, had collided with Dexter Fowler in the third game of the season, wrecking his knee. He was not supposed to be back till the spring. But the thought of getting this close only to miss the first Cubs World Series since 1945 was too much. It drove him toward a miraculous recovery. He worked and worked. We heard the first murmurs a few days before. Schwarber has been hitting off a tee! Schwarber has been hitting in the cage! As the Cubs were beating the Dodgers, Schwarber was playing tune-up games in the Arizona Fall League. The doctors cleared him to hit but not field. He could only pinch-hit in Chicago but made an ideal designated hitter in Cleveland. His mere presence in the lineup, the power and charisma of it, changed the equation. Bryant, Rizzo, Schwarber—that's a murderers' row.

At first, the analysts did not see Schwarber as a factor—it struck many as a gimmick. Even if he really were healthy—which was doubtful—it had been months since he'd faced major league pitching. Which brings up another piece of conventional wisdom: For every week a hitter misses, he will need a week of games to get back his timing. It's half the reason for spring training— you slowly pick up rhythm and pace, until you reach big league speed. How could Schwarber step into the batter's box when the game was at its most taut and expect to do anything but flail? His first major league swing in months would come in the World Series, where he'd be facing the best pitchers with their best stuff. It'd be like taking the wheel in the last lap of the Indianapolis

500. Nothing like it had been attempted. Pete Rose scoffed at the notion, saying, in essence, I'll tell you what to expect from Schwarber—three strikeouts.

Schwarber did strike out in his first at bat, but the way he looked doing it—how grooved in he was, the sweet swing and the long foul that just missed—made you reevaluate the conventional wisdom. "There was Kyle Schwarber," Epstein wrote, "who should not have even been playing after his horrific knee injury . . . raking as always."

How good did Schwarber look?

Good enough to give birth to conspiracy theories. Some said Schwarber had never been injured, that it had been an act, that he'd been playing secretly in Mexico all along, held back as a secret weapon. When the narrative does not fit belief—you can't start your season in the World Series—it's not the belief that changes.

Schwarber went 1 for 3: walk, two strikeouts, and an off-the-wall double that just missed being gone. He was one of the few Cubs who did not look out of sorts against Kluber or the pitchers who came on in relief: Andrew Miller, Cody Allen. Chicago was shut out but at least forced those Cleveland relievers to throw a lot of pitches. It was a silver lining. In a long series, small Game 1 decisions—leaving a pitcher in an extra inning—can determine what happens in Game 7.

Final score: Cleveland 6, Chicago 0.

GAME 2

Trevor Bauer started for the Indians. He was a twenty-five-year-old pitcher who'd never been much better than decent. Three weeks before the World Series, he'd injured the pinkie on his pitching hand while goofing around with a toy drone. This was thereafter referred to as "a drone injury." Asked about it, Indians manager Terry Francona said, "Everyone has suffered a drone injury at some point." In the days that followed, Bauer worked with a bandage on his pinkie. He threw a lot of complicated pitches—four-seam fastball, sinker, curve, cutter, splitter, change, slider—which put pressure on every finger. By the middle innings, the bandage was often red with blood.

Bryant singled with one out in the first. Then Rizzo—his left-handed swing is classic but he can look funny in the box—crowds the plate, bat held away from his belt, barrel perpendicular, pointing at the sky. He moves as he waits, sways his hips in search of a heavenly groove. He is like a hula dancer without a hoop. Then the ball comes and he strides, all that kinetic energy searching for contact.

Rizzo works a pitcher—fouling off ball after ball after ball, like a poker player examining and rejecting cards till he gets just what he wants. It was Bauer's seventh pitch. Rizzo's swing was beautiful, Shoeless Joe by way of the Splendid Splinter. You see it frozen in the camera flash, the follow-through carrying the bat all the way to the ground as the ball travels on a perfect arc to deep right field. Bryant was running with the pitch—never looked back, never slowed, just kept going. They clocked him—first to home in fourteen seconds.

Bryant struck out to open the fifth. Rizzo walked. Zobrist tripled, driving in Rizzo. Schwarber singled, driving in Zobrist. And that was more than enough. Arrieta was on the mound, cruising. He gave up just two hits before turning the game over to his relievers: Mike Montgomery, Aroldis Chapman. Mike

Napoli, the Indians' first baseman, later said Arrieta had been effective because he seemed a little wild. While part of you is thinking about getting a hit, another part is thinking about survival. You want to help your team but don't want to spend the rest of your life eating out of a straw.

Final score: Chicago 5, Cleveland 1.

GAME 3

Most of us had never been to Wrigley Field this late in the season. The 1945 World Series was over by October 10. In 2016, the World Series did not even start till October 25. It was like the sun coming up at 2 a.m. In fact, the first thing I noticed as I approached the park on foot from the south was an old man carrying a huge sign that said, THE HOUR IS AT HAND. REPENT. THE WAGES OF SIN ARE DEATH. I thought to myself: *That guy carries that sign every day and one day he will be right.*

I'd flown from New York via Westchester County Airport, which is as cozy as an airport in the Caribbean. A little plane rolling through the clouds. Half the people on the flight were Cubs fans. You could tell by their hats and jerseys, by their key chains, which they dropped in a dish before they went through security, by their ringtones—"Go Cubs Go, Go Cubs Go." We made eye contact, acknowledging each other, but did not make a big thing about it; we did not have to, because it was a big thing. We were exiles returning to our small island nation in a time of celebration or war. We'd always known we'd go back.

The crowd was so thick around Wrigley Field I had to push my way through. Even people without tickets had come. They wanted to be close to the park when the trumpets sounded—feel the holy emanations, sit in the holy taverns, and drink holy Schlitz beer. The streets had been closed to traffic. There was a thirty-minute wait to get into the train station. No one cared. This was a nation on parade. There was happiness, but solemnity too. Everyone had a list of people who had not lived long enough. Those known to all of us: Ernie Banks, Ron Santo, Harry Caray. Those known to just some of us: Todd Johnston, Phil Thomas, Morris Liebman.

The players felt it too, and it screwed up their minds: all those fans, all those expectations, the frustrations of all the futile seasons. This too was the curse—the pressure the drought itself generated, the way it mounted as the years went by. You saw it from the first innings in Game 3—how tight the Cubs looked at the plate, how hard they pressed. Hitting well is like being cool in high school. The more you want it, the worse it gets.

Josh Tomlin started for the Indians. He's a good pitcher, but not as good as the box score suggests. The guy had a 4.40 ERA in 2016 and won just thirteen games, but the Cubs made him look like Nolan Ryan. They simply could not get going—two hits off Tomlin, who then gave way to those relievers.

Kyle Hendricks kept Chicago in it. Tall and goofy in a studious way, Hendricks majored in economics at Dartmouth, which is only one reason they call him the Professor. The other is the way he pitches. Hendricks, who has no great fastball—he tops out at 87 mph—gets by on location and change of speed—that 87 mph fastball is followed by a 72 mph curve. If he puts the ball anywhere close to where a hitter wants, it's a mistake. "Pinpoint" is the book on Hendricks. By the numbers, he was the best Cubs starter in 2016: 16–8, 2.13 ERA, which led the league. He was even better in the playoffs: a .71 ERA over twelve innings in the NLCS. Yet Maddon and pitching coach Chris Bosio never seemed to trust him, especially to get out of a jam. Because he did not throw hard. In a pinch, management always prefers power to finesse.

Hendricks got into trouble in the fifth. Gave up a single to Tyler Naquin, walked Carlos Santana, hit Jason Kipnis. Bases loaded and Hendricks was gone, replaced by Justin Grimm, who got the Cubs through the crisis. It was still scoreless in the bottom of the seventh. By then, the Cubs had the lanky, hard-throwing twenty-five-year-old Carl Edwards, Jr., on the mound. He's skinny as a beam (6′3″, 170 pounds) and his motion is loose and easy—I show more effort tossing my keys—but the ball explodes out of his hand—a 95 mph fastball, a slow curve. But *he* got in trouble in the seventh: gave up a single to start the inning, then threw a wild pitch, then walked Rajai Davis, then hung a curve that Coco Crisp hammered into right, scoring the game's only run.

The night ended with Javier Báez at the plate. His had been one of the great stories of the playoffs, a wildly talented, wonder-performing infielder who'd gotten big hits in the clutch. His personal story was even more moving. His family had relocated from Puerto Rico to the United States when Báez was in junior high. They were seeking treatment for Javier's sister, who'd been born with spina bifida. Javier's father, Angel—a landscaper—died in a fall soon after. Javier's mother held the family together, moving them to Florida so her son could play baseball year-round. Báez said he'd worked hard to make the majors so he could take care of his sister—she died in April 2015. Her name—NOELY—is stitched inside his glove. Because he'd been hitting so well, Maddon moved him up in the order. But he expressed reservations as he did it. He worried that the expectations of the new slot would cause Báez to press. He indeed looked lost in that final at bat. Chase and miss. He went down on five pitches, swinging wildly, his body twisted into a pretzel of futility.

Final score: Cleveland 1, Chicago 0.

GAME 4

It was one of the toughest choices I've ever had to make. I'm a contributing editor at *Vanity Fair* magazine. Had I been graded more fairly in school, I might have been a doctor. I was graded unfairly and am a writer instead. I have a job to do. I'm a professional. My editor left me a message while I was at Game 3. He said the magazine wanted me to fly to L.A. the following afternoon. Chris Pratt would be on the cover of the next issue and they needed me to go out and interview him. "It's the only time he can meet." I had agreed to do the story long before I knew the timing of the interview or the World Series. It meant I'd have to miss Games 4 and 5.

"We're counting on you," said my editor.

I went back and forth all night. On the one hand, not since 1945. On the other hand, isn't this what being an adult is all about? I made up my mind to go to L.A., then changed my mind, then changed it again. I packed my bag and got a car to O'Hare. No decision is final till I'm actually on the plane, I told myself. I can always turn around and go back. The fact that the Cubs were in the World Series and that I had a credential and was not going to use it made me nauseous. I was spitting in the face of my fifteen-year-old self. And yet, I had made a promise. Back and forth, back and forth, right up to the moment the plane was racing down the runway and it was too late—too goddamn late.

That night, soon after I landed, I went by a theater to see a Rolling Stones cover band. For reasons I won't go into, I ended up backstage, talking to Fake Mick, Fake Keith, Fake Ron Wood, Fake Charlie Watts. That's how I came to get the news of Game 5 from ersatz rockers in leather pants, black eyeliner, sequin shirts. I'm not sure if the accents were real, or if they were just in character.

Mick: It was a blowout, mate, an ugly thing.

Keith: Lackey against Kluber, so you know you had no chance going in.

Woody: The Klubot!

Charlie: Lackey was a disappointment.

Mick: Chicago scored the first run, then nothing from your boys. Where is the old Chicago power?

Keith: Chicago is the home of Muddy Waters. Plenty of power there, Mick.

Charlie: I think you've missed the point, Keith.

Mick: Carlos Santana hit a home run for Cleveland. Won't call 'em Indians. Offensive, that is.

Keith: Carlos Santana?

Mick: Not that one.

Woody: That mascot . . . what is it? Chief Wahoo. With the grinning face? Disgusting.

Mick: Cleveland scored again in the third. Kipnis, bloody fantastic.

Keith: It was Kluber from there. Shut down your Cubs, he did.

Woody: Two-seam.

Charlie: Four-seam.

Mick: Kipnis broke your back with a drive into the seats.

Keith: Your boys are on the brink.

Woody: Your boys are toast.

Mick: One more loss, and it's score another for the billy goat.

Charlie: Down three games to one in the series? Not many come back from that, mate.

Final score: Cleveland 7, Chicago 2.

GAME 5

I thought I was going to miss it. I'd be at Chris Pratt's house when the first pitch was thrown. He'd be cooking tacos made with the meat of a wild boar he himself had killed. I'd be eating those tacos and interviewing him. That was the conceit of the story. But after twenty minutes, I could tell that he was a good guy and would understand, so I told him everything—the press pass, the tough choice, the Cubs, the precipice—"Down three games to one in the series? Not many come back from that, mate"—and he insisted we drink tequila, turn on the big TV, and watch the game. He said he was partial to the Cubs, "because if they win, anything is possible."

Jon Lester was on the mound. He had his best stuff—you could tell right away. The ball was jumping. He struck out the first batter (Rajai Davis, six pitches), struck out the second (Jason Kipnis, three pitches), struck out the third (Francisco Lindor, four pitches). He looked like John Wayne heading back to the dugout, cool but exhilarated, pumping a fist.

Trevor Bauer was pitching for Cleveland. His finger must have healed, because he got the Cubs one, two, three in the first. Pratt shook his head sadly, saying, "I don't know, man. I don't know. Cleveland looks good."

Lester sailed through the first two-thirds of the second, in complete control. He was like a trucker behind the wheel of a big rig, working the stick, blazing through open country. Then, with two outs and no one on, a squirrel ran out onto the road. Shifting gears and screeching tires, the driver screaming, *Oh, fuuuuck!* An 0–1 pitch, low and inside, that José Ramírez sent into Wrigley's left-field bleachers, where it landed amid a sea of resentful fans. A moment later, the ball was thrown back onto the field. It's a tradition. We don't want your stinking home run. We vomit it back, reject it like a bad kidney. You see it tumbling back onto the grass, unloved and unwanted. In the 1980s, I saw an out-of-town slugger hit a ball onto Waveland Avenue, where it was picked up by a mailman making his rounds. He turned it over in his hands, looked up, and asked, "Ours or theirs?"

"Theirs," we shouted.

"Sons of bitches," he said, heaving the ball over the bleachers and onto the field.

Lester got right back into the game, as if the home run had never happened. Possibly because he knew there was nothing wrong with his pitching. In fact, David Ross, who was catching for the Cubs, took the blame. "That one was one hundred percent my fault," he said. "I got greedy. I called one too many pitches inside and Ramírez was waiting for it."

Lester got the next hitter to ground out to end the inning, then walked calmly back to the dugout. He seemed confident despite the home run. Chris Pratt did not. He knew about the Cubs and about the curse and baseball. He knew about psychology and the importance of scoring that first run. In three of the previous four games, the team that scored first went on to win—it's just tougher to chase.

Pratt is a devout Christian. That surprised me—because, you know, movie star—and I admired him for it. He believes that his life is in the hands of God, and his God is the sort that gets involved. Sizing up the situation, Pratt said—this was just after he'd served his tacos but before we'd started to eat—"Let's say a prayer for the Cubs." We got on our knees, around the table, beside the big TV, held hands with our eyes closed. Pratt thanked Jesus for the food and friends and life, then put in a word for the Cubs— "this afflicted team and its long-suffering fans that need your help now more than ever"—then said amen.

During the third inning, we realized that I had to get back to my hotel. Pratt had a dinner and I had a call, so we timed it. He drove me down the hill in his Tesla, which was as fast and silent as a shark, dropping me off just in time for the first pitch in the bottom of the fourth.

Kris Bryant led off. He's tall, as are many of the Cubs. Rizzo is 6'3". Fowler is 6'5". Zobrist is 6'3". Heyward is 6'5". Lester is 6'4". Walking through an airport, they look less like a baseball team than a basketball team. Bryant is 6'5". He bends his knees at the plate—a deep and significant bend that gives him the aspect of a tall man trying to fit through a low doorway. He's patient in the batter's box. Players like that, players prophesized before they arrive, usually don't pan out. It's the law of averages, the difficulty of recruiting—a scout first sees a player when he's sixteen, seventeen years old. It's not enough to decide if that player is good enough to play in the majors—none are at that age. He has to decide if he *will* be good enough in five or eight years. He predicts the future and is usually wrong. But the scouts were right about Bryant. He won the Rookie of the Year in 2015, the MVP in 2016. Only a handful of careers have started that way. He's always fun to watch and often comes through in big situations. To those who dismiss the clutch hitter as myth, I say, Look at what Bryant did in the fourth inning of Game 5, when his team was down and facing elimination.

Third pitch: Bauer missed, Bryant pounced. You can almost feel the air leave his body as he connects, driving the ball as you drive a nail all the way into the wood. *Boom!* As the Cleveland center fielder drifts back, back, an old Cubs fan will hear the trademark home run call of the great broadcasters: "Hey, hey!" (Jack Brickhouse); "It might be, it could be, it is!" (Harry Caray).

Tie game.

The camera goes from the bleachers to the dugout, where Maddon looks on in a winter cap; to the stands, where a fan is laughing and coughing up beer; to Bryant, who is exchanging high fives at home plate; to Bill Murray, who is wiping away a tear; to Rizzo, who is doing his hula, waiting for his pitch, which he gets and hammers into deep right. The Cleveland outfielder races back, and for a moment you think it too is gone, but it lands in the ivy, which makes a crunchy sound that you've never heard at Wrigley Field before because it means the leaves are dying and it's the end of autumn. Rizzo slides into second, pops up and points to the sky, then starts throwing punches.

That was it—the piñata had been busted open, the candy was spilling across the floor. Zobrist singled. Russell singled. Báez singled. Ross sacrificed. The Cubs were up 3–1. The Indians scored in the sixth, keeping it close. Carl Edwards, Jr., who'd come on in relief, got in trouble in the seventh. A single and a passed ball put a Cleveland player in scoring position. Maddon called for Chapman. This marked the beginning of a debate: Did the manager overwork the closer during the World Series? As a rule, a pitcher like Chapman doesn't come in before the eighth inning. Like uranium, he's most effective when used sparingly. By sending out Chapman with one out in the seventh, Maddon was making a counterargument: What are we saving him for? If we lose this game in the seventh, the season is over and the best-rested reliever in the world won't help us.

Chapman was throwing those surreal fastballs. Struck out Ramírez, hit Guyer, got Roberto Perez to ground out to end the inning. Into and out of a jam in the eighth, back for the ninth, striking out Ramírez a second time to close it. Chapman had been through the entire Cleveland batting order and had thrown forty-five pitches, far more work than he's accustomed to.

I ran into Chris Pratt a few months later. He was surrounded by reporters and focused on selling a movie, but he shouted when he saw me: "Hey, dude! The Cubs! The Cubs! Our prayer worked!"

Final score: Cleveland 2, Chicago 3.

GAME 6

Many of the Cubs were still wearing Halloween costumes when they got on the plane for Cleveland. Addison Russell was dressed as a Teenage Mutant Ninja Turtle. David Ross was a jester. Carl Edwards, Jr., was Mr. Incredible. "When we were making travel plans for our trip back to Cleveland after Game 5, we all got this text message about a change in plans," Dexter Fowler wrote. "We normally would've flown out in the morning. But it turned out that our travel day was going to be Halloween, and Joe wanted us to be able to trick-or-treat with our families. He let us know that we were going to stay in Chicago until 7 p.m. so that we could all enjoy some family time and have fun with our kids. I mean, for real: Who does that? The two biggest games of our careers are on the horizon, and we're out trick-or-treating until nighttime rolls around. I'll never forget that. Thanks to Joe, my wife and I took our daughter out and had fun together—she was a tiny little elephant!"

Perhaps as a result, the pregame mood in the clubhouse was loose, easy. According to Fowler, the Cubs passed the downtime listening to the *Rocky* soundtrack (Rizzo's favorite) and playing *Mario Kart*. "Joe Maddon gets it," Fowler wrote. "He just does. He knew we'd all be better off if we spent some time with our families and just living life, instead of stewing about 108 years and curses and having to win the next two games."

I'd flown from L.A. to New York, then turned right around and flew to Cleveland. It was 70 degrees at game time—70 in Cleveland in November.

Jake Arrieta started for Chicago. I could see him, bearded and burly, stretching on the outfield grass. The stands were filled with Cubs fans—I imagined all of them, closed in their cars, decked in their gear, making their way along I90 East. Nothing past South Bend but the vastness of Indiana and Ohio. They wore jerseys from every era—like a conclave of all-time greats: Reuschel, Sandberg, Holtzman, Dawson, Buckner, Grace, Shawon Dunston—everyone but Sosa.

The game began with a burst of fireworks. Tomlin was out there for Cleveland, throwing his array—four-seam, two-seam, cut fastball, curve, changeup. He'd shut down the Cubs in Game

3 but didn't seem like the same pitcher tonight. Or maybe the Cubs were different. They looked so much looser away from home, calm and focused. As if getting out of Wrigley Field had been a relief. As if the weight of the past, legends and ghosts, had twisted their innards. It's the way you sometimes sleep better in a hotel. No backstory in a hotel—no deeper meaning or historical resonance. You saw it right away—the top of the first. Fowler lined out and Schwarber grounded out but both hit the ball hard—"Hard, but at people," as Harry would say.

Bryant had seen mostly curveballs in the World Series. Cleveland pitchers did not want to throw him anything that he could drive. It worked on pitch one (slider, strike) and pitch two (slider, strike), but he hammered pitch three. A God ball. Gone. It stilled the crowd just as they were getting into the game. Then Rizzo singled. Zobrist singled. Addison Russell, the Cubs' twenty-two-year-old All-Star shortstop, doubled, bringing in two more runs.

The Cubs drove Tomlin out of the game in the third. Dan Otero came on in relief with one out, bases loaded, Addison Russell at the plate. At that point, you think: *Whatever they're paying this guy, it's not enough.* Otero pitched from the stretch. Ball one. Ball two. Watch Russell on the third pitch. He's made up his mind before it's left Otero's hand. It hangs, time suspends, Russell steps into it, turning his hips. He ends with his leg bent, standing on the toe of his back foot. The ball goes out in left center where the wall is twenty feet high. Grand slam. Cubs 7, Indians 0. On the broadcast—I went back and watched all these games again—you see Javier Báez celebrating beside the dugout, Indians manager Terry Francona stuffing sunflower seeds into his mouth, and Cleveland fans, in T-shirts that say BELIEVE, stone-faced, as if they believe in nothing.

In Chicago, fans crowded the bars of Wrigleyville. They wanted to be near the park, though the game was being played far away. They wanted to experience the thing in its proper atmosphere. They wanted to do it because they wanted to do it and because they wanted to say, years hence, it was something they had done. They wanted to mark the occasion as unprecedented. It's why people take pictures of scenes that are already being photographed by multitudes. Because taking a picture is like placing a check mark beside a moment, acknowledging its importance. I took a picture of the players, the stadium, and the sky in the bottom of the sixth. The scene was sharp but the picture came out smeary, a bleed of color. It wasn't a good picture, but it was exactly how I felt.

Arrieta seemed to be dominating: two runs, three hits, struck out nine, but Maddon must have seen something because, just like that, in the bottom of the sixth, Arrieta was gone. Mike Montgomery finished that inning, then gave up a walk and a hit in the seventh, which should have been no big deal. A general rule: Any lead in excess of four runs is safe because even a grand slam won't tie the game. The Cubs were up five with two outs and a bullpen filled with strong arms. And it's here that Joe Maddon, perhaps showing nerves, made the second in his string of controversial moves. The first had been letting Chapman throw more than forty pitches in Game 5. Now, with two outs in the seventh inning and a huge lead, Maddon once again called on Chapman. He ended the inning with two pitches but was back for the eighth—he threw thirteen more pitches—then back at the start of the ninth, which was a surprise. Chapman is a specialist, best suited to come in with one or two outs in the ninth. Now and then, in an important game, you might bring him on in the eighth, then give him extra rest. But the seventh? Two games in a row? Why did Maddon do it? What if he was needed in Game 7? Would he have anything left?

Chapman later said he felt he'd been mishandled. "I don't think I needed to come into [Game 6]," he explained through an interpreter. "The important game was going to be Game 7 and basically we had that game almost won."

Maddon later said that sending Chapman out to start the ninth had been a mistake—not a lapse in judgment but an actual mistake. He did not mean to do it. He got so caught up, he forgot to warm up a pitcher for the bottom half. Then, when the inning started, only Chapman was ready, and he had to send him back out while the other guys got warm.

Travis Wood closed it for Chicago—final score: Cubs 9, Indians 3—and so our thoughts switched from Aroldis Chapman to the big thing at hand. Game 7!

■ ■ ■

I came out of the press box as if I'd been shot from a cannon. I went everywhere and high-fived everyone, then headed back to my hotel. It had been warm in the middle innings, but at some point a cold front blew in. Dark clouds, lashing rain. It came on so fast. I zipped up my coat and hugged myself and that's when it hit me: What if the Cubs win? Losing would be easy. I'd spent my whole life losing. But what would winning mean? Being for the Cubs had always seemed special—we were different from other fans. The curse and the years of futility had given us a unique role. We were emissaries from a higher realm, warning of hubris and vanity. We were holier—better, pure. We knew life was more than pennants and percentages. Wearing a Yankees hat meant corporate excellence. Wearing a Mets hat meant miracles. But wearing a Cubs hat meant loving the game on its most humdrum afternoon—September 13, 1979, fourteen games out of first place, Larry Biittner driving Ivan DeJesus in to score. Would we lose that? Would being a Cubs fan become ordinary? There'd be the initial euphoria, of course. The party and the glow that would linger as long as the core of this particular team survived. But, after a while, these players would age and give way to others and the fans who are young would become old and those who are being born would grow up in a strange world, with the fantastical belief that the Cubs are a good baseball team. Being a Cubs fan would become just like everything else.

There's only one solution, I decided. If the Cubs win the World Series, the playing of the sport must be discontinued. The leagues disbanded, the players sent home, the stadiums destroyed. Professional baseball really began with the team that became the Cubs. Early in the twentieth century, that team won and won and won, and then, for whatever reason, stopped winning. They set off on a 108-year trek through the wilderness, plumbed the depths of defeat, then somehow found their way back. 2016 was 1908 all over again. The historic arc of the game could finally be recognized. It's a story that begins and ends in Chicago. If they won Game 7, that story would reach its obvious conclusion. Disband and go home. Anything beyond this point is postscript.

At 8:02, Dexter Fowler stood in the box, swinging a bat, staring out at Corey Kluber. The Cubs had yet to solve the Cleveland ace, who was attempting to win his third game of the World Series. That's exceedingly rare. No one had done it since Randy Johnson in 2001. By the third start, a pitcher is tired and the opposition hitters have faced him five or six times, learned every habit and trick. Kluber's first pitch was a called strike, but you could tell he'd worn thin. Even at the beginning, he was throwing junk. Fowler waited for the fastball and the fastball came—he drove it to the deepest part of the park. Center fielder Rajai Davis had a bead on it, went back and back, jumped, but it slipped over his glove into the bullpen. A leadoff home run.

Fowler turned all the way around between first and second, ran backward, then righted himself. It seemed like a preplanned celebration—an impression he later corrected. "Here's the real story," he wrote. "So every time I hit a homer, I dap up my first base coach, Brandon Hyde. It's just something I do after I hit a bomb. Just showing some love. But this time things were a bit different, because, during the biggest game of my life, after the biggest hit of my career . . . I got caught in no man's land. It was like I was floating as I left the batter's box and the next thing I knew, the ball cleared the wall . . . and I'd already passed first. So when I turned to my first base coach, I was already way past him. I had to improvise. And that's what you saw. I just kind of turned around too late and had to wing it. I mean, I'd love to take credit for doing something cool, but in reality, it was just that simple."

You noticed something when Fowler hit that home run: the crowd. Not that it was quiet or demoralized—it seemed invigorated. If the crowd had been 20 percent Cubs fans in Game 6, it was more like 50 percent tonight. How did all these Cubs fans get tickets? You could not help but come to the conclusion that Indians fans had sold their seats to Chicagoans. On the one hand, you could understand—by game time, a grandstand seat was going for upward of $5,000. On the other hand, *How could you?* It made you think that Cleveland did not deserve to win. Kluber got through the rest of the first unscathed, but even the outs came on hard-hit balls.

The Indians tied the game in the third. Bryant singled in the fourth. Rizzo was hit by a pitch. Russell sacrificed. Contreras, the rookie catcher, doubled off the wall. The score was 3–1. Báez led off the fifth inning with a solo home run that knocked Kluber out of the game. Andrew Miller came on in relief—another Cleveland untouchable. He's a six-foot-seven left-hander with a sidearm delivery that confounds hitters. He'd been with the Yankees the first half of the season. As a Yankee, he was clean-cut—that's the Yankee rule. He stopped shaving when he reached the Indians and a main thought on seeing him was amazement at how quickly he'd been able to grow a thick beard. The Cubs flailed at him most of the series; they'd need to beat him now. First Kluber, then Miller.

Bryant drew a walk with two outs. Rizzo came up. He crowds the plate. Miller threw inside and Rizzo turned on the pitch, sending it into right field. Bryant, running for as long as I've been writing this sentence, scored from first base.

Cubs 5, Indians 1.

Five Cubs pitchers walked across the outfield, five big pitchers on a great green sward, five big pitchers heading to the bullpen.

Hendricks got the first Cleveland batter of the fifth to ground out and struck out the next, but Lester was already warming up. When Hendricks walked the third batter, the door in center field opened and out came the reliever, making the slow walk. He replaced Hendricks and Ross replaced Contreras. It was the third controversial move in Maddon's string: Why replace Kyle Hendricks? He was up 5–1, had thrown only sixty-three pitches, and seemed to be in control. It looked like he could go all the way. Maddon later said he'd seen the first signs of fatigue. It was his third time through the batting order and he was about to face Kipnis, Cleveland's best hitter. It seemed like the moment to shut it down. But bringing in Lester with a man on base violated a rule. According to Tom Verducci, Epstein and Maddon had agreed that Lester should come in only with a clean canvas—no men on base. Because of the yips.

Kipnis fouled his way to Lester's sixth pitch, then swung, topping the ball, squibbing it between home and the mound. Ross yanked off his mask, grabbed the ball, and threw to Rizzo. But the throw went off target. It pulled Rizzo away from the bag, where he collided with Kipnis, who went flying as the ball got away. On TV, you can hear Ross yell something that sounds like, "Dang it." Kipnis ended up at second, Santana at third. Men on base, taking leads, in motion—as dust mites are to hay fever, this situation is to the yips. Francisco Lindor came to the plate. A small player from Puerto Rico, a tough hitter making close to the league minimum—not relevant but interesting, the disparities. Twenty million pitching to $540K. With first base open, Lester pitched carefully, maybe too carefully. He bounced a curveball meant to make Lindor chase. It came up and hit Ross in the face mask, knocking him off his haunches. You can hear Ross scream. This time it sounds like "Ouch!" He gets up, stumbles as if concussed, then runs for the ball. Santana scores. Ross throws to Lester, who is covering home, but throws to the wrong side of the bag—Kipnis, sliding headfirst, gets in just before the tag. In a moment, you'd gone from Hendricks being boringly efficient to this whirligig of insanity. "I'm like, 'Wait a minute, I've been in here five minutes and now I've given up two runs—this is not my thing,'" Ross said on TV later. "I come in to prevent runs. This is what I do. I've been here two seconds and I feel like I've given the momentum back to Cleveland." No one in the press box had seen anything like it in a World Series: two runs scored on a wild pitch. Lester struck out Lindor, but the game had tightened.

Ross was the second batter up in the sixth. You wondered if he was all there—had that wild pitch knocked him silly? ("I was fine," he said later. "I'd just tripped over my own feet.")

Ross facing Miller. He'd caught for Miller in Boston. He knew his style, the nature of his stuff. He took the first pitch—a curveball. "I wanted to see one," Ross explained, "just get my feet wet." Then came the slider, "so nasty," called for a strike. Ross fouled off the next pitch. Then, with two strikes, choked up, hoping to make contact. The pitch was high and outside—"That's the first one that I saw really well," said Ross, "and I decided, if he throws another one of those, let it eat," meaning his bat. Ross was watching Miller carefully. He saw him look in at the catcher and shake off a sign. He knew that he was shaking off the slider. "I had done my homework and I'd seen him shake a lot and when he shakes he shakes to the [fastball]," Ross explained. "He threw it down, where I like the ball, and I'd choked up and I got really good wood on it. It went out and I felt like I floated around the bases."

A few minutes after the home run, a camera caught Ross in the dugout talking to Tommy La Stella, a utility infielder. "Hey, Tommy," says Ross, matter-of-fact. "I just went deep in the World Series in Game 7."

Lester found his groove in the bottom of the sixth and rode it through the seventh, into the eighth, when he gave up a ground ball single to José Ramírez. At that point, it was Cubs 6, Indians 3, one man on, two gone. I'd begun counting down outs on Facebook. How many more did we need? Nine, eight, seven, six, five. I was not the only one. "I found myself counting outs," Bryant said later, "but then I thought this is too easy. This is way too easy."

Lester was cruising, but Chapman is the closer, the assassin. The door swung open and out he came, jogging across center field with a cameraman on his heels, the eyes of the world. Yet another of Maddon's controversial moves: Why bring in Chapman, who'd thrown so many pitches in the last few days, when Lester was going good?

Friends watching at home later told me that it seemed clear, even as he threw warm-ups, that Chapman was not at his best. His fastball did not have that otherworldly extra gear, that kick that turns the ball into vapor. But I don't believe them. You'd have to be a pro player to tell the difference. Even off his game, Chapman is still throwing in the high 90s.

Brandon Guyer was the first hitter to face Chapman. *That's* when you could tell something was wrong. When facing Chapman, hitters usually look nervous, even scared, but Guyer—all eye black and chew—looked comfortable, as if he was enjoying himself. He drove Chapman's second pitch into center field, a stand-up double. Ramirez scored. Chapman looked irritated. Now it was 6 to 4 and there was that old feeling again, the dread bubbling up, the chill of the curse, the sense that our destiny is not to win but to almost win then lose as we are idiotically counting outs. I was not supposed to root in the press box—I had been warned twice—and was not rooting but was instead banging my head with my hand and saying over and over, "Stupid, stupid, stupid."

The next batter? Rajai Davis. Who was he? Nobody, nothing—a thirty-six-year-old journeyman who'd never hit better than .284 and never hit more than twelve home runs in a season. But that's the way of the gods—not just to defeat us but to defeat us with everyday tools. Not merely beaten, but beaten by Tim Flannery. Davis ran the count to two balls, two strikes. He was choking up on the bat, waving it, eyes as wide as eyes can be. You could almost hear his heart. The pitch was low and flat—then gone, hit on a rope down the left-field line, up onto the concourse where they sell hot dogs and beer, sending the TV camera spinning wildly as its operator dove for cover. "When Rajai hit that shot, . . . I just kept saying to myself: *Please hit off the wall. Please hit off the wall. Please hit off the wall,*" Dexter Fowler wrote. "But it didn't hit off the wall. To his credit, it was a great [at bat]—Rajai kept fouling Chapman off over and over again. So you could tell that something might go down. But a home run there? Against one of the best closers in baseball, to tie up Game 7? Really? When the ball cleared the fence in left, I remember thinking to myself, *You've gotta be f***ing kidding right now.* And for the second time in the game, I couldn't believe what I was seeing. I literally couldn't believe it."

The cheering crowd makes the camera vibrate. Everything is vibrating, buzzing, spinning. Davis rounds the bases with arm raised, as if possessed by the demon ghost of Steve Garvey. Everywhere I look, I see Cubs fans—disbelieving, deflated, ruined, wrecked, each thinking the same thing: *Of course.* The game is tied, though I do not believe it. I turn to the sportswriter next to me and say, "Well, at least we still have the lead."

He says, "No you don't. Look at the scoreboard."

I do, but it still won't register.

I say, "There's something wrong with the scoreboard. It says the game is tied."

"It is tied."

"No, it can't be tied," I say. "We're winning."

Only later will I realize that I was watching one of the greatest baseball games of all time—the back-and-forth scoring, the big home runs, now this. But I was too freaked to care about history. The writers in the press box seemed freaked out too—not excited but confused. We all felt it. Something strange had happened, some otherworldly force had come into play. "Like everyone else who cared about the Cubs, I was in a daze," Theo Epstein wrote. "A three-run lead in Game 7 with four outs to go, nobody on, bottom of the order coming up—and it was gone in the blink of an eye. The stunning homer by Rajai Davis was impossible to process in real time. We sat silent, shaken and surrounded by the thunderous roar of the home crowd."

"We were up three runs, we had a guy throwing a hundred miles an hour. How does this happen?" said Zobrist, who later admitted to thinking, in this bleak moment, about the curse.

Chapman looked angry, bewildered. He got through the inning, then came back to pitch in the bottom of the ninth. This was the Hemingway moment, grace under pressure—it was not how he performed when everything was good and he had his best stuff, but how he did after the disaster when he had nothing that tells you the kind of player he is. It was the grittiest inning of his career—Game 7, bottom of the ninth, when all the momentum was with Cleveland. "Most guys, when they're dead tired, and they've just given up a World Series–tying homer, don't come back for the next inning," Epstein told me. "Chapman insisted on it. He said, 'No, this is on me.' And he got us through the ninth. That was huge."

It began to rain. Autumn coming in. The broadcasters were talking to the weathermen, who were studying the radar. The umps made the call before the top of the tenth. The strangest rain delay in history, the Cubs frozen in midcollapse. I sat in the press box, watching the ground crew cover the infield with a tarp, wishing someone would cover me with a tarp.

The rain delay lasted just under twenty minutes. I wandered around the park. I felt strange, as if I had a flu coming on. This was the nadir, rock bottom, the place where, on every other occasion, the path forked and we went the wrong way. On TV, there was a shot of Chapman in the dugout, staring through the rain, tears on his face. Meanwhile, Jason Heyward was gathering the team, calling everyone to a players-only meeting in the weight room off the dugout tunnel—the first such meeting of the season. Heyward was the big bust of 2016, the one Epstein move that did not work. He'd been given a huge contract, then fizzled at the plate. But here he was, in the pinch, taking charge. In this moment, he earned all that money, proving that everyone who was there had to be there—that every player had a role.

"Our minds were just . . . spinning," Fowler wrote. "As we came off the field and walked back through the tunnel, some guys were mad, other guys were sad, some guys were *waaaaay* too pumped. It was almost like we were thinking of everything all at once, and we needed something to snap us back to reality. We needed to get our focus back. Of course, as you know, after we went up the tunnel, J-Hey called a meeting. He brought us together as a team, and he was just real with it. He saw that there were a lot of emotions swirling for us, and he said what needed to be said: *We've come too far to let it slip away like this. We're the better team. So let's turn up and just go out and play like we know how.* It wasn't anything we hadn't heard before, but it was something that we *needed* to hear at that exact moment. And it was *how* he said it that really had an impact. You could see it in his eyes, you could hear it in his voice. It was really something. I'll never forget it. After J-Hey spoke, everyone sort of chimed in and everything just seemed to snowball in a really positive way. Rossy spoke a little bit. Then Riz said something. Then I spoke up. And all of a sudden we were rolling again. We couldn't get out of that clubhouse and onto the field fast enough."

"Turning a corner, I saw, through the window of the weight room door, the backs of our players' blue jerseys, shoulder to shoulder and packed tightly, all 25 guys squeezed into a space designed for half that many," Epstein wrote. "It was an unusual sight. We hardly ever had meetings and never during a game. Was this a group lament? A bitch session? A last-minute strategic meeting? Did someone pass out?

"Now, before extra innings in the biggest game they will ever play in, the players gathered in the dank weight room." The door was ajar and so Epstein eavesdropped:

"We are the best team in baseball!" shouted one of the players.

"We've got you, Chappy, we've got you!" said another.

"We've worked so hard all year just for this moment."

"This is only going to make it sweeter, boys!"

"Keep grinding, keep grinding!"

"The rain delay came at the exact right moment," Epstein told me. "It gave us time to stop and think about the magnitude of the situation."

Many Cubs fans will tell you that the rain was sent by God—that it was like a big storm in the Bible, a fierce cleansing rain that ushered in a new season. When the tarp was rolled back, the field looked new, as if remade by the storm. Schwarber led off with a single to right field. He looked into the Cubs dugout as he went by, pumping a fist. Albert Almora, Jr., came in to pinch-run. He was the first player Epstein acquired as president of the Cubs. Bryant got hold of a pitch and drove it to deep center. It just missed going out. Almora tagged and reached second—scoring position. It was a heady play for a rookie; runners hardly ever tag up at first. The Indians walked Rizzo intentionally. Putting men on first and second was smart, as it set the Indians up to turn a double play, but walking a hitter to get to Zobrist never seems to work out. He wanted to be patient and watched the first two pitches go by—strike one, strike two. He swung at third, got around late, slicing down the left-field line. The Indians' third baseman dove for it and just missed. A double—Almora scored.

Zobrist is screaming and pointing at second. Rizzo, with his hands on his helmet at third, looks stunned as he says, "Oh, my God!" Montero came in to pinch-hit. He singled. Another run, insurance. Cubs 8, Indians 6.

Three outs to go. I called my wife in that interregnum between the top and the bottom half of the tenth. I was so nervous, I did not know what to do.

"The Cubs can actually win this thing," I told her.

She said, "I know."

"Well, what if we do win?"

"Maybe you should stop talking—they haven't won anything yet."

"But will that mean there never really was a curse?" I asked.

"Have we been watching the same game?" she said. "Did that look to you like a team that isn't cursed? Rajai Davis hits a two-run home run off Aroldis Chapman in the bottom of the eighth inning? I've never seen better evidence of a curse in my life. That team is cursed. We've just seen the strength of the curse and how good the Cubs have had to be to overcome it. It's like watching someone fight off bird flu."

Carl Edwards, Jr., started the bottom of the tenth. He got Mike Napoli swinging. One out. Got Ramirez on a grounder.

Two outs. He walked Brandon Guyer. Then Rajai Davis again. He hit a laser into center field. Guyer scored. The Cubs converged on the mound—one more wave of nausea, one more taste of flu. Mike Montgomery came in to get the final out. The Indians had used just about everyone on their bench. At the last moment, the best Cleveland could do was Michael Martínez, a career minor leaguer who'd had only four at bats all season. He swung on an 0–1 pitch, hitting a weak grounder to third. It's a play that's already burned into the collective consciousness: Kris Bryant slipping as he gets to the ball, making the long throw, Rizzo stretching and catching and completing the final play for the final out.

Final score: Chicago 8, Cleveland 7.

Rizzo tucked the ball into his back pocket, the team raced to the mound. Pandemonium. The celebration seen on TV. Fans in front of Wrigley, players on the field. A quick shot of the Indians' dugout, stony faces. I've always identified less with the winners than with the losers. It comes from my upbringing, a decision, made a million years ago, to cast my lot with the Cubs. Fans were hanging on each other and singing "Go Cubs Go" when I got out of the press box. I had my pass and could go onto the field and partake in the party but was not in the mood. I wanted to sit in a dark room. I was happy but sad too. A whole period of my life had ended. My childhood suddenly seemed much farther away. I walked back to my hotel alone.

If this were the ultimate Cubs book, it would have included several people and events that I either had and cut or never had at all—because a book is finite but the Cubs go on forever. It would have had the catcher Gabby Hartnett hitting the decisive home run in late September 1938, the walk off that put the Cubs into the World Series, the Homer in the Gloaming, so-called because he hit it in the bottom of the ninth when it was dark. It would have had Dizzy Dean, who came in a trade from the Cardinals after he'd wrecked his arm—he got out of jams with a new pitch, cooked up late in life, that he called a nothing ball. It would have had Andre Dawson, who, in essence and because he so badly wanted to play at Wrigley, presented Dallas Green with a blank contract and said, I'll play for whatever you pay me. In 1987, working for close to the league minimum, Dawson had one of the best seasons in franchise history, hitting 49 home runs and 137 RBIs, winning the MVP. They called him Hawk. When he took his position in right field at the top of an inning, the bleacher bums would bow and genuflect before his greatness. It would have had the game I dragged Jerry Schmelter to at Wrigley in 1985, when Billy Hatcher hit for the cycle. It would have had the way it is at Wrigley when it's just started to rain, and it's August, and you can smell woodsmoke, and the other fans run for cover so you sit alone in the sea of green seats beneath your Cubs poncho. It would have had the Sandberg Game, in which Ryno, on June 23, 1984, emerged on the national stage, hitting a home run off the great Bruce Sutter to tie the game in the bottom of the ninth, then hitting another off Sutter in the bottom of the tenth to tie it again. The Cubs won in the eleventh. It would have had the hard-drinking Mike Kelly, the first baseball superstar, who, before he died in a Boston hospital room, said, "Well, boys, it looks like this is my last slide into home." It would have had Billy Sunday, who went from the field to the pulpit but never gave up the language of baseball. "Lord, we got souls stranded on third and need your help bringing them in to score." It would have had Game 3 of the 1932 World Series, in which Babe Ruth, being mercilessly heckled by the Cubs bench, pointed either at the players in the Chicago dugout, at Cubs pitcher Charlie Root, or at center field, then hit a home run to the place he'd been pointing—the famous called shot. It would have had those summer afternoons when Harry Caray and Steve Stone broadcast from the right-field bleachers, the beer flowing. It would have had Bill Veeck, Jr., dying of cancer, spending some of his last days in the left-field bleachers, smoking cigarettes, talking to fans, shirtless, tapping ash into the ashtray built into his wooden leg, looking out at the field as if looking back at his own past. It would have had the afternoon when I happened upon Keith Magnuson, the great Blackhawks defenseman, in the stands and talked to him for twenty minutes about Stan Mikita and Bobby Hull and the similarities between baseball and hockey. It would have had Billy Jurges, the other Cubs infielder shot by a crazed person in a hotel—room 509 of the Hotel Carlos, the showgirl Violet Valli (née Popovich) blasting away with a .25 caliber handgun because the shortstop wanted to break up with her. He survived and was soon back on the field and she went on to perform under the name "Violet (What I did for love) Valli, the Most Talked About Girl in Chicago." It would have had Kiki Cuyler just for his nickname. Also just for their nicknames: "Pop" Schriver, "Dad" Clarke, "Jiggs" Parrott, "Buttons" Briggs, "Shadow" Pyle, "Bubbles" Hargrave, "Cupid" Childs, "Wildfire" Schulte, "Zip" Zabel, "Rube" Waddell, "Hippo" Vaughn, "High Pockets" Kelly, "Rabbit" Maranville, "Dim Dom" Dallessandro, "Jumbo" Brown, "Tiny" Osborne, "Sweetbread" Bailey. It would have had Ronnie "Woo Woo" Wickers, the self-fashioned ultimate Cubs fan, who spent year after year in the bleachers, chanting "Cubs-Woo, Cubs-Woo, Cubs-Woo," or, if the team was about to sweep, "Sweep-Woo, Sweep-Woo, Sweep-Woo." Asked how he invented this cheer, Wickers told the *Chicago Tribune*, "It just came to be." It would have had Shawon Dunston when he first took over at shortstop in 1985, with that wild cannon of an arm that sent the ball either across the infield on a line or into the tenth row of the stands.

It would have had everything that's ever happened and is happening and will happen. It would have had what it felt like when you were eight and came through the tunnel and saw the field for the first time. It would have had the ground crew raking the dirt between innings and the billows of dust that blew across the outfield. It would have had the electricity the moment before a storm, a single ray of sunlight coming through the overcast to illuminate a spot on a building across Waveland like a heavenly suggestion to Jody Davis—hit it here. The big catcher swinging as the lightning flashed, the ball going out, the rain coming down. It would have had what happened but also what it felt like and what it meant. It would have had my mother who died. It would have had the foul ball my friend Mark caught and the other foul ball my friend Andrew missed, inciting boos from the crowd.

It would have had everything, but it can't because it's just a book.

BIBLIOGRAPHY

BOOKS

Alexander, Charles C. *Our Game: An American Baseball History.* New York: Henry Holt, 1991.

———. *Ty Cobb.* New York: Oxford University Press, 1984.

Angell, Roger. *Five Seasons: A Baseball Companion.* New York: Simon & Schuster, 1977.

———. *Game Time: A Baseball Companion.* New York: Harcourt, 2003.

———. *The Summer Game.* New York: Viking, 1972.

Banks, Ernie, with Jim Enright. *"Mr. Cub."* Chicago: Follett, 1971.

Believe It! Chicago Cubs World Series Champions. Chicago: Chicago Sun-Times, 2016.

Berkow, Ira. *Wrigley Field: An Oral and Narrative History of the Home of the Chicago Cubs.* New York: Stewart, Tabori & Chang, 2014.

Bogen, Gil. *The Billy Goat Curse: Losing and Superstition in Cubs Baseball Since World War II.* Jefferson, NC: McFarland & Company, 2015.

Boswell, Thomas. *Why Time Begins on Opening Day.* New York: Penguin, 1984.

Bouton, Jim. *Ball Four.* New York: Wiley, 1970.

Breslin, Jimmy. *Can't Anybody Here Play This Game? The Improbable Saga of the Mets' First Year.* Chicago: Ivan R. Dee, 1963.

Brown, Warren. *The Chicago Cubs.* New York: Putnam, 1946.

Caray, Harry, with Bob Verdi. *Holy Cow!* New York: Villard, 1989.

Chastain, Bill. *Hack's 191: Hack Wilson and His Incredible 1930 Season.* Guilford, CT: Lyons Press, 2012.

Chicago Tribune. Won for the Ages: How the Chicago Cubs Became the 2016 World Series Champions. Chicago: Triumph Books, 2016.

Cobb, Ty. *My Twenty Years in Baseball.* 1925. Reprint, Mineola, NY: Dover, 2002.

Cobb, Ty, with Al Stump. *My Life in Baseball.* Garden City, NY: Doubleday, 1961.

Dawson, Andre, with Alan Maimon. *If You Love This Game . . . : An MVP's Life in Baseball.* Chicago: Triumph Books, 2012.

Deveney, Sean. *The Original Curse: Did the Cubs Throw the 1918 World Series to Babe Ruth's Red Sox and Incite the Black Sox Scandal?* New York: McGraw-Hill, 2010.

Durocher, Leo, with Ed Linn. *Nice Guys Finish First.* New York: Simon & Schuster, 1975.

Ehrgott, Roberts. *Mr. Wrigley's Ball Club: Chicago and the Cubs During the Jazz Age.* Lincoln: University of Nebraska Press, 2013.

Eskenazi, Gerald. *The Lip: A Biography of Leo Durocher.* New York: William Morrow, 1993.

Evers, John J., and Hugh S. Fullerton. *Touching Second: The Science of Baseball.* 1910. Reprint, Jefferson, NC: McFarland & Company, 2005.

Farrell, James T. *My Baseball Diary: A Famed American Author Recalls the Wonderful World of Baseball . . . Yesterday and Today.* New York: A. S. Barnes, 1957.

Feldman, Doug. *Miracle Collapse: The 1969 Chicago Cubs.* Lincoln: University of Nebraska Press, 2006.

Frascella, John. *Theology: How a Boy Wonder Led the Red Sox to the Promised Land.* New York: Sterling & Ross, Cambridge House Press, 2009.

Gatto, Steve. *Da Curse of the Billy Goat: The Chicago Cubs, Pennant Races, and Curses.* Lansing, MI: Porter House, 2004.

Gold, Eddie, with Art Ahrens. *The Golden Era Cubs, 1876–1940.* Chicago: Bonus Books, 1985.

Gollenbock, Peter. *Wrigleyville: A Magical History Tour of the Chicago Cubs.* New York: St. Martin's Press, 1996.

Gould, Stephen Jay. *Triumph and Tragedy in Muddville.* New York: W. W. Norton, 2003.

Hample, Zack. *Watching Baseball: A Professional Fan's Guide for Beginners, Semi-experts, and Deeply Serious Geeks.* New York: Vintage, 2007.

Holtzman, Jerome. *The Jerome Holtzman Baseball Reader.* Chicago: Triumph Books, 2003.

Honig, Donald. *Baseball When the Grass Was Real: Baseball from the Twenties to the Forties Told by the Men Who Played It.* Lincoln: University of Nebraska Press, 1975.

James, Bill. *The New Historical Baseball Abstract.* New York: Free Press, 2001.

Jenkins, Fergie, with Lew Freedman. *Fergie: My Life from the Cubs to Cooperstown.* Chicago: Triumph Books, 2009.

Kavanagh, Jack. *Ol' Pete: The Grover Cleveland Alexander Story.* South Bend, IN: Diamond Communications, 1996.

Koca, Gary. *Great Chicago Cub Baseball Players Since 1876.* Self-published, 2015.

Kogan, Rick. *A Chicago Tavern: A Goat, a Curse, and the American Dream.* Chicago: Lake Claremont Press, 2006.

Lardner, John. *The John Lardner Reader: A Press Box Legend's Classic Sportswriting.* Lincoln: University of Nebraska Press, 2010.

Lardner, Ring. *Lardner on Baseball.* Guilford, CT: Lyons Press, 2002.

———. *Ring Lardner: Stories and Other Writings.* New York: Library of America, 2013.

Lewis, Michael. *Moneyball: The Art of Winning an Unfair Game.* New York: W. W. Norton, 2003.

Lund, John. *1908: A Look at the World Champion 1908 Chicago Cubs.* Self-published, 2008.

Major League Baseball, eds. *Chicago Cubs: 2016 World Series Champions.* New York: Random House, 2016.

Malamud, Bernard. *The Natural*. New York: Farrar, Straus and Cudahy, 1952.

Mathewson, Christy. *Pitching in a Pinch: Baseball from the Inside*. 1912. Reprint, New York: Penguin, 2013.

Mnookin, Seth. *Feeding the Monster: How Money, Smarts, and Nerve Took a Team to the Top*. New York: Simon & Schuster, 2006.

Parker, Clifton Blue. *Fouled Away: The Baseball Tragedy of Hack Wilson*. Jefferson, NC: McFarland & Company, 2000.

Pepitone, Joe, with Barry Stainback. *"Joe, You Coulda Made Us Proud."* Chicago: Playboy Press, 1975.

Pernot, Laurent. *Before the Ivy: The Cub's Golden Age in Pre-Wrigley Chicago*. Urbana: University of Illinois Press, 2015.

Remnick, David, ed. *The Only Game in Town: Sportswriting from* The New Yorker. New York: Random House, 2010.

Rice, Grantland. *The Tumult and the Shouting: My Life in Sport*. New York: A. A. Barnes, 1954.

Richler, Mordecai. *Dispatches from the Sporting Life*. Toronto: Knopf Canada, 2002.

Ritter, Lawrence S. *The Glory of Their Times: The Story of the Early Days of Baseball Told by the Men Who Played It*. New York: Macmillan, 1966.

Roberts, Randy, and Carson Cunningham. *Before the Curse: The Chicago Cubs' Glory Years, 1870–1945*. Urbana: University of Illinois Press, 2012.

Rogers, Phil. *Ernie Banks: Mr. Cub and the Summer of '69*. Chicago: Triumph Books, 2011.

Ross, David, with Don Yaeger. *Teammate: My Journey in Baseball and a World Series for the Ages*. New York: Hachette, 2017.

Roth, Philip. *The Great American Novel*. New York: Holt, Rinehart and Winston, 1973.

Sandberg, Ryne, with Barry Rozner. *Second to Home: Ryne Sandberg Opens Up*. Chicago: Bonus Books, 1995.

Santo, Ron, with Randy Minkoff. *Ron Santo: For the Love of Ivy*. Chicago: Bonus Books, 1993.

Skipper, John C. *Wicked Curve: The Life and Troubled Times of Grover Cleveland Alexander*. Jefferson, NC: McFarland & Company, 2004.

Sosa, Sammy, with Marco Breton. *Sammy Sosa: An Autobiography*. New York: Grand Central Publishing, 2000.

Sowell, Mike. *The Pitch That Killed: The Story of Carl Mays, Ray Chapman, and the Pennant Race of 1920*. New York: Macmillan, 1989.

Stout, Glenn. *The Cubs: The Complete Story of Chicago Cubs Baseball*. New York: Houghton Mifflin, 2007.

Theodore, John. *Baseball's Natural: The Story of Eddie Waitkus*. Lincoln: University of Nebraska Press, 2006.

Thomson, Cindy, and Scott Brown. *Three Finger: The Mordecai Brown Story*. Lincoln: University of Nebraska Press, 2006.

Van Dyck, Dave, Mark Gonzales, Paul Sullivan, K. C. Johnson, Steve Rosenbloom, David Haugh, Phil Rogers, and Phil Valasquez. *When Theo Met Tom: A Cubs Story*. Chicago: Amazon Books, Chicago Tribune Press, 2011.

Veeck, Bill, with Ed Linn. *Veeck—As in Wreck*. Chicago: University of Chicago Press, 1962.

Weisberger, Bernard A. *When Chicago Ruled Baseball: The Cubs–White Sox World Series of 1906*. New York: William Morrow, 2006.

Will, George F. *A Nice Little Place on the North Side: A History of Triumph, Mostly Defeat, and Incurable Hope at Wrigley Field*. New York: Three Rivers Press, 2014.

Williams, Billy, with Fred Mitchell. *Billy Williams: My Sweet-Swinging Lifetime with the Cubs*. Chicago: Triumph Books, 2008.

Williams, Ted, and John Underwood. *The Science of Hitting*. New York: Simon & Schuster, 1970.

Wind, Herbert Warren, ed. *The Realm of Sport: A Classic Collection of the World's Greatest Sporting Events and Personalities as Recorded by the Most Distinguished Writers*. New York: Simon & Schuster, 1966.

ARTICLES

Adames, Yoel. "Sosa Reflects on MLB Career." ESPN Deportes, June 4, 2009.

Axelrod, David. "The Most Pleasing Campaign of 2016: The Chicago Cubs

Look Poised to End the Longest Championship Drought in American Sports." *The New Yorker*, September 15, 2016.

Axson, Scooby. "World Series Game 7 Ticket Sells for $19,500." *Sports Illustrated*, November 2, 2016.

Berkow, Ira. "Eric Show's Solitary Life, and Death." *The New York Times*, March 27, 1994.

———. "Sports of The Times; 'I Didn't Know' Is Familiar Refrain." *The New York Times*, June 7, 2003.

Bruck, Connie. "Rough Rider: Where Will Sam Zell Take the Struggling Tribune Company?" *The New Yorker*, November 12, 2007.

Burkholder, Ed. "Three-Fingered Immortal." *Sport*, November 1953.

Corcoran, Cliff, and Jay Jaffe. "How the Cubs Were Built: Turning Baseball's Longest-Running Losers into Winners." SI.com, August 10, 2016.

Davey, Monica. "Curses, Old and New, Haunt the Cubs' Fans." *The New York Times*, October 16, 2003.

Dealbook. "Ricketts Family Emerges as Cubs' Top Bidder." *The New York Times*, January 23, 2009.

Fowler, Dexter. "You Go, We Go." *The Players' Tribune*, November 11, 2016.

Foxsports. "Major League Baseballs Have a Short Life." Foxsports.com, June 30, 2013.

Friend, Tom. "The Tortured Life of Eric Show." ESPN.com, September 7, 2010.

Frierson, Eddie. "Christy Mathewson." Society for American Baseball Research.

"Hack Wilson Dies; Baseball Star, 48." *The New York Times*, November 24, 1948.

Holtzman, Jerome. "'King' Kelly Gave Players Reason to Think." *Chicago Tribune*, November 6, 1994.

Jones, Robert F. "Chicago, Chicago, That Tottering Town." *Sports Illustrated*, October 27, 1969.

Keown, Tim. "Party Room of the Century? A Week Inside the Cubs' Clubhouse." *ESPN The Magazine*, September 23, 2016.

Lamberty, Bill. "Harry Pulliman." Society for American Baseball Research, 2004.

Leavy, Jane. "Dave Kingman." *The Washington Post*, June 15, 1980.

Lipsyte, Robert. "In Year 7 of Game 6, Buckner Retaliates." *The New York Times*, July 16, 1993.

McGrath, Ben. "The Professor of Baseball." *The New Yorker,* July 14, 2004.

Newman, Bruce. "Kong!" *Sports Illustrated,* August 20, 1979.

Reichard, Kevin. "#TBT: Zachary Taylor Davis." Ballparkdigest.com, April 16, 2015.

Rogers, Tom. "Leo Durocher, Fiery Ex-Manager, Dies at 86." *The New York Times,* October 8, 1991.

Sanborn, I. E. "Cubs Champions; Beat Giants in Final Game, 4–2." *The Chicago Daily Tribune,* October 9, 1908.

Schmidt, Michael S. "Sosa Is Said to Have Tested Positive in 2003." *The New York Times,* June 16, 2009.

Sullivan, Paul. "Cubs Fire Wrigley Field DJ for Playing Inappropriate Song." *Chicago Tribune,* August 15, 2016.

———. "Final Game Not 1st Time Sosa Left Clubhouse Early." *Chicago Tribune,* June 9, 2005.

Verducci, Tom. "C of Joy: The End of the Cubs' Title Drought Has Unleashed a Flood of Emotions." *Sports Illustrated,* November 15, 2016.

———. "Reign Men: The Storm, the Speech and the Inside Story of the Cubs' Game 7 Triumph." *Sports Illustrated,* November 3, 2016.

———. "Timeless: World Series Between the Cubs and the Indians is One for the Ages." *Sports Illustrated,* November 7, 2016.

Weber, Bruce. "Ruth Ann Steinhagen Is Dead at 83; Shot a Ballplayer." *The New York Times,* March 23, 2013.

Witz, Billy. "At Yale, Theo Epstein Made a Splash as Newspaper's Sports Editor." *The New York Times,* October 29, 2016.

Yellon, Al. "An Updated Comprehensive List of 2016 Cubs Walkup/Intro Music." *The Bleacher Report,* July 14, 2016.

Yoder, Chad. "How Theo Epstein Built the Cubs: 140 Players, 37 Trades, 80 Signings and 85 Departures." *Chicago Tribune,* October 17, 2016.

ACKNOWLEDGMENTS

Writing acknowledgments for this book is like standing drunk at the end of a long game, trying to thank every person who argued and analyzed and enjoyed it with you in the bleachers, even those bastards in right field.

Well, here goes: Jennifer Rudolph Walsh, Dana Brown, Sam Walker, Leslie Epstein, Theo Epstein, Tom Ricketts, Josh Karp, Neil Steinberg, Rick Kogan, Rick Telander, Sandy Frazier, Gary Fencik, Doug Plank, Dan Dorfman, Jim McMahon, Mr. (Steve) Hilsabeck. David Lipsky, who remembers exactly what it felt like; Roger Bennett, who remembers Jody Davis; Spitz and Mark and Jamie and Dennis and Todd Johnston and Duffy and Katie and Lisa and the vendor who sold me beer even though he could get fired for it, which I knew because he kept saying, "Hey, man, I can get fired for it." Matt Levin, who helped with research. Julie Tate, who helped with fact-checking. Pete Wilson, who gave it an early, Cubs' fan read. We met at New Trier freshman year in

Radio Workshop. He was smarter than me then and is smarter than me now—just ask Frank Mattuci. Kevin Baker, who gave it an early, baseball-scholar read. Jeff Seroy at FSG, who once suggested I throw out the first pitch at a Bears game. Pete Burnside, who was a great role model and the only teacher who could tell me what it was like to pitch to Mickey Mantle. Jon Miller, who could not hit my whiffle sinker even in his prime. Special thanks to Julie Grau for understanding my deep love for this team. Graydon Carter, for his friendship and support. Ben Metcalf, who sent me on the road with the Cubs when there was nothing in the world I'd rather do. Stephen Cannella, who assigned and edited the Cubs pieces I wrote for *Sports Illustrated* and was good to his word—he got me the pass that let me see the thing when the thing finally happened. Emma Span, also at *SI*, who helped me make those pieces work. Chris Pratt, for the prayer that put the engine back on the tracks. Jerry Schmelter—where are your Padres now? My father, Herbie—Herbela, Handsomo—who took me to my first Cubs game, never failed to tell me what DiMaggio would hit in this park ("355 down the line, are you kidding me?"), told the parking guy he needed a space with "easy egress" as he was a doctor (he wasn't) who might, at any moment, be called to surgery, and taught me how to throw a screwball, which he advised me to use only in the pinch. My mother, who did not care about baseball but nonetheless wanted to see the Cubs win because "it's enough already." My sister, Sharon, who has looked out for me since I was in danger of oncoming traffic. My brother, Steven, whose sensibility was deeply formed by the Cubs even if he doesn't know it.

As the Cubs made their run, he sent me the record "Cubs Power" along with the following note, dated 10-17-16:

Richard—
I located this to remind you that the fates are *not* to be tempted. Ever! Be mindful of history but more mindful that there is a cosmic consciousness that hovers over everything.
"We asked for signs. The signs were sent," Leonard Cohen.
Be wise and aware of how you proceed. We've been here before.

Steven

Jonathan Galassi, who was with me at Soldier Field when Mike Ditka's number was retired and who I hope will be with me at Wrigley when the Cubs win their next championship. He called me shortly after Chicago got past Los Angeles in the NLCS and said, You have been preparing—now is the time. Jessica Medoff, who lived this with me. She was not there in 1979 and 1984 but was there for Sosa and the Bartman Ball, Epstein and Bryant and the rest. Jessica read every page first, second, third, tenth. It's Jessica I imagine reading whatever I write as I am writing it.

We did it, baby! We finally did it!